Travellers' **Scandinavian**

Pan Books London, Sydney and Auckland

Other titles in the series

Whilst the advice and information in this book is believed to
be true and accurate at the time of going to press, neither the
authors nor the publishers can accept any legal responsibility for
any errors or omissions that may be made

The publishers would like to thank the various national tourist
offices for their help during the preparation of this book

First published 1984 by Pan Books Ltd
Cavaye Place, London SW10 9PG
9 8 7 6 5 4 3
© L. Bernadotte, D. L. Ellis, M. Hoddevik, B. Stokvis 1984
ISBN 0 330 28276 X

Phototypeset by Input Typesetting Ltd., London SW19 0DR.
Printed and bound in Great Britain by
Hazell Watson & Viney Limited
Member of BPCC plc
Aylesbury Bucks

Contents

Using the phrase book and a note on the pronunciation system

- This phrase book is designed to help you get by in Denmark, Norway and Sweden, to get what you want or need. It concentrates on the simplest but most effective way you can express these needs in an unfamiliar language.
- The CONTENTS for each different language section gives you a good idea of which pages to consult for the phrase you need.
- The INDEX at the end of each language section gives more detailed information about where to look for your phrase. When you have found the right page you will be given:
  - either – the exact phrase
  - or – help in making up a suitable sentence
  - and – help in getting the pronunciation right
- The English sentences in **bold type** will be useful for you in a variety of different situations, so they are worth learning by heart.
- In some cases you will find help in understanding what people say to *you*, in reply to your questions.
- Note especially these two sections:
  Everyday expressions
  Shop talk
  You are sure to want to refer to them most frequently.
- When you arrive in the foreign country make good use of the tourist information offices.

- The pronunciation system in this book is founded on three assumptions: firstly, that it is not possible to describe in print the sounds of a foreign language in such a way that the English speaker with no phonetic training will produce them accurately, or even intelligibly; secondly, that perfect pronunciation is not essential for communication; and lastly that the average visitor abroad is more interested in achieving successful communication than in learning how to pronounce new speech sounds. Observation and experience have shown these assumptions to be justified. The most important characteristic of the present system, therefore, is that it makes no attempt whatsoever to teach the sounds of the other language, but uses instead the nearest English sounds to them. The sentences transcribed for pronunciation are designed to be read as naturally as possible, as if they were ordinary English (of a generally south-eastern variety) and with no attempt to make the words sound 'foreign'. In this way you will still sound quite English but you will at the same time be understood. Practice always helps performance and it is a good idea to rehearse out loud any of the sentences you know you are going to need. When you come to the point of using them, say them with conviction.

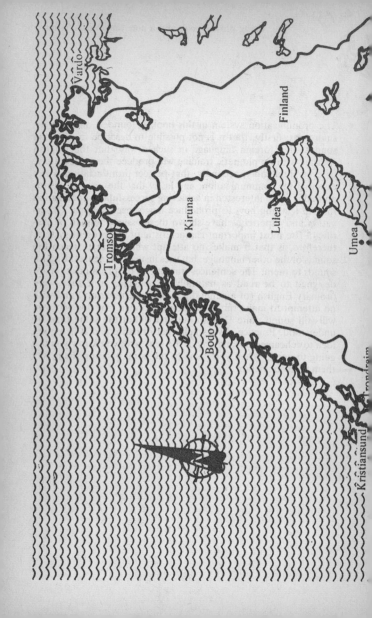

Travellers' **Danish**

David Ellis is Director of the Somerset Language Centre and co-author of a number of language books

Benthe Stokvis has lived in England for a number of years and teaches Danish to adults

Dr John Baldwin is Lecturer in Phonetics at University College, London

Travellers' Danish

D. L. Ellis, B. Stokvis

Pronunciation Dr J. Baldwin

Useful address
Danish Tourist Board
Sceptre House
169 Regent Street
London W1

Danish

Contents

Everyday expressions

[*See also 'Shop talk', p. 50*]

- Although you will find the correct greetings listed below, the Danes commonly use the informal **dav** (dow) to express all of these.

Hello	**Dav/hej**
	dow/hi
Good morning	**Godmorgen**
	go-morn
Good day	**Goddag**
	go-day
Good evening	**Godaften**
	go-aften
Good night	**Godnat**
	go-nat
Goodbye	**Farvel**
	far-vel
Yes	**Ja**
	ya
Thank you	**Tak**
	tuck
Thank you very much	**Mange tak**
	mung-er tuck
That's right	**Det er rigtigt**
	day air regtit
No	**Nej**
	nigh
No thank you	**Nej tak**
	nigh tuck
I disagree	**Det er ikke rigtigt**
	day air igger regtit
Excuse me	**Undskyld**
	on-skool
That's good	**Det er godt**
	day air got
That's no good	**Det er ikke godt**
	day air igger got
I know	**Det ved jeg**
	day vethe yigh

It doesn't matter	**Det gør ikke noget**
	day gur igger no-et
Where's the toilet please?	**Hvor er toilettet?**
	vor air toilet-tet
Do you speak English?	**Taler De engelsk?**
	tayler dee eng-elsk
I'm sorry . . .	**Desværre . . .**
	desvair . . .
I don't speak Danish	**Jeg taler ikke dansk**
	yigh tayler igger dansk
I only speak a little Danish	**Jeg taler kun lidt dansk**
	yigh tayler kon lit dansk
I don't understand	**Jeg forstår det ikke**
	yigh forstor day igger
Please can you . . .	**Vil De være så venlig at . . .**
	vil dee vair saw venlee at . . .
repeat that?	**gentage det?**
	ghen-tay day
speak more slowly?	**tale langsommere?**
	tayler lung-sommer-er
write it down?	**skrive det ned?**
	skreever day nethe
What is this called in Danish?	**Hvad hedder det på dansk?**
[*point*]	va hither day paw dansk

Crossing the border

ESSENTIAL INFORMATION

- Don't waste time before you leave rehearsing what you are going to say to the border officials – the chances are that you won't have to say anything at all, especially if you travel by air. It is more useful to check that you have all your documents handy for the journey: passports, tickets, money, travellers' cheques, insurance documents, driving licence and car registration documents.

  Look out for these signs: **TOLD** (customs)
  GRÆNSE (border) **GRÆNSEPOLITI** (frontier police)

- You may be asked routine questions by the customs officials [*see below*]. If you have to give personal details see 'Meeting people' p. 16. The other important answer to know is 'Nothing': **Ingenting** (ing-on-ting).

ROUTINE QUESTIONS

Passport?	**Pas?** p*as*
Insurance?	**Forsikring?** for-s*ee*k-ring
Registration document? (logbook)	**Indregistreringsattest?** in-reggee-stray-rings-att*est*
Ticket, please?	**Deres billet?** d*ai*r-es billet
Have you anything to declare?	**Har De noget at fortolde?** har dee n*o*-et at for-t*o*ller
Where are you going?	**Hvor skal De hen?** v*or* skal dee h*e*n
How long are you staying?	**Hvor længe bliver De?** v*or* leng-er bl*ee*r dee
Where have you come from?	**Hvor Kommer De fra?** v*or* k*o*mmer dee fra

Meeting people

[*See also 'Everyday expressions', p. 14*]

Breaking the ice

How are you?	**Hvordan har De det?** vor-d*a*n har dee day
I am here . . .	**Jeg er her . . .** y*igh* air hair . . .
on holiday	**på ferie** paw f*ai*ree
on business	**på forretningsrejse** paw forretnings-rye-ser

Can I offer you . . .	**Må jeg tilbyde Dem . . .**
	maw yigh til-b*oo*ther dem . . .
a drink?	**en drink?**
	ain drink
a cigarette?	**en cigaret?**
	ain cigar*et*
a cigar?	**en cigar?**
	ain cig*a*r
Are you staying long?	**Bliver De her længe?**
	bleer dee hair leng-er

Name

What's your name?	**Hvad hedder De?**
	va hither dee
My name is . . .	**Jeg hedder . . .**
	yigh hither . . .

Family

Are you married?	**Er De gift?**
	air dee gift
I am . . .	**Jeg er . . .**
	yigh air . . .
married	**gift**
	gift
single	**ugift**
	oo-gift
This is . . .	**Det er . . .**
	day air . . .
my wife	**min kone**
	mean k*o*ner
my husband	**min mand**
	mean man
my son	**min søn**
	mean sern
my daughter	**min datter**
	mean d*a*tter
my boyfriend	**min ven**
	mean ven
my girlfriend	**min veninde**
	mean ven-*een*-ner
my colleague (male or female)	**min kollega**
	mean koll*ay*-ga
Do you have any children?	**Har De børn?**
	har dee burn

I have . . .
         Jeg har . . .
         yigh har . . .

 one daughter
         en datter
         ain datter

 one son
         en søn
         ain sern

 two daughters
         to døtre
         toe der-trer

 three sons
         tre sønner
         tray sern-er

No, I haven't any children
         Nej, jeg har ingen børn
         nigh yigh har *eeng*-en burn

Where you live

Are you . . .
         Er De . . .
         air dee . . .

 Danish?
         dansker?
         dan-sker

 German?
         tysker?
         too-sker

 Swedish?
         svensker?
         sven-sker

I am . . .
         Jeg er . . .
         yigh air . . .

 American
         amerikaner
         amair-ee-k*ay*ner

 English
         englænder
         eng-len-ner

[*For other nationalities see p. 104*]

I live . . .
         Jeg bor . . .
         yigh bore . . .

 in London
         i London
         ee lon-don

 in England
         i England
         ee eng-lan

 in the north (of England)
         i Nordengland
         ee nor-eng-lan

 in the south (of England)
         i Sydengland
         ee sooth-eng-lan

 in the west (of England)
         i Vestengland
         ee vest-eng-lan

 in the east (of England)
         i Østengland
         ee urst-eng-lan

| in the centre (of England) | **i Midtengland** |
| | ee mid-*eng*-lan |

[*For other countries, p. 102*]

For the businessman and woman

I'm from . . . (firm's name)	**Jeg er fra . . .**
	yigh air fra . . .
I have an appointment with . . .	**Jeg har en aftale med . . .**
	yigh har ain *ow*-tayler methe . . .
This is my card	**Her er mit visitkort**
	hair air meet vee-s*ee*t-kort
I'm sorry, I'm late	**Undskyld jeg kommer for sent**
	*o*n-skool yigh kommer for sent
Can I fix another appointment?	**Kan jeg få en anden aftale?**
	kan yigh faw ain *a*n-on *ow*-tayler
I'm staying at the hotel . . .	**Jeg bor på hotel . . .**
	yigh bore paw hot*e*l . . .

Asking the way

ESSENTIAL INFORMATION

- Keep a look out for all these place names as you will find them on shops, maps and notices.

WHAT TO SAY

Excuse me, please	**Undskyld**
	*o*n-skool
How do I get . . .	**Hvordan kommer jeg . . .**
	vor-d*a*n kommer yigh . . .
to the airport?	**til lufthavnen?**
	til l*oo*ft-how-nen
to Copenhagen?	**til København?**
	til ker-ben-h*ow*n
to the beach?	**til stranden?**
	til str*u*n-nen

Danish

How do I get . . .
    Hvordan kommer jeg . . .
    vor-d*a*n k*o*mmer yigh . . .

to the bus station?
    til busterminalen?
    til b*oo*s-tair-mee-nay-len

to the hotel (Ritz)?
    til hotel (Ritz)?
    til hotel (reets)

to the market?
    til markedet?
    til m*a*r-kethet

to the police station?
    til politistationen?
    til poli-*tee*-stash-yonen

to the port?
    til havnen?
    til h*ow*-nen

to the post office?
    til posthuset?
    til posst-h*oo*-set

to the railway station?
    til banegården?
    til b*a*ner-gaw-en

to the sports stadium?
    til stadion?
    til st*a*y-dee-on

to the Tivoli?
    til Tivoli?
    til *tee*-vo-lee

to the tourist information office?
    til turistkontoret?
    til tour*i*st-kon-toe-ret

to the town centre?
    til byens centrum?
    til b*oo*-ens c*e*n-trum

to the town hall?
    til rådhuset?
    til rothe-h*oo*-set

Excuse me, please
    Undskyld
    *o*n-skool

Is there . . . near by?
    Er der . . . i nærheden?
    air dair . . . ee n*ai*r-hethen

an art gallery
    et kunstgalleri
    it konst-galler*ee*

a baker's
    en bager
    ain bay-er

a bank
    en bank
    ain bunk

a bar
    en bar
    ain bar

a botanical garden
    en botanisk have
    ain bo-*tay*-nisk h*a*ver

a bus stop
    et busstoppested
    it b*oo*s-st*o*p-per-stethe

a butcher's	**en slagter**
	ain sl*a*gter
a café	**en café**
	ain café
a cake shop	**et konditori**
	it con-dee-toe-r*ee*
a campsite	**en campingplads**
	ain c*a*mpingplas
a car park	**en parkeringsplads**
	ain par-k*ai*r-ringsplas
a chemist's	**et apotek**
	it uppo-t*a*ke
a church	**en kirke**
	ain k*ee*r-ker
a cinema	**en biograf**
	ain bee-o-gr*a*hf
a delicatessen	**en viktualieforretning**
	ain vic-too-*ay*-lee-er-forretning
a dentist's	**en tandlæge**
	ain t*a*n-layer
a department store	**et stormagasin**
	it store-ma-ga-s*ee*n
a disco	**et diskotek**
	it disco-t*a*ke
a doctor's surgery	**en læge/doktor**
	ain l*a*yer/d*o*ctor
a dry cleaner's	**et renseri**
	it ren-ser-r*ee*
a fishmonger's	**en fiskehandler**
	ain f*i*sker-hanler
a garage (for repairs)	**et autoværksted**
	it *ow*-toe-va*i*rk-stethe
a greengrocer's	**en grønthandler**
	ain gr*u*nt-hanler
a grocer's	**en købmand**
	ain k*u*r-man
a hairdresser's	**en frisør**
	ain free-s*er*
a hardware shop	**en isenkram**
	ain *ee*-sern-krum
a hospital	**et hospital/sygehus**
	it h*oe*-speet*a*l/s*oo*-yer-hoos

Is there . . . near by?   **Er der . . . i nærheden?**
                                      air dair . . . ee nair-hethen
a hotel   **et hotel**
                                      it hotel
an ice-cream shop   **en iskiosk**
                                      ain *ees*-kiosk
a laundry   **et vaskeri**
                                      it vasker-r*ee*
a local sickness insurance   **et sygesikringskontor**
  office   it s*oo*-yer-*seek*-rings-kon-t*o*r
a museum   **et museum**
                                      it moo-s*ay*-oom
a night club   **en natklub**
                                      ain n*a*t-kloob
a park   **en park**
                                      ain park
a petrol station   **en tankstation**
                                      ain t*u*nk-stash-yon
a post box   **en postkasse**
                                      ain p*o*sst-kasser
a public toilet   **et offentligt toilet**
                                      it *o*ffent-lit toilet
a restaurant   **en restaurant**
                                      ain restor*u*ng
a (snack) bar   **en (snack) bar**
                                      ain (sn*a*ck) bar
a sports ground   **en sportsplads**
                                      ain sportsplas
a supermarket   **et supermarked**
                                      it s*u*per-markethe
a sweet shop   **en chokoladeforretning**
                                      ain shoko-l*ai*ther-forretning
an (indoor) swimming pool   **en svømmehal**
                                      ain sver-mer-hal
a telephone (booth)   **en telefonboks**
                                      ain teleph*o*ne-box
a theatre   **et teater**
                                      it tee-*ai*rt-ter
a tobacconist's   **en tobakshandler**
                                      ain toe-b*u*ks-hanler
a travel agent's   **et rejsebureau**
                                      it r*y*e-ser-bee-r*o*

a youth hostel	**et vandrerhjem**
	it v*u*n-drer-yem
a zoo	**en zoologisk have**
	ain so-o-*lo*-gisk haver

DIRECTIONS

- Asking where a place is, or if a place is near by, is one thing; making sense of the answer is another.
- Here are some of the most important key directions and replies.

Left	**Venstre**
	ven-strer
Right	**Højre**
	h*oy*-rer
Straight on	**Lige ud**
	lee-er *oo*the
There	**Der**
	dair
First left/right	**Første vej til venstre/højre**
	f*i*rst-er vy til v*e*n-strer/h*oy*-rer
Second left/right	**Anden vej til venstre/højre**
	*a*n-on vy til v*e*n-strer/hoy-rer
At the crossroads	**Ved krydset**
	vethe kr*oo*-set
At the traffic lights	**Ved trafiklyset**
	vethe traf-f*i*k-*loo*-set
At the roundabout	**Ved rundkørslen**
	vethe r*o*n-kerslen
At the level crossing	**Ved jernbaneoverskæringen**
	vethe y*air*baner-*o*-er-skair-ing-en
It's near/far	**Det er nær ved/langt væk**
	day air n*air* vethe/langt vek
One kilometre	**En kilometer**
	ain kilom*ait*-ter
Two kilometres	**To kilometer**
	t*oe* kilom*ait*-ter
Five minutes . . .	**Fem minutters . . .**
	fem mee-n*oo*ters . . .
on foot	**gang**
	gung
by car	**kørsel**
	k*e*r-sel

Danish

Take . . .	**Tag** . . .
	tay . . .
the bus	**bussen**
	boossen
the train	**toget**
	toe-et

[For public transport, see p. 90]

The tourist information office

ESSENTIAL INFORMATION

- Most towns in Denmark have a tourist information office; in smaller towns the local travel agent (**REJSEBUREAU**) provides the same information and services.
- Key word to look for: **TURISTINFORMATION** and this sign
- If your main concern is to find and book accommodation, **VÆRELSEANVISNING** is the best place to go to.
- Tourist offices offer you free information in the form of printed leaflets, fold-outs, brochures, lists and plans.
- For finding a tourist office, see p. 24.

WHAT TO SAY

Please, have you got . . .	**Har De** . . .
	har dee . . .
a plan of the town?	**et bykort?**
	it boo-kort
a list of hotels?	**en liste over hoteller?**
	ain lee-ster o-er hotel-ler
a list of campsites?	**en liste over campingpladser?**
	ain lee-ster o-er camping-plasser

a list of restaurants?	**en liste over restauranter?**
	ain *lee*-ster o-er restor*u*ng-er
a list of events?	**en liste over begivenheder?**
	ain *lee*-ster o-er beg*ee*ven-hether
a leaflet on the town?	**en brochure om byen?**
	ain broch*u*re om b*oo*-en
a leaflet on the region?	**en brochure om egnen?**
	ain brochure om *eye*-nen
a railway/bus timetable?	**en tog/buskøreplan?**
	ain t*oe*/b*oo*s-ker-er-pl*a*n
In English, please	**På engelsk**
	paw *eng*-elsk
How much do I owe you?	**Hvor meget bliver det?**
	vor *my*-et bl*ee*r day

LIKELY ANSWERS

You need to understand when the answer is 'No'. You should be able to tell by the assistant's expression, tone of voice and gesture but there are some language clues, such as:

No	**Nej**
	nigh
I'm sorry	**Desværre**
	des*vair*
I don't have a list of hotels	**Jeg har ikke en liste over hoteller**
	yigh h*a*r igger ain *lee*-ster o-er hotel-ler
I haven't got any left	**Jeg har ikke flere**
	yigh h*a*r igger fl*ee*-er
It's free	**Det er gratis**
	day air gr*a*tis

Danish

Accommodation

Hotel

ESSENTIAL INFORMATION

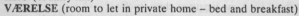

- If you want hotel-type accommodation, all the following words in capital letters are worth looking for on name boards:
  HOTEL
  MISSIONSHOTEL (comfortable accommodation at a reasonable price – no alcohol served)
  PENSIONAT (boarding house)
  MOTEL
  KRO (country inn)
  VÆRELSE (room to let in private home – bed and breakfast)
- A list of hotels in the town or district can usually be obtained at the local tourist office (see p. 24).
- Hotels in Denmark are not graded by stars but the price level is a fair guide to the standard.
- Not all hotels provide meals apart from breakfast; inquire about this, on arrival, at the reception.
- The price quoted for the room is for the room itself, per night and not per person. It usually includes service charges and taxes, but quite often does not include breakfast.
- Breakfast is continental style with coffee or tea and rolls, butter and jam and mild Danish cheese. Some larger hotels also offer a **MORGENBUFFET** where you can help yourself to cereal, yoghurt, juice and the Danish breakfast pastry **WIENERBRØD**.
- Upon arrival you may be asked to fill in a registration form which most often bears an English translation.
- Finding a hotel, see p. 26.

WHAT TO SAY

I have a booking

Jeg har reserveret et værelse
yigh har reser-vairt it vair-el-ser

Have you any vacancies, please?	**Har De et ledigt værelse?**
	har dee it lay-theet vair-el-ser
Can I book a room?	**Har De et værelse?**
	har dee it vair-el-ser
It's for . . .	**Det er til . . .**
	day air til . . .
one person	**en person**
	ain pair-sone
two people	**to personer**
	toe pair-so-ner
[*For numbers, see p. 96*]	
It's for . . .	**Det er . . .**
	day air . . .
one night	**en overnatning**
	ain o-er-natning
two nights	**to overnatninger**
	toe o-er-natning-er
one week	**en uges overnatning**
	ain oo-ers o-er-natning
two weeks	**to ugers overnatning**
	toe oo-ers o-er-natning
I would like . . .	**Jeg vil gerne have . . .**
	yigh vil gair-ner ha . . .
a room	**et værelse**
	it vair-el-ser
two rooms	**to værelser**
	toe vair-el-ser
a room with a single bed	**et enkeltværelse**
	it ain-kelt-vair el-ser
a room with two single beds	**et værelse med to senge**
	it vair-el-ser methe toe seng-er
a room with a double bed	**et dobbeltværelse**
	it dobbelt-vair-el-ser
I would like a room . . .	**Jeg vil gerne have et værelse . . .**
	yigh vil gair-ner ha it vair-el-ser. . .
with a toilet	**med toilet**
	methe toilet
with a bathroom	**med bad**
	methe bathe
with a shower	**med brusebad**
	methe broo-ser-bathe
with a cot	**med en barneseng**
	methe ain barner-seng

Danish

I'd like . . . | **Jeg vil gerne have . . .**
yigh vil gair-ner ha . . .

full board | **fuld pension**
full pungs-yon

half board | **halv pension**
hal pungs-yon

Do you serve meals? | **Er her restaurant?**
air hair restorung

At what time is . . . | **Hvornår serveres der . . .**
vornor sevvairs dair . . .

breakfast? | **morgenmad?**
morn-mathe

lunch? | **frokost?**
fraw-kost

dinner? | **middag?**
medda

How much is it? | **Hvor meget koster det?**
vor my-et koster day

Can I look at the room? | **Må jeg se værelset?**
maw yigh say vair-el-set

I'd prefer a room . . . | **Jeg foretrækker et værelse . . .**
yigh fortrekker it vair-el-ser . . .

at the front/back | **mod gaden/gården**
mothe gathen/gaw-en

OK, I'll take it | **Det tager jeg**
day tar yigh

No thanks, I won't take it | **Nej tak, jeg vil ikke have det**
nigh tuck yigh vil igger ha day

The key to number (10) please | **Nøglen til nummer (ti)**
noy-len til noom-mer (tee)

Please, may I have . . . | **Jeg vil gerne have . . .**
yigh vil gair-ner ha . . .

a coat hanger? | **en bøjle?**
ain boiler

a glass? | **et glas?**
it glas

a towel? | **et håndklæde?**
it hon-klerthe

some soap? | **et stykke sæbe**
it stookker say-ber

an ashtray? | **et askebæger?**
it asker-bayer

another pillow?	**en hovedpude til** ain ho-ethe-*poo*-ther til
Come in!	**Kom ind!** kom in
One moment, please!	**Et øjeblik!** it *oy*-er-blik
Please can you . . .	**Vil De være så venlig at . . .** vil dee *vai*i saw *ven*lee at . . .
do this laundry/dry-cleaning?	**sende dette til vask/rensning?** *sen*ner *det*ter til *va*sk/*rens*-ning
help me with my luggage?	**hjælpe mig med bagagen?** *yel*per my *me*the bag*ay*she
call me a taxi for . . .?	**bestille en taxa til klokken . . .?** best*il*ler ain *ta*xa til *clo*cken . . .
call me at . . .?	**vække mig klokken . . .?** *vek*ker my *clo*cken . . .
[*For times, see p. 98*] The bill, please	**Må jeg få regningen?** maw yigh faw *rye*-ningen
Is service included?	**Er det med betjening?** air day *me*the bech*ai*ning
I think this is wrong	**Jeg tror, der er en fejl** yigh tror dair air ain *fi*le
May I have a receipt?	**Må jeg få en kvittering?** maw yigh *fa*w ain kveett*ai*ring

At breakfast

Some more . . ., please	**Jeg vil gerne have mere . . .** yigh vil *ga*ir-ner ha *me*re . . .
coffee	**kaffe** *ku*ffer
tea	**the** tay
bread	**brød** *bre*rthe
butter	**smør** smer
jam	**syltetøj** *si*lter-toy
May I have a boiled egg?	**Må jeg få et blødkogt æg?** maw yigh *fa*w it *ble*rthe-kogt aig

LIKELY REACTIONS

Have you an identity document?	**Har Det ID-kort eller pas?** har day ee-day-kort eller pas
What is your name? [see p. 17]	**Hvad er Deres navn?** va air dair-es noun
Sorry, we're full	**Desværre, alt er optaget** desvair alt air op-tay-et
I haven't any rooms left	**Jeg har ingen ledige værelser** yigh har eeng-en lay-thee-er vair-el-ser
Do you want to have a look?	**Vil De se det?** vil dee say day
How many people is it for?	**Hvor mange personer er det til?** vor mung-er pair-soner air day til
From (7 o'clock) onwards	**Fra (klokken syv)** fra (clocken soo)
From (midday) onwards	**Fra (klokken tolv middag)** fra (clocken tol medda)
[For times, see p. 98]	
It's (30) kroner	**Det koster (tredive) kroner** day koster (trethe-ver) kroner
[For numbers, see p. 96]	

Camping and youth hostelling

ESSENTIAL INFORMATION

Camping

- Look for the words: **CAMPINGPLADS** and **TELTPLADS**.
- Danish campsites are divided into 1, 2 and 3 star categories. 3 star sites have every facility; about a hundred are so well equipped that they stay open all year.
- An international camping carnet, obtainable from motoring organizations, national camping clubs etc., is obligatory but the campsite manager is also authorized to issue temporary passes for those who have left home without one.
- If you cannot find a campsite and wish to use private land be sure to get the landowner's permission.

Youth hostels

- Look for the word:
  VANDRERHJEM or this sign
- You must have a YHA card.
  You can buy a guest card, however,
  if you have not obtained one
  but these are comparatively
  expensive.
- Danish youth hostels are also open
  to tourists with cars. Many have
  family rooms to take 4 to 8 people;
  these are very popular and
  should be booked in advance.
- Blankets and pillows are provided but guests must supply their
  own sheets. Most hostels have cooking facilities but it is also
  possible to buy meals at reasonable prices.
- For buying and replacing camping equipment, see p. 48.

WHAT TO SAY

Have you any vacancies?	**Har De ledige pladser?**
	har dee *lay*-thee-er pl*a*sser
It's for . . .	**Det er til . . .**
	day air til . . .
one adult/person	**en voksen/person**
	ain v*o*ksen/pair-s*o*ne
two adults/people	**to voksne/personer**
	t*oe* voks*ne*r/pair-s*o*-ner
and one child	**og et barn**
	o *i*t barn
and two children	**og to børn**
	o t*oe* burn
It's for . . .	**Det er for . . .**
	day air for . . .
one night	**en nat**
	*ai*n nat
one week	**en uge**
	*ai*n *oo*-er
How much is it . . .	**Hvor meget koster det . . .**
	vor my-et k*o*ster day . . .
for the tent?	**for teltet?**
	for t*e*ltet

Danish

How much is it . . .	**Hvor meget koster det . . .**
	vor my-et koster day . . .
for the caravan?	**for campingvognen?**
	for camping-vonen
for the car?	**for bilen?**
	for beelen
for the electricity?	**for elektricitet?**
	for elektree-seetate
per person?	**per person?**
	pair pair-sone
per day/night?	**per dag/nat?**
	pair day/nat
May I look around?	**Må jeg se mig omkring?**
	maw yigh say my omkreng
Do you provide anything . . .	**Kan man få noget . . .**
	kan man faw no-et . . .
to eat?	**at spise?**
	at spee-ser
to drink?	**at drikke?**
	at dregger
Do you have . . .	**Er her . . .**
	air hair . . .
a bar?	**en bar?**
	ain bar
hot showers?	**brusebad?**
	broo-ser-bathe
a kitchen?	**et køkken?**
	it kerg-en
a laundry?	**et vaskeri?**
	it vasker-ree
a restaurant?	**en restaurant?**
	ain restorung
a shop?	**en forretning?**
	ain forretning
a swimming pool?	**et svømmebassin?**
	it svermer-basseng

[*For food shopping, see p. 54, and for eating and drinking out, see p. 66*]

Where are . . .	**Hvor er . . .**
	vor air . . .
the dustbins?	**affaldsspandene?**
	ow-fels-spanner-ner

the showers?	**brusebadet?**
	broo-ser-bathet
the toilets?	**toiletterne?**
	toiletter-ner
At what time must one . . .	**Hvornår skal man . . .**
	vornor skal man . . .
go to bed?	**gå i seng?**
	gaw ee seng
get up?	**stå op?**
	staw op
Please, have you got . . .	**De har vel ikke . . .**
	dee har vel igger . . .
a broom?	**en kost?**
	ain koast
a corkscrew?	**en proptrækker?**
	ain prop-trekker
a drying-up cloth?	**et viskestykke?**
	it veesker-stookker
a fork?	**en gaffel?**
	ain gaffel
a fridge?	**et køleskab?**
	it curler-skab
a frying pan?	**en stegepande?**
	ain sty-er-panner
an iron?	**et strygejern?**
	it stroo-yer-yairn
a knife?	**en kniv?**
	ain k-neev
a plate?	**en tallerken?**
	ain tallair-ken
a saucepan?	**en gryde?**
	ain groo-the
a teaspoon?	**en teske?**
	ain tay-skay
a tin-opener?	**en dåseåbner?**
	ain dawser-awbner
a bottle opener?	**en samfundshjælper?**
	ain samfoons-yelper
any washing-up liquid?	**noget opvaskemiddel?**
	no-et opvasker-meethel
any washing powder?	**noget vaskepulver?**
	no-et vasker-poolver

Problems

The toilet	**Toilettet**
	toilet-tet
The shower	**Bruseren**
	broo-ser-ren
The tap	**Hanen**
	hay-nen
The razor point	**Stikkontakten til barbermaskinen**
	stick-kon-tuckten til barbeer-maskeenen
The light	**Lyset**
	loo-set
. . . is not working	**. . . virker ikke**
	. . . veerker igger
My camping gas has run out	**Jeg har ikke mere campinggas**
	yigh har igger mere camping-gas

LIKELY REACTIONS

Have you an identity document?	**Har De legitimation?**
	har dee lay-gheet-ee-mashown
Your membership card, please	**Deres medlemskort**
	dair-es methe-lems-kort
What's your name?	**Hvad er Deres navn?**
[see p. 17]	va air dair-es noun
Sorry, we are full	**Desværre, alt er optaget**
	desvair alt air optay-et
How many people is it for?	**Hvor mange personer er det til?**
	vor mung-er pair-son-er air day til
How many nights is it for?	**Hvor mange nætter bliver De?**
	vor mung-er netter bleer dee
It's (20) kroner . . .	**Det koster (tyve) kroner . . .**
	day koster (too-ver) kroner . . .
per day/night	**per dag/nat**
	pair day/nat

[For numbers, see p. 96]

Rented accommodation:
problem solving

ESSENTIAL INFORMATION

- If you are looking for accommodation to rent, look out for:
  TIL LEJE (to let)
  LEJLIGHED (flat)
  VÆRELSE (room)
  HUS (house)
  SOMMERHUS (summer house)
- For arranging details of your let, see 'Hotel' p. 26.
- Key words you will need if renting on the spot:
  depositum (deposit)
  nøgle (key)
- Having arranged your own accommodation and arrived with the key, check the obvious basics that you take for granted at home.
  Electricity: The electric current is 220V AC (50 Hz). Sockets are the standard 2-pin continental type.
  Gas: Town gas or bottled gas? Butane gas must be kept indoors, propane gas must be kept outdoors.
  Cooker: Don't be surprised to find the grill inside the oven, or no grill at all.
  Toilet: Mains drainage or septic tank? Don't flush disposable nappies or anything else down the toilet if you are on a septic tank.
  Water: Find the stopcock. Check taps and plugs – they may not operate in the way you are used to. Check how to turn on (or off) the hot water.
  Windows: Check the method of opening and closing windows and shutters.
  Insects: Is an insecticide spray provided? If not, get one locally.
  Equipment: For buying or replacing equipment, see p. 48.
- You will probably have an official agent, but be clear in your own mind who to contact in an emergency, even if it is only a neighbour in the first instance.

WHAT TO SAY

My name is . . .   **Jeg hedder** . . .
                                yigh hither . . .

I'm staying at . . .	**Jeg bor . . .**
	yigh bore . . .
They've cut off . . .	**Der er lukket for . . .**
	dair air look-ket for . . .
the electricity	**elektriciteten**
	elektree-see-taten
the gas	**gassen**
	gassen
the water	**vandet**
	vannet
Is there . . . in the area?	**Er der . . . i nærheden?**
	air dair . . . ee nair-hethen
an electrician	**en elektriker**
	ain elektree-ker
a plumber	**en VVS mand**
	ain VVS man
a gas fitter	**en gasarbejder**
	ain gas-ar-byder
Where is . . .	**Hvor er . . .**
	vor air . . .
the fuse box?	**elmåleren?**
	el-maw-lern
the stopcock?	**hovedhanen?**
	ho-ethe-hay-nen
the boiler?	**fyret?**
	foo-ret
the water heater?	**varmtvandsbeholderen?**
	varmt-vans-beholleren
Is there . . .	**Er der . . .**
	air dair . . .
bottled gas?	**flaskegas?**
	flasker-gas
a septic tank?	**septisk tank?**
	septisk tunk
central heating?	**centralvarme?**
	centrahl-varmer
The cooker	**Komfuret**
	komfooret
The hairdrier	**Hårtørreren**
	hor-tern
The heating	**Varmeanlægget**
	varmer-an-lay-get

The iron	**Strygejernet**
	stroo-yer-yairnet
The pilot light	**Vågeblusset**
	vo-er-bloosset
The refrigerator	**Køleskabet**
	curler-skabet
The telephone	**Telefonen**
	telefonen
The toilet	**Toilettet**
	toilet-tet
The washing machine	**Vaskemaskinen**
	vasker-maskeenen
. . . is not working	**. . . virker ikke**
	. . . veerker igger
Where can I get . . .	**Hvor kan jeg få . . .**
	vor kan yigh faw . . .
a bottle of butane gas?	**noget flaskegas?**
	no-et flaskergas
a fuse?	**en sikring?**
	ain sikring
an insecticide spray?	**en insektspray?**
	ain insektspray
a light bulb?	**en pære?**
	ain pair
The drain	**Afløbet**
	ow-lerbet
The sink	**Vasken**
	vasken
The toilet	**Toilettet**
	toilet-tet
. . . is blocked	**. . . er stoppet**
	. . . air stoppet
The gas is leaking	**Gasledningen er utæt**
	gas-lethe-ningen air oo-tet
Can you mend it straightaway?	**Kan De reparere det nu?**
	kan dee reparair day noo
When can you mend it?	**Hvornår kan De reparere det?**
	vornor kan dee reparair day
How much do I owe you?	**Hvor meget bliver det?**
	vor my-et bleer day
When is the rubbish collected?	**Hvornår hentes affaldet?**
	vornor hen-tes ow-fallet

Danish

LIKELY REACTIONS

What's your name?	**Hvad er Deres navn?**
	va air dair-es noun
What's your address?	**Hvad er Deres adresse?**
	va air dair-es adresser
There's a shop . . .	**Der er en forretning . . .**
	dair air ain forretning . . .
in town	**i byen**
	ee boo-en
in the village	**i landsbyen**
	ee lans-boo-en
I can't come . . .	**Jeg kan ikke komme . . .**
	yigh kan igger kommer . . .
today	**i dag**
	ee day
this week	**i denne uge**
	ee denner oo-er
until Monday	**før mandag**
	fur manda
I can come . . .	**Jeg kan komme . . .**
	yigh kan kommer . . .
on Tuesday	**på tirsdag**
	paw teers-da
when you want	**når De ønsker det**
	nor dee ernsker day
Every day	**Hver dag**
	vair day
Every other day	**Hveranden dag**
	vair-annen day
On Wednesdays	**Om onsdagen**
	om ons-day-en

[*For days of the week, see p. 99*]

General shopping

The chemist's

ESSENTIAL INFORMATION

- Look for the word
  APOTEK (chemist's)
  or this sign:
- There are two kinds of chemist in
  Denmark. The **APOTEK** (dispensing
  chemist) is the place to go for
  prescriptions, medicines, etc; toilet and
  household articles as well as patent
  medicines are sold at the **MATERIALIST**

  (chemist's shop) as well as at department stores and supermarkets.
- The **APOTEK** is open Monday to Thursday 9.00 a.m. – 5.30 p.m.,
  Friday 9.00 a.m. – 7.00 p.m. and Saturday 9.00 a.m. – 1.00 p.m.
- Chemists take it in turn to stay open over the weekend and all
  night. If the chemist is shut, a notice on the door will give the
  address of the nearest chemist on duty (**APOTEKERVAGT**).
- Finding a chemist, see p. 39.

WHAT TO SAY

I'd like . . .	**Jeg vil gerne have . . .** yigh vil g*air*-ner h*a* . . .
a box of aspirin	**en æske aspirin** ain esker aspir*in*
some Alka Seltzer	**nogle Alka Seltzer** n*o*-ler *a*lka seltzer·
some antiseptic	**et antiseptisk middel** it antiseptisk meethel
some bandage	**en bandage** ain band*air*-sher
some cotton wool	**noget vat** n*o*-et v*a*t
some eye drops	**nogle øjendråber** n*o*-ler *o*yen-draw-ber

Danish

I'd like . . .	**Jeg vil gerne have . . .**
	yigh vil gair-ner ha . . .
some inhalant	**et indhaleringsmiddel**
	it in-ha-lairings-meethel
some insect repellent	**en myggebalsam**
	ain moogger-bal-sam
some lip salve	**en læbepomade**
	ain lay-ber-pomay-ther
some sticking plaster	**noget hæfteplaster**
	no-et hefter-pluster
some throat pastilles	**nogle halspastiller**
	no-ler halss-pastill-er
some Vaseline	**noget Vaseline**
	no-et vaseleener
I'd like something for . . .	**Jeg vil gerne have noget mod . . .**
	yigh vil gair-ner ha no-et mothe
	. . .
bites (dog)	**bid**
	beethe
burns	**forbrændinger**
	forbrenning-er
a cold	**forkølelse**
	forker-lel-ser
constipation	**forstoppelse**
	forstoppel-ser
a cough	**hoste**
	ho-ster
diarrhoea	**diarré**
	dee-aray
earache	**ørepine**
	err-er-pee-ner
'flu	**influenza**
	influenza
sore gums	**ømme gummer**
	err-mer gommer
stings (mosquitoes, bees)	**stik**
	stick
sunburn	**solskoldning**
	sole-skol-ning
travel sickness	**køresyge**
	ker-er-soo-yer
I need . . .	**Jeg skal bruge . . .**
	yigh skal broo-er . . .

some baby food	**noget baby mad**
	no-et baby mathe
some contraceptives	**noget prævention**
	no-et pray-venshown
a deodorant	**en deodorant**
	ain day-o-dorunt
some disposable nappies	**nogle papirbleer**
	no-ler papeer-blee-er
some handcream	**en håndcreme**
	ain hon-craim
some lipstick	**en læbestift**
	ain lay-berstift
some make-up remover	**en rensecreme**
	ain ren-ser-craim
some paper tissues	**papirlommetørklæder**
	papeer-lommer-ter-klether
some razor blades	**barberblade**
	barbeer-blather
some safety pins	**sikkerhedsnåle**
	sikker-hethes-naw-ler
some sanitary towels	**en pakke bind**
	ain pukker bin
some soap	**et stykke sæbe**
	it stookker say-ber
some suntan oil/lotion	**en sololie/lotion**
	ain sole-oo-lee-er/lo-shown
some talcum powder	**noget talkum**
	no-et talkum
some Tampax	**en pakke Tampax**
	ain pukker tampax
some (soft) toilet paper	**(blødt) toiletpapir**
	(blert) toilet-papeer
some toothpaste	**en tube tandpasta**
	ain toober tann-pasta

[*For other essential expressions, see 'Shop talk', p. 50*]

Holiday items

ESSENTIAL INFORMATION

- Places to shop at and signs to look for:
  BOGHANDEL (bookshop, stationer)
  FOTO (films) **GAVEARTIKLER** (gift shop)
- In Copenhagen there are three major department stores:
  MAGASIN DU NORD, ILLUM and **DAELLS VAREHUS**

WHAT TO SAY

I'd like . . .	**Jeg vil gerne have . . .**
	yigh vil g*air*-ner h*a* . . .
a bag	**en taske**
	ain t*a*ssker
a beach ball	**en badebold**
	ain b*a*ther-bolld
a bucket	**en spand**
	ain sp*a*n
an English newspaper	**en engelsk avis**
	ain *e*ng-elsk av*ee*s
some envelopes	**nogle konvolutter**
	n*o*-ler konvo-l*oo*tter
a guide book	**en rejsehåndbog**
	ain r*y*e-ser-hon-bo
a map (of the area)	**et kort (over egnen)**
	it k*o*rt (o-er *eye*-nen)
some postcards	**nogle postkort**
	n*o*-ler p*o*sskort
a spade	**en spade**
	ain sp*ay*-ther
a sun hat	**en solhat**
	ain s*o*le-hat
some sunglasses	**et par solbriller**
	it par s*o*le-breller
an umbrella	**en paraply**
	ain parapl*oo*
some writing paper	**noget skrivepapir**
	n*o*-et skr*ee*ver-pap*ee*r

I'd like . . . [*show the camera*]	**Jeg vil gerne have . . .**
	yigh vil *gair*-ner ha . . .
a colour film	**en farvefilm**
	ain *far*ver-film
a black and white film	**en sort-hvid film**
	ain sort-*vee*the film
for prints	**til papirbilleder**
	til pa*peer*-beellether
for slides	**til lysbilleder**
	til *loos*-beellether
Please can you . . .	**Vil De være så venlig at . . .**
	vil dee *vair* saw venlee at . . .
develop/print this?	**fremkalde/lave aftryk?**
	fremkaller/*lay*-ver *ow*-trook
load the camera for me?	**sætte filmen i for mig?**
	setter filmen *ee* for my

[*For other essential expressions, see 'Shop talk' p. 50*]

The tobacconist's

ESSENTIAL INFORMATION

- Tobacco is sold where you see the signs:
  CIGARHANDLER and **TOBAKSHANDEL**
- To ask if there is one near by, see p. 22.
- Most usual brands of tobacco, cigars and cigarettes may be bought at supermarkets, kiosks and station restaurants.

WHAT TO SAY

A packet of cigarettes . . .	**En pakke cigaretter . . .**
	ain *pukker* cigar-*re*tter . . .
with filters	**med filter**
	methe filter
without filters	**uden filter**
	oo-then filter

Danish

A packet of cigarettes . . .	**En pakke cigaretter . . .**
	ain pukker cigar-retter . . .
king size	**king size**
	king size
menthol	**med menthol**
	methe mentol
Those up there . . .	**De der . . .**
	dee dair . . .
on the right	**til højre**
	til hoy-rer
on the left	**til venstre**
	til venstrer
These [*point*]	**De her**
	dee hair
Have you got . . .	**Har De . . .**
	har dee . . .
English cigarettes?	**engelske cigaretter?**
	eng-elsker cigar-retter
rolling tobacco?	**rulletobak?**
	rooller-tobuk
A packet of pipe tobacco	**En pakke pibetobak**
	ain pukker peeber-tobuk
This one [*point*]	**Den her**
	den hair
A cigar, please	**En cigar**
	ain cigar
Some cigars, please	**Nogle cigarer**
	no-ler cigar-er
Those [*point*]	**De der**
	dee dair
A box of matches	**En æske tændstikker**
	ain esker ten-sticker
A packet of pipe cleaners	**En pakke piberensere**
	ain pukker peeber-ren-ser
A packet of flints [*show lighter*]	**Nogle sten**
	no-ler sten
Lighter fuel	**Noget tændvæske**
	no-et ten-vesker
Lighter gas	**En gaspatron**
	ain gas-patroone

[*For other essential expressions, see 'Shop talk' p. 50*]

Buying clothes

ESSENTIAL INFORMATION

- Look for:
  DAMETØJ (women's clothes)
  HERRETØJ (men's clothes)
  BØRNETØJ (children's clothes)
  SKOTØJSFORRETNING (shoe shop)
- Don't buy without being measured first or without trying things on.
- Don't rely on conversion charts of clothing sizes (see p. 335).
- If you are buying for someone else, take their measurements with you.

WHAT TO SAY

I'd like . . .	**Jeg vil gerne have . . .**
	yigh vil g*ai*r-ner h*a* . . .
an anorak	**en anorak**
	ain anor*u*ck
a belt	**et bælte**
	it b*e*lter
a bikini	**en bikini**
	ain bik*i*ni
a bra	**en BH**
	ain beh*aw*
a pair of briefs	**et par trusser**
	it par tr*oo*sser
a swimming cap	**en badehætte**
	ain b*a*ther-hetter
a cardigan	**en cardigan**
	ain c*a*rdigan
a coat	**en frakke**
	ain fr*a*kker
a dress	**en kjole**
	ain k-y*o*ler
a hat	**en hat**
	ain h*a*t
a jacket	**en jakke**
	ain y*a*kker

I'd like . . .	Jeg vil gerne have . . .
	yigh vil gair-ner ha . . .
a pair of jeans	**et par cowboybukser**
	it par cowboy-bawkser
a jumper	**en strikket bluse**
	ain strikket bloo-ser
a nightdress	**en natkjole**
	ain nat-k-yoler
a pullover	**en pullover**
	ain pullo-er
a pair of pyjamas	**et pyjamas**
	it pee-ya-mas
a raincoat	**en regnfrakke**
	ain rine-frakker
a blouse	**en bluse**
	ain bloo-ser
a shirt (men)	**en skjorte**
	ain sk-yorter
a suit (women)	**en dragt**
	ain drukt
a suit (men)	**en habit**
	ain habeet
a swimsuit	**en badedragt**
	ain bather-drukt
a T-shirt	**en T-shirt**
	ain T-shirt
a pair of tights	**et par strømpebukser**
	it par stroom-per-bawkser
a pair of trousers	**et par bukser**
	it par bawkser
I'd like a pair of . . .	Jeg vil gerne have et par . . .
	yigh vil gair-ner ha it par . . .
gloves	**handsker**
	hansker
socks (short/long)	**sokker (korte/lange)**
	sokker (korter/lun-ger)
stockings	**strømper**
	stroomper
shoes	**sko**
	sko
canvas shoes	**lærredssko**
	laireths-sko

sandals	**sandaler**
	sand*ay*-ler
beach shoes	**strandsko**
	str*u*n-sko
smart shoes	**elegante sko**
	eleg*a*nter sk*o*
moccasins	**mokkasiner**
	mokkas*ee*ner
My size is . . .	**Jeg bruger størrelse . . .**
	yigh br*oo*-er st*i*rl-ser . . .

[*For numbers, see p. 96*]

Can you measure me, please?	**Vil De tage mine mål?**
	vil dee t*ay* meaner m*aw*l
Can I try it on?	**Må jeg prøve den?**
	maw yigh pr*oo*ver den
It's for a present	**Det er til en gave**
	day air til ain g*ay*-ver
These are the measurements. . .	**Her er målene . . .**
[*show written*]	hair air m*aw*ler-ner . . .
bust/chest	**brystmål**
	br*oo*st-m*aw*l
collar	**halsvidde**
	h*a*lss-veeder
hip	**hoftemål**
	h*o*fter-mawl
leg	**benlængde**
	b*ee*n-leng-der
waist	**taljemål**
	t*a*l-yer-mawl
Have you got something . . .	**Har De noget . . .**
	har dee n*o*-et . . .
in black?	**i sort?**
	ee s*o*rt
in white?	**i hvidt?**
	ee v*ee*t
in grey?	**i gråt?**
	ee gr*o*t
in blue?	**i blåt?**
	ee bl*o*t
in brown?	**i brunt?**
	ee br*oo*nt
in pink?	**i lyserødt?**
	ee l*oo*-ser-r*oo*t

Danish

Have you got something . . .	Har De noget . . .
	har dee no-et . . .
in green?	i grønt?
	ee grernt
in red?	i rødt?
	ee root
in yellow?	i gult?
	ee goolt
in this colour? [point]	i den farve?
	ee den farver
in cotton?	i bomuld?
	ee bom-ool
in denim?	i cowboystof?
	ee cowboy-stof
in leather?	i skind?
	ee skin
in nylon?	i nylon?
	ee nylon
in suede?	i ruskind?
	ee roo-skin
in wool?	i uld?
	ee ool
in this material? [point]	i det stof her?
[For other essential expressions, see 'Shop talk', p. 50]	ee day stof hair

Replacing equipment

ESSENTIAL INFORMATION

- Look for these shop signs:
  ISENKRAM (hardware)
  EL-INSTALLATØREN (electrical goods)
- In a supermarket look for this display:
  HUSHOLDNINGSARTIKLER (household cleaning materials)
- To ask the way to a shop, see p. 000.
- At a campsite try their shop first.

WHAT TO SAY

Have you got . . .	Har De . . .
	har dee. . .
an adaptor?	**et mellemstik?**
[show appliance]	it mellemstick
a bottle of butane gas?	**flaskegas/butan?**
	flasker-gas/bootan
a bottle of propane gas?	**flaskegas/propan?**
	flasker-gas/propan
a bottle opener?	**en samfundshjælper?**
	ain samfoons-yelper
a corkscrew?	**en proptrækker?**
	ain prop-trekker
any disinfectant?	**et disinfektionsmiddel?**
	it disinfek-shown-smeethel
any disposable cups?	**engangskrus?**
	ain-gungs-kroos
a drying-up cloth?	**et viskestykke?**
	it veesker-stookker
any forks?	**nogle gafler?**
	no-ler gafler
a fuse? [show old one]	**en sikring?**
	ain sik-ring
an insecticide spray?	**en insektspray?**
	ain insektspray
a paper kitchen roll?	**en køkkenrulle?**
	ain kerg-en-rooller
any knives?	**nogle knlve?**
	no-ler k-neever
a light bulb? [show old one]	**en pære?**
	ain pair
a plastic bucket?	**en plast spand?**
	ain plast-span
a scouring pad?	**en grydesvamp?**
	ain groo-the-svump
a spanner?	**en skruenøgle?**
	ain skroo-er-noy-ler
a sponge?	**en svamp?**
	ain svump
any string?	**noget snor?**
	no-et snor

Danish

Have you got . . .	Har De . . .
	har dee. . .
any tent pegs?	**nogle teltpløkke?**
	no-ler telt-plookker
a tin-opener?	**en dåseåbner?**
	ain daw-ser-awbner
a torch?	**en lommelygte?**
	ain lommer-loog-ter
any torch batteries?	**lommelygtebatterier?**
	lommer-loog-ter-batteree-er
a universal plug (for the sink)?	**en bundprop?**
	ain boonprop
a washing line?	**en tøjsnor?**
	ain toy-snor
any washing powder?	**vaskepulver?**
	vasker-poolver
a washing-up brush?	**en opvaskebørste?**
	ain opvasker-burster
any washing-up liquid?	**et opvaskemiddel?**
[*For other essential expressions, see 'Shop talk', p. 50*]	it opvasker-meethel

Shop talk

ESSENTIAL INFORMATION

- Danish coins: see illustration
  Danish notes: 20, 50, 100, 500 and 1,000 kroner.
- Know how to say the important weights and measures.
  You will hear grams, kilos and pounds in shops and markets.
  [*For numbers, see p. 96*]

50 grams	**halvtreds gram**
	hal-tress grum
100 grams	**hundrede gram**
	hoonrer-ther grum
200 grams	**to hundrede gram**
	toe hoonrer-ther grum

½ lb (250 grams)	**et halvt pund**
	it h*u*lt p*oo*n
1 lb	**et pund**
	it p*oo*n
1 kilo	**et kilo**
	it k*i*lo
2 kilos	**to kilo**
	t*oe* k*i*lo
½ litre	**en halv liter**
	ain hal l*ee*ter
1 litre	**en liter**
	ain l*ee*ter
2 litres	**to liter**
	t*oe* l*ee*ter

- In small shops don't be surprised if customers, as well as the shop assistant, say 'hello' and 'goodbye' to you.

CUSTOMER

I'm just looking	**Jeg kigger bare**
	yigh k*i*gger b*a*r-er
Excuse me	**Undskyld**
	*o*n-skool
How much is this/that?	**Hvor meget koster den her/den der?**
	vor my-et k*o*ster den h*ai*r/den d*ai*r
What's that/those?	**Hvad er det?**
	v*a* air day
Is there a discount?	**Er der rabat?**
	air dair ra-b*a*t
I'd like that, please	**Jeg vil gerne have den/det**
	yigh vil g*ai*r-ner ha den/d*a*y
Not that	**Ikke den/det**
	*i*gger den/d*a*y
Like that	**Ligesom den/det**
	l*ee*-er-som den/d*a*y
That's enough, thank you	**Det er nok**
	day air nok
More, please	**Lidt mere**
	lit m*e*re
Less, please	**Lidt mindre**
	lit m*i*ndrer

That's fine	**Det er fint**
	day air *fe*ent
OK	**Godt**
	got
I won't take it, thank you	**Jeg vil ikke have den/det**
	yigh vil *igg*er h*a* den/day
It's not right	**Det er ikke det rigtige**
	day air *igg*er day r*e*gtee-er
Have you got something . . .	**Har De noget . . .**
	har dee n*o*-et . . .
better?	**bedre?**
	b*e*the-rer
cheaper?	**billigere?**
	b*i*llee-er
different?	**andet?**
	*a*nnet
larger?	**større?**
	st*i*rrer
smaller?	**mindre?**
	m*i*ndrer
At what time do you . . .	**Hvornår . . .**
	vorn*o*r . . .
open?	**åbner De?**
	*aw*bner dee
close?	**lukker De?**
	l*oo*kker dee
Can I have a bag, please?	**Jeg vil gerne have en bærepose**
	yigh vil g*ai*r-ner h*a* ain b*a*re-po-ser
Can I have a receipt?	**Jeg vil gerne have en kvittering**
	yigh vil g*ai*r-ner h*a* ain kveett*ai*ring
Do you take . . .	**Tager De . . .**
	tar dee . . .
English/American money?	**engelske/amerikanske penge?**
	*e*ng-elsker/amerik*a*nsker p*e*ng-er
travellers' cheques?	**rejsechecks?**
	r*ye*-ser-shecks
credit cards?	**kreditkort?**
	kred*i*tkort
I'd like . . .	**Jeg vil gerne have . . .**
	yigh vil g*ai*r-ner h*a* . . .
one like that	**sådan en**
	s*u*dden ain

Danish

SHOP ASSISTANT

Can I help you?	**Kan jeg hjælpe Dem?**
	kan yigh yelper dem
What would you like?	**Hvad skulle det være?**
	va skooller day vair
Will that be all?	**Var der ellers andet?**
	var dair ellers annet
Anything else?	**Ellers andet?**
	ellers annet
Would you like it wrapped?	**Skal det pakkes ind?**
	skal day pukkes in
Sorry, none left	**Jeg beklager, der er ikke flere**
	yigh beklay-er dair air igger flee-er
I haven't got any	**Jeg har ingen**
	yigh har ing-en
I haven't got any more	**Jeg har ikke flere**
	yigh har igger flee-er
How many do you want?	**Hvor mange ønsker De?**
	vor mung-er ern-sker dee
How much do you want?	**Hvor meget ønsker De?**
	vor my-et ern-sker dee
Is this enough?	**Er det nok?**
	air day nok

Shopping for food

Bread

ESSENTIAL INFORMATION

- Finding a baker's, see p. 20.
- Key words to look out for:
  BAGERI (baker's)
  BAGER (baker)
  BRØD OG KAGER (bread and cakes)

- Supermarkets of any size and general stores nearly always sell bread.
- Bakeries are open from 7.00 a.m. to 5.30 p.m. weekdays, 7.00 a.m. to 2.00 p.m. on Saturdays. Bakers in a given area take it in turn to open very early on Sundays when many people buy **MORGENBRØD** – special rolls and Danish pastries.

WHAT TO SAY

A loaf (like that)	**(Sådan) et brød**
	(su_dden) it br_erthe_
A white loaf	**Et franskbrød**
	it fr_u_nsk-br_erthe_
a large one	**et stort**
	it st_o_rt
a small one	**et lille**
	it l_i_ller
A loaf of rye bread	**Et rugbrød**
	it r_oo_-br_erthe_
a whole one	**et helt**
	it h_e_lt
half a one	**et halvt**
	it h_u_lt
A bread roll	**Et rundstykke**
	it r_oo_n-st_oo_kker
A bun	**En bolle**
	ain b_o_ller
Four buns	**Fire boller**
	f_ee_rer b_o_ller
A French stick	**En flute**
	ain fl_oo_ter
A wholemeal loaf	**Et grovbrød**
	it gr_ow_-br_erthe_

[*For other essential expressions, see 'Shop talk' p. 50*]

Danish

Cakes

ESSENTIAL INFORMATION

- Key words to look for:
  BAGERI (baker's)
  BAGER (baker)
  KONDITORI (cake shop, often with tea/coffee shop attached)
- To find a cake shop, see p. 21.

WHAT TO SAY

The type of cakes you find in the shops may vary from region to region but the following are the most common; cake is *not* bought per slice but gâteau is.

wienerbrød	Danish pastry
veener-brerthe	
kringle	yeast pastry
krengler	
en smørkage	butter cake/pastry
ain smer-kayer	
en tærte	tart
ain tairter	
en formkage	plain/fruit cake (to slice)
ain form-kayer	
en lagkage	layercake/gâteau
ain la-oo-kayer	
et stykke kransekage	almond cake
it stookker kran-ser-kayer	
en flødekage	cream cake
ain flerther-kayer	
småkager	biscuits
smokkayer	

Ice-cream and sweets

ESSENTIAL INFORMATION

- Key words to look for:
  IS (ice-cream)
  ISKIOSK (ice-cream shop)
  CHOKOLADEFORRETNING (sweet shop)
  BAGERI (baker's)
- Best known ice-cream brands are:
  FRISKO
  PREMIERE
- When buying ice-cream, specify what price cone or tub you want.
- Pre-packed sweets are available in general stores and supermarkets.

WHAT TO SAY

A . . . ice, please	**En . . . is**
	ain . . . *ee*s
caramel	**nougat**
	n*oo*ga
chocolate	**chokolade**
	shoko-l*ai*ther
lemon	**citron**
	citr*o*ne
mocha	**mokka**
	m*o*kka
strawberry	**jordbær**
	y*o*r-bear
vanilla	**vanille**
	van*i*lla
One (5 kr) cone	**En vaffel til fem kroner**
	ain v*u*ffel til f*e*m kr*o*ner
Two (7 kr) tubs	**To bægre til syv kroner**
	t*oe* b*a*re til s*oo* kr*o*ner
A lollipop	**En slikkepind**
	ain sl*i*kker-pin
A packet of . . .	**En pakke . . .**
	ain p*u*kker . . .

Danish

100 grams of . . .	**Hundrede gram . . .**
	hoonrer-ther gr*u*m . . .

[*For further details of Danish weights, see 'Shop talk' p. 50*]

chewing gum	**tyggegummi**
	t*oo*gger-g*oo*mmee
chocolates	**chokolade**
	shoko l*ai*thcr
liquorice	**lakrids**
	lakr*i*s
mints	**pebermynte**
	pev-er-m*oo*nter
sweets	**bolsjer**
	b*o*ll-sher
toffees	**karameller**
	karam*e*ller

[*For other essential expressions, see 'Shop talk' p. 50*]

Picnic food

ESSENTIAL INFORMATION

- Key words to look out for:
  DELIKATESSEN
  PÅLÆG   delicatessen
  SLAGTER (butcher)

WHAT TO SAY

Two slices of . . .	**To skiver . . .**
	t*oe* sk*ee*ver . . .
roast beef	**roast beef**
	roast beef
roast pork	**flæskesteg**
	fl*e*sker-sty
ham (cooked)	**skinke**
	sk*i*nker
ham (smoked)	**røget skinke**
	rer-yet sk*i*nker

saveloy sausage	**cervelatpølse**
	ser-verlat-pullser
salami	**spegepølse**
	spy-er-pullser
150 grams of . . .	**Hundredeoghalvtreds gram . . .**
	hoonrer-ther-o-hal-tress grum. . .
potato salad	**kartoffelsalat**
	kartoffel-salat
herring salad	**sildesalat**
	siller-salat
Russian salad	**italiensk salat**
	ee-tay-lee-ensk salat
mackerel salad	**makrelsalat**
	makrel-salat

You might also like to try some of these:

en røget makrel
ain rer-yet makrel
a smoked mackerel

en røget ål
ain rer-yet awl
a smoked eel

en røget sild
ain rer-yet sill
a smoked herring

en frikadelle
ain frikka-deller
tasty pork and veal meat ball

en fiskefrikadelle
ain fisker-frikka-deller
as above, made with fish

et stykke medisterpølse
it stookker medister-pullser
piece of pork sausage

**en rødspættefilet med
remoulade**
ain rerthe-spetter-fee-lay
 methe rem-o-laither
fried plaice fillet with tangy
 mayonnaise dressing

rullepølse
roollcr-pullser
rolled pork

leverpostej
laverpo-sty
liver pâté, often sold warm

Havarti ost
havarti oast
Havarti cheese (mild and mature)

Samsø ost
samser oast
Samsø cheese

Castello ost
castello oast
Castello, soft blue-veined cheese

Fruit and vegetables

ESSENTIAL INFORMATION

- Key words to look out for:
  FRUGT (fruit)
  GRØNTHANDLER (greengrocer)
  GRØNTSAGER (vegetables)
[*For details of Danish weights, see 'Shop talk' p. 50*]

WHAT TO SAY

1 kilo (2 lbs) of . . .	**Et kilo . . .**
	it kilo . . .
apples	**æbler**
	eb-ler
bananas	**bananer**
	ba-*nai*ner
cherries	**kirsebær**
	k*eer*-ser-bear
grapes	**vindruer**
	v*een*-droo-er
oranges	**appelsiner**
	appel-*see*ner
pears	**pærer**
	p*ear*
peaches	**ferskner**
	f*airs*k-ner
plums	**blommer**
	bl*omm*er
raspberries	**hindbær**
	h*in*-bear
strawberries	**jordbær**
	y*or*-bear
A pineapple, please	**En ananas**
	ain *ann*anas
A grapefruit	**En grapefrugt**
	ain gr*ape*-frookt
A melon	**En melon**
	ain mel*one*

A watermelon	**En vandmelon**
	ain van-melone
½ kilo of . . .	**Et halvt kilo . . .**
	it hult kilo . . .
carrots	**gulerødder**
	gooller-rerther
green beans	**grønne bønner**
	grerner burnner
leeks	**porrer**
	pore
mushrooms	**champignoner**
	sham-peen-yong-er
onions	**løg**
	loy
peas	**ærter**
	air-ter
potatoes	**kartofler**
	kartofler
red cabbage	**rødkål**
	rerthe-kawl
spinach	**spinat**
	spee-nat
tomatoes	**tomater**
	toe-mater
A bunch of . . .	**Et bundt . . .**
	it boont . . .
chives	**purløg**
	poor-loy
radishes	**radiser**
	ra-disser
A head of garlic	**Et hvidløg**
	it veethe-loy
A lettuce	**Et salathoved**
	it salat-ho-ethe
A cauliflower	**Et blomkål**
	it blom-kawl
A cabbage	**Et hvidkål**
	it veethe-kawl
A cucumber	**En agurk**
	ain agoork
Like that, please	**Sådan en/et**
	sudden ain/it

[*For other essential expressions, see 'Shop talk' p. 50*]

Danish

Meat

ESSENTIAL INFORMATION

- Key words to look out for:
  SLAGTER (butcher)
- The diagrams opposite are to help you make sense of labels on counters and supermarket displays and decide which cut or joint to have. Translations do not help and you don't need to say the Danish word involved.
- You will find that lamb and especially mutton are much less popular in Denmark. The butcher's display will tell you what is available.

WHAT TO SAY

For a joint, choose the type of meat and then say how many people it is for:

I'd like . . .	**Jeg vil gerne have . . .**
	yigh vil *gair*-ner ha . . .
some beef	**noget oksekød**
	no-et *o*kser-kethe
some lamb	**noget lammekød**
	no-et *lu*mmer-kethe
some pork	**noget flæskekød**
	no-et *fle*sker-kethe
some veal	**noget kalvekød**
	no-et *ka*l-ver-kethe
A joint . . .	**En steg . . .**
	ain sty . . .
for four people	**til fire personer**
	til *fe*erer pair-*so*-ner
I'd like . . .	**Jeg vil gerne have . . .**
	yigh vil *gair*-ner ha . . .
some steak	**noget oksesmåkød**
	no-et *o*kser-smaw-kerthe
some liver	**noget lever**
	no-et *la*ver
some kidneys	**nogle nyrer**
	no-ler *noo*-rer
some sausages	**nogle pølser**
	no-ler *pu*llser

Beef Oksekød

1 Mellemskært	6 Bov
2 Tykkam	7 Tværreb
3 Højreb	8 Bryst
4 Tyndsteg	9 Låret
5 Tyksteg	10 Skank

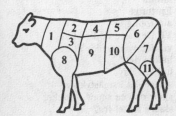

Veal Kaluekød

1 Mellemskært	8 Skank
2 Mellemkam	9 Bryst
3 Tyndbov	10 Slaget
4 Kam	11 Skank
5 Nyresteg	
6 Mellemkølle	
7 Skankekølle	

Pork Flæskekød

1 Nakkekam	6 Stegeflæsk
2 Koteletstykket	7 Kogeflæsk
3 Kam	8 Skinke
4 Halssnitte	9 Skank
5 Bov	

Lamb Lammekød

1 Hals med nakke
2 Kam (koteletter)
3 Sadel (nyrestykke)
4 Bov
5 Bryst
6 Kølle

Danish

Two veal escalopes	**To kalveschnitzler**
	t*o*e k*a*l-ver-sn*ee*ts-ler
Three pork chops	**Tre svinekoteletter**
	tray sv*ee*ner kotter-letter
Four lamb chops	**Fire lammekoteletter**
	f*ee*rer l*u*mmer-kotter-letter

You may also want:

A chicken	**En kylling**
	ain k*oo*-ling
A duck	**En and**
	ain *a*n
A tongue	**En tunge**
	ain t*oo*ng-er
Please can you . . .	**Vil De være venlig at . . .**
	vil dee v*ai*r v*e*nlee at . . .
mince it?	**hakke det?**
	h*u*kker day
dice it?	**skære det i småstykker?**
	sk*ai*r day ee smaw-st*oo*kker
trim the fat?	**skære fedtet fra?**
	sk*ai*r f*i*t-tet fra

[*For other essential expressions see 'Shop talk' p. 50*]

Fish

ESSENTIAL INFORMATION

- The word to look out for: **FISKEHANDLER** (fishmonger's)
- Some supermarkets have a fresh fish counter.

WHAT TO SAY

Purchase large fish and small shellfish by weight:

½ kilo of . . .	**Et halvt kilo . . .**
	it h*u*lt k*i*lo . . .
cod	**torsk**
	torsk

eel	**ål** *aw*l
haddock	**kuller** k*oo*ller
herring	**sild** sill
plaice	**rødspætte** rerthe-spetter
turbot	**pighvarre** p*i*g-var
mussels	**muslinger** m*oo*sling-er
prawns	**Nordsørejer** n*or*-sir-*rye*-er
shrimps	**rejer** *rye*-er
A piece of . . .	**Et stykke . . .** it st*oo*kker . . .
salmon	**laks** luks

For some shellfish and 'frying pan' fish specify the number you want:

A crab, please	**En krabbe** ain kr*u*bber
A lobster	**En hummer** ain h*oo*mmer
A trout	**En ørred** ain *e*rthe
A sole	**En søtunge** ain s*ir*-toong-er
A mackerel	**En makrel** ain makrel

Other essential expressions [*see also p. 50*]

Please can you . . .	**Vil De være venlig at . . .** vil dee v*air* venlee at . . .
take the head off?	**skære hovedet af?** sk*air* ho-er-thet *ay*
clean them?	**rense dem?** ren-ser dem
fillet them?	**filere dem?** feel*air* dem

[*For other essential expressions, see 'Shop talk' p. 50*]

Danish

Eating and drinking out

Ordering a drink

ESSENTIAL INFORMATION

- The places to ask for:
  EN BAR/PUB/CAFÉ/KRO (in the country)
  EN BODEGA/VINSTUE (wine bar)
  ET KONDITORI (coffee/pastry shop)
- There is waiter service in all pubs, cafés and wine bars. In many places you can also drink at the bar if you wish.
- When the bill is presented the amount will be inclusive of service and **VAT (MOMS)**.
- Pubs, cafés and bars serve drinks and cold food and are open all day and often until the early hours of the morning.
- Wine bars serve non-alcoholic and alcoholic drinks and a choice of simple meals.
- Coffee shops serve coffee/tea and very good Danish pastries. Cream/milk is always served separately with coffee or tea.
- Children are allowed into bars.

WHAT TO SAY

I'll have . . ., please	**Jeg vil gerne have . . .**
	yigh vil ga*i*r-ner ha . . .
a black coffee	**en kop kaffe**
	ain kop k*u*ffer
a tea	**en kop te**
	ain kop t*a*y
with milk	**med mælk**
	methe m*e*lk
with lemon	**med citron**
	methe citr*o*ne
a glass of milk	**et glas mælk**
	it glas m*e*lk
a hot chocolate	**en kop (varm) chokolade**
	ain kop (varm) shoko-l*ai*ther
a mineral water	**en mineralvand**
	ain miner*a*l-van

a lemonade	**en limonade**
	ain leemo-*nai*ther
a Coca Cola	**en Coca Cola**
	ain coca *co*la
an orangeade	**en appelsinvand**
	ain appelseenvan
an orange juice	**en appelsinjuice**
	ain appel-*see*njuice
a grape juice	**en druesaft**
	ain *droo*er-saft
an apple juice	**en æblemost**
	ain *eb*ler-mosst
a beer	**en øl**
	ain *erl*
a draught beer	**en fadøl**
	ain *fa*the-erl
a half	**en lille**
	ain *lil*ler
an alcohol-free beer	**en lys øl**
	ain loos erl
a lager	**en pilsner**
	ain *pil*sner
A glass of . . .	**Et glas . . .**
	it glas . . .
Two glasses of . . .	**To glas . . .**
	toe glas . . .
red wine	**rødvin**
	rerthe-*veen*
white wine	**hvidvin**
	veethe-*veen*
rosé wine	**rosévin**
	rosé-*veen*
dry	**tør**
	ter
sweet	**sød**
	serthe
A bottle of . . .	**En flaske . . .**
	ain *flas*ker . . .
sparkling wine	**mousserende vin**
	moos-*sai*ren-ner veen
champagne	**champagne**
	shampan-*yer*

Danish

A whisky	**En whisky**
	ain whisky
with ice	**med is**
	methe *ees*
with water	**med vand**
	methe v*a*n
with soda	**med dansk vand**
	methe dansk v*a*n
A gin	**En gin**
	ain gin
with tonic	**med tonic**
	methe tonic
with bitter lemon	**med bitter lemon**
	methe bitter lemon
A brandy/cognac	**en cognac**
	ain cognac

The following are local drinks you may like to try:

snaps/akvavit snaps/akva-v*ee*t	a strong spirit distilled from potatoes and almost always enjoyed with food. There are many different kinds of snaps, flavoured with various herbs and spices
Cherry Heering cherry h*ee*ring	a famous cherry liqueur named after the Heering family.
Kirsebærvin K*ee*rser-bear-v*ee*n	a cherry-based dessert wine
Solbærrom solbear-rom	a blackcurrant-based dessert wine: both these wines are often served with ice as an apéritif
Malt øl m*a*l-terl	a dark, sweet malt beer
Carlsberg Elefant øl c*a*rlsbear elef*a*nt erl	
Tuborg Guld Export t*oo*bore g*oo*l export	extra strong beers
Påskebryg p*a*w-sker-br*oo*k	a strong beer brewed only at Easter
Julebryg y*oo*le-br*oo*k	a strong beer brewed only at Christmas

Other essential expressions:

Miss! [*this does not sound abrupt in Danish*]	**Frøken!** frer-ken
Waiter!	**Tjener!** ch*ai*ner
The bill, please	**Må jeg betale?** maw yigh bet*a*ler
How much does that come to?	**Hvor meget bliver det?** vor my-et bl*ee*r day
Is service included?	**Er det med betjening?** air day methe bech*ai*ning
Where is the toilet, please?	**Hvor er toilettet?** vor air toilet-tet

Ordering a snack

ESSENTIAL INFORMATION

- Look for any of these places:
  PØLSEVOGN (a street kiosk selling warm snacks)
  CAFETERIA
  GRILLBAR
- Apart from snacks, the cafeterias and grill bars also sell soft drinks, bottled beer, coffee and tea.
- If you want a 'take-away' sandwich lunch look out for **SMØRRE-BRØDSFORRETNING**. Here you can buy an assortment of Danish open sandwiches from the display.
- For cakes, see p. 56; for ice-cream, see p. 57; for picnic-type snacks, see p. 58.

WHAT TO SAY

I'll have . . . please	**Jeg vil gerne have . . .** yigh vil g*ai*r-ner h*a* . . .
a cheese sandwich	**et stykke brød med ost** it st*oo*kker br*er*the methe *oa*st
a ham sandwich	**et stykke smørrebrød med skinke** it st*oo*kker smerrer-br*er*the methe skinker

I'll have . . . please	**Jeg vil gerne have . . .**
	yigh vil *gair*-ner h*a* . . .
toasted cheese and ham sandwich	**toast med skinke og ost**
	t*oa*st methe sk*i*nker aw *oa*st
an omelet	**en omelet**
	ain omel*e*t
with mushrooms	**med champignoner**
	methe shampeen-*yo*ng-er

These are some other snacks you might like to try:

en rød pølse	red pork sausage
ain *re*rthe p*u*llser	
en stegt pølse	fried pork sausage
ain stegt p*u*llser	
en frikadelle	pork meat ball
ain frikka-d*e*ller	
en rødspætte filet	fried plaice fillet
ain *re*rthe-spetter fill*ay*	
en halv kylling	half a (roast) chicken
ain .hal k*oo*-ling	
en dansk bøf med løg	large hamburger with fried onions
ain dansk berf methe l*oy*	
et spejlæg	a fried egg
it spy-leg	
pommes frites	portion of chips
pom frits	
kartoffelsalat	potato salad
kartoffel-sal*a*t	

[*For other essential expressions see 'Ordering a drink', p. 66*]

In a restaurant

ESSENTIAL INFORMATION

- The place to ask for: **EN RESTAURANT** [*see p. 22*]
- You can eat at the following places:

RESTAURANT
HOTEL-RESTAURANT
BANEGÅRDSRESTAURANT (railway station restaurant)
MOTEL
CAFE-RESTAURANT (limited choice here)

- Most restaurants display the menu in the window and that is the only way to judge if a place is right for your needs.
- A service charge of 12–15% is always added to the bill.
- Most restaurants have children's portions.
- Many restaurants offer a set dinner **DAGENS RET** at a reasonable price.
- Restaurants displaying the sign **DAN MENU**! serve a 2-course traditional Danish meal – often some local speciality – at a fixed price throughout the country. A brochure with names and addresses of restaurants participating in the scheme is available from the Danish Tourist Board in London.

- Hot meals are served from 12.00 p.m. – 2.00 p.m. at lunchtime and from 6.00 p.m. – 9/10.00 p.m. at night. After that many restaurants offer snacks for latecomers.

WHAT TO SAY

May I book a table?	**Jeg vil gerne bestille et bord** yigh vil gair-ner bestiller it bor
I've booked a table	**Jeg har bestilt et bord** yigh har bestilt it bor
A table . . .	**Et bord . . .** it bor . . .
for one	**til en person** til ain pair-sone
for three	**til tre personer** til tray pairso-ner
The à la carte menu, please	**A la carte menuen** a la carte menoo-en
Today's special menu, please	**Dagens ret** day-ens ret

Danish

What's this, please? *[point to menu]*	**Hvad er det?** va air day
The wine list	**Vinkortet** veenkortet
A glass of wine	**Et glas vin** it glas veen
A half bottle	**En halv flaske** ain hal flasker
A bottle	**En flaske** ain flasker
A litre	**En liter** ain leeter
Red/white/rosé/house wine	**Rødvin/hvidvin/rosévin/husets vin** rerthe-veen/veethe-veen/rosé-veen/hoo-sets veen
Some more bread, please	**Noget mere brød** no-et mere brerthe
Some more wine	**Noget mere vin** no-et mere veen
Some dressing	**Noget dressing** no-et dressing
Some salt	**Noget salt** no-et selt
Some pepper	**Noget peber** no-et paver
With/without garlic	**Med/uden hvidløg** methe/oothen veethe-loy
Some water	**Noget vand** no-et van
How much does that come to?	**Hvor meget bliver det?** vor my-et bleer day
Is service included?	**Er det med betjening?** air day methe bechaining
Miss! *[this does not sound abrupt in Danish]*	**Frøken!** frer-ken
Waiter!	**Tjener!** chainer
The bill, please	**Må jeg betale?** maw yigh betailer

Key words for courses, as seen on some menus. [*Only ask this question if you want the waiter to remind you of the choice*]

What have you got in the way of . . .	Hvilke . . . har De?
	veelker . . . har dee
STARTERS?	**FORRETTER?**
	for-retter
SOUP?	**SUPPER?**
	soopper
EGG DISHES?	**ÆGGERETTER?**
	egger-retter
FISH?	**FISKERETTER?**
	fisker-retter
MEAT?	**KØDRETTER?**
	kerthe-retter
GAME?	**VILDTRETTER?**
	vilt-retter
FOWL?	**FJERKRÆRETTER?**
	f-yair-kray-retter
VEGETABLES?	**GRØNTSAGER?**
	grernt-sayer
CHEESE?	**OSTE?**
	oaster
FRUIT?	**FRUGT?**
	frookt
ICE-CREAM?	**IS?**
	ees
DESSERT?	**DESSERTER?**
	dessairter

UNDERSTANDING THE MENU

- You will find the names of the principal ingredients of most dishes on these pages:

Starters p. 58	Fruit p. 60
Meat p. 62	Cheese p. 59
Fish p. 64	Ice-cream p. 57
Vegetables p. 61	Dessert p. 56

- Used together with the following lists of cooking and menu terms, they should help you to decode the menu.
- These cooking and menu terms are for understanding – not for speaking aloud.

Cooking and menu terms

bagt	baked
blandet	mixed
bouillon	broth, clear soup
brunet i smør	sautéed
dampet	steamed
filet	fillet
fløde	cream
flødeskum	whipped cream
fyldt	stuffed
garneret	garnished
gennemstegt (steak)	well done
glaseret	glazed
gratineret	au gratin
grydestegt	braised
hjemmelavet	homemade
jævnet	thickened
kogt	boiled
marineret	marinated
paneret	dressed with egg and breadcrumbs
pikant	savoury
puré	purée
ragout	stew
revet	grated
ristet	toasted
rød	rare (steak)
røget	smoked
rå	raw
sovs	sauce
stegt	fried
sur	sour
sød	sweet

Further words to help you understand the menu

æggekage	Danish omelette garnished with tomatoes, bacon and chives
agurkesalat	cucumber in sweet/sour dressing
and	duck
aspargessuppe	asparagus soup
boller i karry	pork meat balls in curry sauce served with rice

bøf med løg	beef hamburger with fried onions and sauce
engelsk bøf	fillet of beef
flæskesteg med svær	roast pork with crackling
flæskesteg med rødkål	roast pork with red cabbage, traditional Sunday dish
frikadeller	pork and veal meat balls
gemyse	vegetables
gule ærter	split pea soup with pork
hachis	minced steak with onions, spices and vinegar
hamburgerryg	smoked, glazed pork
hindbær	raspberries
hofdessert	meringue, whipped cream and chocolate sauce
hønsekødssuppe	clear chicken soup with meat balls and vegetables
jordbærgrød	strawberry dessert served with fresh cream
kalvefrikasse	veal stew with vegetables
karamelbudding	crème caramel
kærnemælkskoldskål	buttermilk dessert served with biscuits
lagkage	layer cake
laks	salmon
lever, stegt med løg	fried liver with onions
medisterpølse	spiced, fried pork sausage
muslinger	mussels
mørbradbøf	fillet of pork
oksefilet	fillet of beef
ørred	trout
pandekager	pancakes
peberrodssovs	horseradish sauce
rejer	shrimps
remoulade	creamy dressing with mustard and herbs
rødbeder, syltede	beetroot in sweet/sour dressing
rødgrød med fløde	dessert made from raspberries, redcurrants and blackcurrants and served with fresh cream
rødkål	red cabbage cooked with sugar and vinegar

Danish

stegt/kogt rødspætte	fried or boiled plaice – sometimes served with shrimp sauce
svinekotelet	pork chop
sylte	brawn
torsk med sennepssovs	cod with mustard sauce
æbleflæsk	fried apples and onions with bacon
æblekage	stewed apples with toasted breadcrumbs and whipped cream
ål, stegt	fried eel

Health

ESSENTIAL INFORMATION

- For details of reciprocal health agreement between the UK and Denmark ask for leaflet E-111 D at your local Department of Health and Social Security a month before leaving or ask your travel agent.
- In addition it is preferable to purchase a medical insurance policy through the travel agent, a broker or a motoring organization.
- Take your own 'first line' first aid kit with you.
- For finding your own way to a doctor, dentist, chemist or Health and Social Security Office (for reimbursement) see p. 00.
- Your UK passport or the E-111 D certificate must be shown to the doctor or pharmacist, who are entitled to payment of the full amount of their bills. If cash payment is demanded, the refund is paid by the nearest municipal or health insurance office: the tourist office will tell you where to go. The refund should be applied for before you leave Denmark.
- If staying in the country, the name of the medical practitioner on duty at weekends and at nights can be found in the local papers. In Copenhagen, ring LÆGEVAGTEN on 0041 if you require medical assistance at weekends or weekdays after 4.00 p.m.

WHAT'S THE MATTER?

I have a pain in my . . .	Jeg har ondt i . . . yigh har *o*nt ee . . .
ankle	**anklen** *a*nk-len
arm	**armen** *a*rmen
back	**ryggen** r*oo*ggen
bowels	**tarmene** *ta*rmerner
breast/chest	**brystet** br*er*-stet
ear	**øret** *e*rert
eyes	**øjnene** *oy*-nerner
foot	**foden** f*oe*-then
head	**hovedet** ho-*er*thet
heel	**hælen** h*ay*-len
jaw	**kæben** k*ay*-ben
leg	**benet** b*ee*net
lung	**lungen** l*oo*ng-en
neck	**nakken** n*u*kken
penis	**min penis** mean p*e*nis
shoulder	**skulderen** sk*oo*llern
stomach/abdomen	**maven** m*ay*-ven
testicle	**testiklerne** test*ee*k-ler-ner
throat	**halsen** h*al*-sen

I have a pain in my . . .	**Jeg har ondt i . . .** yigh har ont ee . . .
vagina	**skeden** sk*ai*then
wrist	**håndledet** h*o*n-lethet
I have a pain here [*point*]	**Jeg har ondt her** yigh har ont h*ai*r
I have toothache	**Jeg har tandpine** yigh har t*a*nn-p*ee*ner
I have broken my dentures	**Min protese er gået i stykker** mean prot*ay*-ser air gaw-et ee st*oo*kker
I have broken my glasses	**Mine briller er gået i stykker** m*ea*ner br*i*ller air gaw-et ee st*oo*kker
I have lost . . .	**Jeg har tabt . . .** yigh har tubt . . .
my contact lenses	**mine kontaktlinser** m*ea*ner kont*a*kt-l*ee*n-ser
a filling	**en plombe** ain pl*o*m-ber
My child is ill	**Mit barn er sygt** meet b*a*rn air s*oo*-oot
He/she has a pain in his/her . . .	**Han/hun har ondt i . . .** h*a*n/h*oo*n har ont ee . . .
stomach [*see list above*]	**maven** m*ay*-ven
How bad is it?	
I'm ill	**Jeg er syg** yigh air s*oo*-oo
It's serious	**Det er alvorligt** day air al-v*o*r-lit
It's not serious	**Det er ikke alvorligt** day air igger al-v*o*r-lit
It hurts (a lot)	**Det gør meget ondt** day gher m*y*-et *o*nt
I have been in pain for . . .	**Jeg har haft ondt i . . .** yigh har haft *o*nt ee . . .
one hour/one day	**en time/en dag** ain t*ee*mer/ain d*a*y

It's a . . .	Det er en . . .
	day air ain . . .
sharp pain	**stikkende smerte**
	st*i*kkener sm*ai*rter
dull ache	**dump smerte**
	d*oo*mp sm*ai*rter
nagging pain	**vedvarende smerte**
	v*e*the-var-en-er sm*ai*rter
I feel dizzy	**Jeg er svimmel**
	y*igh* air sv*i*mmel
I feel sick	**Jeg har kvalme**
	y*igh* har k-v*a*lmer
I have a temperature	**Jeg har feber**
	y*igh* har f*a*ber

Already under treatment for something else?

I take . . . regularly [*show*]	**Jeg tager regelmæssigt . . .**
	y*igh* tar r*a*y-el-messit . . .
this medicine	**denne medicin**
	denner medic*i*n
these pills	**disse tabletter**
	d*i*sser tabletter
I have . . .	**Jeg har . . .**
	y*igh* har . . .
a heart condition	**dårligt hjerte**
	d*o*r-lit y*ai*r-ter
haemmorrhoids	**haemorroider**
	hemmo-r*ee*ther
rheumatism	**gigt**
	gh*ee*gt
I think I have . . .	**Jeg tror, jeg har . . .**
	y*igh* tror y*igh* har . . .
food poisoning	**madforgiftning**
	mathe-for-gh*i*ft-ning
sunstroke	**hedeslag**
	h*ai*ther-slay
I'm . . .	**Jeg er . . .**
	y*igh* air . . .
diabetic/pregnant	**diabetiker/gravid**
	dee-ab*ai*tiker/gra-v*ee*the
allergic to penicillin	**allergisk over for penicillin**
	al-air-gisk o-er for penicill*ee*n

Danish

I'm asthmatic	**Jeg har astma**
	yigh har ast-ma

Other essential expressions

Please can you help?	**Kan De hjælpe mig?**
	kan dee yelper my
A doctor, please	**En læge/doktor**
	ain layer/doktor
A dentist	**En tandlæge**
	ain tann-layer
I don't speak Danish	**Jeg taler ikke dansk**
	yigh tayler igger dansk
What time does . . . arrive?	**Hvornår kommer . . . ?**
	vornor kommer . . .
the doctor	**lægen/doktoren**
	layen/doktoren
the dentist	**tandlægen**
	tann-layen

From the doctor: key sentences to understand

Take this . . .	**De skal tage dette . . .**
	dee skal ta detter . . .
every day/hour	**hver dag/time**
	vair day/teemer
four times a day	**fire gange daglig**
	feerer gung-er dowlee
Stay in bed	**Bliv i sengen**
	bleev ee seng-en
Don't travel . . .	**De må ikke rejse . . .**
	dee maw igger rye-ser . . .
for . . . days/weeks	**i de næste . . . dage/uger**
	ee dee nester . . . day-er/oo-er
You must go to the hospital	**De skal på hospitalet**
	dee skal paw ho-speetay-let

Problems: complaints, loss, theft

ESSENTIAL INFORMATION

- Problems with:
  camping facilities, see p. 30.
  household appliances, see p. 48.
  health, see p. 76.
  the car, see p. 87.
- If the worst comes to the worst, find a police station.
  To ask the way, see p. 20.
- Look for:
  POLITI
- If you lose your passport report the loss to the nearest police station and go to the British Consulate.
- In an emergency dial 0-0-0 and state which service you require. Emergency calls from public telephone boxes are free.

COMPLAINTS

I bought this . . .	**Jeg købte det/den . . .**
	yigh kerbter day/den . . .
today	**i dag**
	ee day
yesterday	**i går**
	ee gor
on Monday [see p. 99]	**i mandags**
	ee mandas
It's no good	**Det/den duer ikke**
	day/den doo-er igger
Look	**Se**
	say
Here [point]	**Her**
	hair
Can you . . .	**Kan De . . .**
	kan dee . . ,
change it?	**bytte det/den?**
	bootter day/den
mend it?	**reparere det/den?**
	reparair day/den

Danish

Here's the receipt	**Her er kvitteringen**
	hair air kveett*air*ing-en
Can I have a refund?	**Kan jeg få pengene tilbage?**
	kan yigh faw *p*eng-en-er tilb*ay*-er

LOSS
[See also 'Theft' below: the lists are interchangeable]

I have lost . . .	**Jeg har mistet . . .**
	yigh har m*i*stet . . .
my bag	**min taske**
	mean t*a*ssker
my bracelet	**mit armbånd**
	m*ee*t *a*rmbon
my camera	**mit kamera**
	m*ee*t k*a*mera
my car keys	**mine bilnøgler**
	m*ea*ner b*ee*l-n*oy*-ler
my logbook	**min indregistreringsattest**
	mean *i*n-reggee-str*ay*-rings-attest
my driving licence	**mit kørekort**
	m*ee*t *ke*r-kort
my insurance certificate	**mit forsikringsbevis**
	m*ee*t fors*ee*k-rings-bev*ee*s

THEFT
[See also 'Loss' above: the lists are interchangeable]

Someone has stolen . . .	**Der er en, der har stjålet . . .**
	dair air *ai*n dair har st-y*aw*-let . . .
my car	**min bil**
	mean b*ee*l
my money	**mine penge**
	m*ea*ner p*e*ng-er
my purse	**min pung**
	mean p*oo*ng
my tickets	**mine billetter**
	m*ea*ner billetter
my travellers' cheques	**mine rejsechecks**
	m*ea*ner r*ye*-ser-shecks
my wallet	**min tegnebog**
	mean t*ie*-ner-bo

my watch	**mit ur**
	meet *oo*r
my luggage	**min bagage**
	mean bag*ay*sher

LIKELY REACTIONS: key words to understand

Wait	**Vent**
	v*e*nt
When?	**Hvornår?**
	vorn*o*r
Where?	**Hvor?**
	v*o*r
Name?	**Navn?**
	n*o*un
Address?	**Adresse?**
	adr*e*sser
I can't help you	**Jeg kan ikke hjælpe Dem**
	yigh kan igger y*e*lper dem

The post office

ESSENTIAL INFORMATION

- To find a post office, see p. 20.
- Key words to look for:
  POSTHUS
  POSTKONTOR
- Look for this sign:
- For stamps look for the word
  FRIMÆRKER on a machine, or at
  a post office counter.
- Many stationers and kiosks selling
  postcards also sell stamps.
- Letter boxes are red.

Danish

WHAT TO SAY

To England, please	**Til England**
	til eng-lan

[*Hand letters, cards or parcels over the counter*]

To Australia	**Til Australien**
	til ow-straw-lee-en
To the United States	**Til Amerika**
	til amair-ee-ka

[*For other countries, see p. 102*]

Airmail	**Luftpost**
	looft-posst
Surface mail	**Overfladepost**
	o-er-flay-ther-posst
I'd like to send a telegram	**Jeg vil gerne sende et telegram**
	yigh vil gair-ner senner it telegrum

Telephoning

ESSENTIAL INFORMATION

- Instructions on how to use the phone are printed inside the directory in several languages.
- The code for the UK is 00944 and for the USA 01144.
- For calls to countries which cannot be dialled direct go to a post office and write the country, town and number on a piece of paper. Add **PERSONLIG SAMTALE** if you want a person-to-person call and **MODTAGEREN BETALER** if you want to reverse the charges. Get them to put the call through for you.
- If you need a number abroad or to reverse the charges ring inquiries (**OPLYSNINGEN**). They speak English.

WHAT TO SAY

I'd like this number . . .	**Vil De give mig dette nummer?**
[*show number*]	vil dee ghee my detter noom-mer

in England	**i England**
	ee eng-lan
in Canada	**i Canada**
	ee canada

[For other countries see p. 102]

Can you dial it for me, please?	**Vil De dreje det for mig?**
	vil dee dry-er day for my
May I speak to . . .?	**Jeg vil gerne tale med . . .**
	yigh vil gair-ner tayler methe . . .
Extension . . .	**Lokal . . .**
	lokal . . .
Do you speak English?	**Taler De engelsk?**
	tayler dee eng-elsk
Thank you, I'll phone back	**Tak, jeg ringer senere**
	tuck yigh ring-er say-nor

LIKELY REACTIONS

That's (15 kroner)	**Det bliver (femten kroner)**
	day bleer (femten kroner)
Cabin number (3)	**Kiosk nummer (tre)**
	kiosk noom-mer (tray)

[For numbers, see p. 96]

Don't hang up	**Læg ikke røret på**
	leg igger rer-ret paw
I'm trying to connect you	**Jeg prøver at få forbindelsen**
	yigh proover at faw for-binnelsen
You're through	**Forbindelsen er klar**
	for-binnelsen air klar
There's a delay	**Der er ventetid**
	dair air venter-teethe
I'll try again	**Jeg prøver igen**
	yigh proover ee-ghen

Changing cheques and money

ESSENTIAL INFORMATION

- Finding your way to a bank, see p. 20.
- Look for these words on buildings:
  BANK (bank)
  SPAREKASSE (savings bank)
- Banks are open weekdays from 9.30 a.m. – 4.00 p.m. On Thursdays or Fridays they stay open until 6.00 p.m. They are closed Saturday and Sunday.
- Small currency exchange offices **VEKSELKONTOR** operate in many tourist centres.
- Exchange rate information might show the pound as:
  £, LONDON, ENGLAND or the British flag.
- Have your passport handy.

WHAT TO SAY

I'd like to cash . . .	**Jeg vil gerne indløse . . .**
	yigh vil gair-ner in-ler-ser . . .
this travellers' cheque	**denne rejsecheck**
	denner rye-ser-sheck
these travellers' cheques	**disse rejsechecks**
	disser rye-ser-shecks
this cheque	**denne check**
	denner sheck

For excursions into neighbouring countries

I'd like to change this . . .	**Jeg vil gerne have vekslet . . .**
[show banknotes]	yigh vil gair-ner ha veks-let . . .
into German marks	**til D-mark**
	til dee-mark
into Norwegian kroner	**til norske kroner**
	til norsker kroner
into Swedish kroner	**til svenske kroner**
	til svensker kroner

LIKELY REACTIONS

Passport, please	**Må jeg se Deres pås** maw yigh say dair-es pas
Sign here	**Vil De skrive under her** vil dee skreever on-ner hair
Your banker's card, please	**Må jeg se Deres checkkort** maw yigh say dair-es sheck-kort
Go to the cash desk	**Gå til 'Kassen'** gaw til kassen

Car travel

ESSENTIAL INFORMATION

- Finding a filling station or garage, see p. 22.
  Is it a self service station? Look out for
  SELVBETJENING
- Grades of petrol:
  NORMAL (standard)
  SUPER (premium)
  DIESEL
- 1 gallon is about 4½ litres (accurate enough up to 6 gallons).
- The minimum sale is 5 litres.
- Filling stations are usually able to help with minor mechanical problems. For major repairs you have to find a garage:
  REPARATIONSVÆRKSTED.

WHAT TO SAY

[*For numbers, see p. 96*]

(20) litres of . . .	**(Tyve) liter . . .** (toover) leeter . . .
(120) kroners of . . .	**For (hundrede og tyve) kroner . . .** for (hoonrer-ther aw toover) kroner . . .

Danish

standard	**normal**
	normal
premium	**super**
	super
diesel	**diesel**
	diesel
Fill it up, please	**Fyld tanken op**
	fool tanken op
Will you check . . .	**Vil De checke . . .**
	vil dee checker . . .
the oil?	**olien?**
	ol-yen
the battery?	**batteriet?**
	batteree-et
the radiator?	**køleren?**
	ker-ler-ren
the tyres?	**dækkene?**
	dekker-ner
I've run out of petrol	**Jeg er løbet tør for benzin**
	yigh air lerbet ter for ben-seen
Can I borrow a can, please?	**Kan jeg låne en dunk?**
	kan yigh lawner ain doonk
My car has broken down	**Min bil er brudt sammen**
	mean beel air brute sammen
Can you help me, please?	**Kan De hjælpe mig?**
	kan dee yelper my
Do you do repairs?	**Laver De reparationer?**
	laver dee repara-showner
I have a puncture	**Jeg er punkteret**
	yigh air poonk-tairt
I have a broken windscreen	**Min forrude er gået i stykker**
	mean for-roothe air gaw-et ee stookker
I think the problem is here . . . [point]	**Jeg tror, problemet er her . . .**
	yigh tror problee-met air hair . . .
Can you . . .	**Kan De . . .**
	kan dee . . .
repair the fault?	**reparere fejlen?**
	reparair fylen
come and look?	**komme og se på den?**
	kommer aw say paw den
estimate the cost?	**give mig en pris?**
	ghee my ain prees

write it down?	**skrive det ned?**
	skreever day nethe
How long will the repair take?	**Hvor lang tid vil det tage?**
	vor lang teethe vil day tay
This is my insurance document	**Her er mit forsikringsbevis**
	hair air meet forseek-rings-bevees

HIRING A CAR

Can I hire a car?	**Kan jeg leje en bil?**
	kan yigh lie-er ain beel
I need a car . . .	**Jeg skal bruge en bil . . .**
	yigh skal broo-er ain beel . . .
for five people	**til fem personer**
	til fem pairsoner
for a week	**i en uge**
	ee ain oo-er
Can you write down . . .	**Vil De skrive . . . ned?**
	vil dee skreever . . . nethe
the deposit to pay?	**depositum**
	depo-see-toom
the charge per kilometre?	**kilometer prisen**
	kilomait-ter pree-sen
the daily charge?	**dagsprisen**
	dows-pree-sen
the cost of insurance?	**forsikringsomkostningerne**
	forseek-rings-om-kostning-erner
Can I leave it in (Esbjerg)?	**Kan jeg aflevere den i (Esbjerg)?**
	kan yigh ow-levair den ee (esh-yer)?
What documents do I need?	**Hvilke papirer behøver jeg?**
	veel-ker papee-er behoover yigh

LIKELY REACTIONS

I don't do repairs	**Jeg foretager ikke reparationer**
	yigh fortayer igger reparas-showner
Where is your car?	**Hvor er Deres bil?**
	vor air dair-es beel
What make is it?	**Hvilket bilmærke er det?**
	veel-ket beel-mairker air day
Come back tomorrow/on Wednesday [*For days of the week, see p. 99*]	**Kom igen i morgen/på onsdag** kom ee-ghen ee morn/paw onsda

Danish

We don't hire cars	**Vi lejer ikke biler ud** vee *lie*-er igger b*ee*ler *oo*the
Your driving licence, please	**Deres kørekort** dair-es k*er*-erkort
The mileage is unlimited	**Ubegrænset kilometerantal** *oo*-begr*e*n-set kil*o*m*ai*t-ter-*a*ntal

Public transport

ESSENTIAL INFORMATION

- Finding the way to the bus station, a bus, the railway station, see p. 20.
- Remember that queueing for buses is unheard of!
- To get a taxi you usually have to telephone the local firm or go to a taxi rank. Hailing a taxi is less common and does not always work.
- Types of trains:
  INTERCITY (long-distance express train, stopping only at principal stations)
  LYNTOG (high-speed train)
  REGIONALTOG (stops at all stations along the route)
  S-TOG (short distance train, suburbs of Copenhagen only)
- Key words on signs:
  BILLETTER (tickets)
  INDGANG (entrance)
  UDGANG (exit)
  FORBUDT (forbidden)
  SPOR (lit. track)
  PERRON (platform)
  OPLYSNINGEN (information)
  DSB (initials of Danish railways)
  GARDEROBESKABE (left luggage)
  BUSSTOPPESTED (bus stop)
  AFGANG (departures)
  ANKOMST (arrivals)

KØREPLAN (timetable)
REJSEGODSKONTOR (forwarding office)
● Buying a ticket?
Buy your train ticket at the ticket office inside the station.
● When travelling on the S-train, Copenhagen only, you can pur-
chase a ticket for use on both the S-train and the ordinary trains.
● When travelling by bus you usually pay as you enter. Most ticket
machines give change.
● In some larger cities a **KLIPPEKORT** can be purchased. This
entitles the buyer to a specific number of journeys at reduced cost
and is obtainable from tobacconists and kiosks.
● Further reductions can be obtained by buying a weekly (**UGE-
KORT**) ticket or a monthly (**MÅNEDSKORT**) ticket.

WHAT TO SAY

Where does the train for (Odense) leave from?	**Hvor går toget til (Odense) fra?** vor gor *toe*-et til (*o*-then-ser) fra
At what time does the train for (Odense) leave?	**Hvornår går toget til (Odense)?** vornor gor *toe*-et til (*o*-then-ser)
At what time does the train arrive in (Odense)?	**Hvornår er toget i (Odense)?** vornor air *toe*-et ee (*o*-then-ser)
Is this the train for (Odense)?	**Er det toget til (Odense)?** air d*ay toe*-et til (*o*-then-ser)
Where does the bus for (Virum) leave from?	**Hvor går bussen til (Virum) fra?** vor gor *boo*ssen til (*vee*-rom) fra
Is this the bus for (Virum)?	**Er det bussen til (Virum)?** air d*ay boo*ssen til (*vee*-rom)
Do I have to change?	**Skal jeg skifte?** skal yigh sk*i*fter
Can you put me off at the right stop, please?	**Vil De sige mig, hvornår jeg skal af?** vil dee *see*-yer my vornor yigh skal *a*
Where can I get a taxi?	**Hvor kan jeg få en taxa?** vor kan yigh *faw* ain t*a*xa
Can I book a seat?	**Kan jeg reservere en plads?** kan yigh reser-v*air* ain pl*a*s
A single	**En enkelt** ain *e*nk-elt
A return	**En retur** ain rer-*tour*
First class	**Første klasse** *fi*rster kl*a*sser

Second class	**Fællesklasse** fel-les-klasser
One adult	**En voksen** ain voksen
Two adults	**To voksne** toe voksner
and one child	**og et barn** o it barn
and two children	**og to børn** o toe burn
How much is it?	**Hvor meget bliver det?** vor my-et bleer day

LIKELY REACTIONS

Over there	**Derovre** dair-o-er
Here	**Her** hair
Platform (1) [*For times, see p. 99*]	**Perron (et)** pairrong (it)
Change at (Roskilde)	**Skift i (Roskilde)** skift ee (ros-killer)
Change at (the town hall)	**Skift ved (rådhuset)** skift vethe (roothe-hoo-set)
This is your stop	**De skal af her** dee skal a hair
There's only first class	**Der er kun første klasse** dair air kon firster klasser
There's a supplement	**Der er et tillæg** dair air it tilleg

Leisure

ESSENTIAL INFORMATION

- Finding the way to a place of entertainment, see p. 21.
- For times of day, see p. 98.
- Important signs, see p. 19.
- No smoking in cinemas, theatres or concert halls and in some restaurants.
- It is customary to leave one's coat in the cloakroom in theatres.

WHAT TO SAY

At what time does . . . open?	**Hvornår åbner . . .**
	vornor *awb*-ner . . .
the museum	**museet?**
	moo-*say*-et
At what time does . . . close?	**Hvornår lukker . . .**
	vornor *look*ker . . .
the skating rink	**skøjtebanen?**
	sk*oy*-ter-baynen
At what time does . . . start?	**Hvornår begynder . . .**
	vornor begern-ner . . .
the cabaret	**kabareten?**
	kaba-*ray*en
the concert	**koncerten?**
	kons*air*-tèn
the film	**filmen?**
	filmen
the match	**kampen?**
	k*u*mpen
the play	**skuespillet?**
	sk*oo*-er-spillet
the race	**væddeløbet?**
	vether-lerbet
How much is it . . .	**Hvor meget koster det . . .**
	vor my-et koster day . . .
for an adult?	**for en voksen?**
	for *ai*n voksen
for a child?	**for et barn?**
	for *i*t barn

Do you have . . .
Har De . . .
har dee . . .

   a programme?
et program?
it program

   a guide book?
en vejledning?
ain vy-lethe-ning

I'd like a lesson in . . .
Jeg vil gerne have undervisning
   i at . . .
yigh vil gair-ner ha oonner-vees-
ning ee at . . .

   sailing
sejle
sigh-ler

   skating
løbe på skøjter
lerber paw skoy-ter

   water skiing
stå på vandski
staw paw van-skee

Can I hire . . .
Kan jeg leje . . .
kan yigh lie-er . . .

   a bicycle?
en cykel?
ain sookel

   a boat?
en båd?
ain bawthe

   a fishing rod?
en fiskestang?
ain fisker-stung

   the necessary equipment?
det nødvendige udstyr?
day nerthe-ven-dee-er oothe-stoor

How much is it?
Hvor meget koster det?
vor my-et koster day

   per day/per hour?
per dag/per time?
pair day/pair teemer

Do I need a licence?
Behøver jeg en tilladelse?
behoover yigh ain til-lay-thel-ser

Asking if things are allowed

ESSENTIAL INFORMATION

- May one smoke here?
  May we smoke here?
  May I smoke here?
  Can one smoke here?
  Can I smoke here?
  Is it possible to smoke here?

  Må man ryge her?
  maw man roo-yer hair

- All these English variations can be expressed in one way in Danish. To save space only the first English version: May one . . .? is shown below.

WHAT TO SAY

Excuse me, please	**Undskyld** on-skool
May one . . .	**Må man . . .** maw man . . .
camp here?	**campere her?** cam-pair hair
dance here?	**danse her?** danser hair
fish here?	**fiske her?** fisker hair
leave one's things here?	**efterlade sine ting her?** efter-layther seener teeng hair
look around?	**se sig omkring?** say sigh omkreng
park here?	**parkere her?** parkair hair
picnic here?	**spise her?** spee-ser hair
sit here?	**sidde her?** sither hair
smoke here?	**ryge her?** roo-yer hair
swim here?	**svømme her?** sver-mer hair

Danish

May one . . .	**Må man . . .**
	maw man . . .
telephone here?	**telefonere her?**
	telefonair hair
wait here?	**vente her?**
	venter hair

LIKELY REACTIONS

Yes, certainly	**Ja, gerne**
	ya gair-ner
Help yourself	**De må gerne selv tage**
	dee maw gair-ner sel tay
I think so	**Det tror jeg**
	day tror yigh
Of course	**Naturligvis**
	natoor-lee-vees
Yes, but be careful	**Ja, men pas på**
	ya men pas paw
No, certainly not	**Nej, bestemt ikke**
	nigh bestemt igger
I don't think so	**Det tror jeg ikke**
	day tror yigh igger
Not normally	**Normalt ikke**
	normalt igger
Sorry	**Desværre**
	desvair

Reference

NUMBERS
Cardinal numbers

0	**nul**	nool
1	**en**	ain
2	**to**	toe
3	**tre**	tray
4	**fire**	feerer

5	**fem**	fem
6	**seks**	sex
7	**syv**	soo
8	**otte**	*aw*-der
9	**ni**	n*ee*
10	**ti**	t*ee*
11	**elleve**	*elver*
12	**tolv**	toll
13	**tretten**	tretten
14	**fjorten**	f-yorten
15	**femten**	femten
16	**seksten**	sigh-sten
17	**sytten**	sootten
18	**atten**	*a*tten
19	**nitten**	n*i*tten
20	**tyve**	t*oo*ver
21	**enogtyve**	*ai*n-o-t*oo*ver
22	**toogtyve**	t*oe*-o-t*oo*ver
23	**treogtyve**	tr*ay*-o-t*oo*ver
24	**fireogtyve**	feerer-o-t*oo*ver
25	**femogtyve**	fem-o-t*oo*ver
30	**tredive**	tr*ai*the-ver
36	**seksogtredive**	sex-o-tr*ai*the-ver
37	**syvogtredive**	soo-o-tr*ai*the-ver
38	**otteogtredive**	*aw*-der-o-tr*ai*the-ver
39	**niogtredive**	n*ee*-o-tr*ai*the-ver
40	**fyrre**	fur-er
41	**enogfyrre**	*ai*n-o-fur-er
50	**halvtreds**	hal-tress
51	**enoghalvtreds**	*ai*n-o-hal-tress
60	**tres**	tress
61	**enogtres**	*ai*n-o-tress
70	**halvfjerds**	hal-f-yers
71	**enoghalvfjerds**	*ai*n-o-hal-f-yers
80	**firs**	feers
81	**enogfirs**	*ai*n-o-feers
90	**halvfems**	hal-fems
91	**enoghalvfems**	*ai*n-o-hal-fems
100	**hundrede**	h*oo*nrer-ther
101	**hundrede og en**	h*oo*nrer-ther o *ai*n
102	**hundrede og to**	h*oo*nrer-ther o t*oe*
125	**hundrede og femogtyve**	h*oo*nrer-ther o fem-*aw*-t*oo*ver

150	**hundrede og halvtreds**	h*oo*nrer-ther o hal-tre*ss*
175	**hundrede og femoghalvfjerds**	h*oo*nrer-ther o fem-ao-hal-f-yers
200	**to hundrede**	t*oe* h*oo*nrer-ther
250	**to hundrede og halvtreds**	t*oe* h*oo*nrer-ther o hal-tre*ss*
300	**tre hundrede**	tray h*oo*nrer-ther
400	**fire hundrede**	f*ee*rer h*oo*nrer-ther
500	**fem hundrede**	fem h*oo*nrer-ther
700	**syv hundrede**	s*oo* h*oo*nrer-ther
1,000	**tusinde**	t*oo*-sinner
1,100	**et tusinde et hundrede**	*it* t*oo*-sinner-*it*-h*oo*nrer-ther
2,000	**to tusinde**	t*oe* t*oo*-sinner
5,000	**fem tusinde**	fem t*oo*-sinner
10,000	**ti tusinde**	t*ee* t*oo*-sinner
100,000	**hundrede tusinde**	h*oo*nrer-ther t*oo*-sinner
1,000,000	**en million**	*ai*n mil-y*oa*n

Ordinal numbers

1st	**første**	f*i*rster
2nd	**anden**	*a*nnen
3rd	**tredje**	tr*a*y-ther
4th	**fjerde**	f-y*ai*r
5th	**femte**	fem-ter
6th	**sjette**	s-yetter
7th	**syvende**	s*oo*venner
8th	**ottende**	*o*t-tenner
9th	**niende**	n*ee*-enner
10th	**tiende**	t*ee*-enner
11th	**ellevte**	*e*lv-ter
12th	**tolvte**	t*o*l-ter

TIME

What time is it?	**Hvad er klokken?**
	v*a* air cl*o*cken
It's . . .	**Den er . . .**
	den air . . .
one o'clock	**et**
	it

two o'clock	**to**
	t*o*e
three o'clock	**tre**
	tr*a*y
It's . . .	**Det er . . .**
	day air . . .
noon	**middag**
	m*e*dda
midnight	**midnat**
	m*ee*the-nat
It's . . .	**Den er . . .**
	den air . . .
five past five	**fem minutter over fem**
	fem mee-n*o*otter o-er fem
twenty past five	**tyve minutter over fem**
	t*o*over-mee-n*o*otter o-er fem
twenty to six	**tyve minutter i seks**
	t*o*over mee-n*o*otter ee s*e*x
ten to six	**ti minutter i seks**
	t*ee* mee-n*o*otter ee s*e*x
At what time . . . (does the train leave)?	**Hvornår . . . (går toget)?**
	vornor . . . (gor t*o*e-et)
At . . .	**Klokken . . .**
	cl*o*cken . . .
13.00	**tretten**
	tretten
18.25	**attenfemogtyve**
	*a*tten-fem-o-t*o*over
23.50	**treogtyvehalvtreds**
	tr*a*y-o-t*o*over-hal-tr*e*ss

DAYS

Monday	**mandag**
	m*a*nda
Tuesday	**tirsdag**
	t*ee*rs-da
Wednesday	**onsdag**
	ons-da
Thursday	**torsdag**
	t*o*rs-da
Friday	**fredag**
	fr*a*y-da

Danish

Saturday	**lørdag**
	ler-da
Sunday	**søndag**
	sern-da
last Monday	**i mandags**
	ee mandas
next Tuesday	**næste tirsdag**
	nerster teers-da
on Wednesday	**på onsdag**
	paw ons-da
on Thursdays	**om torsdagen**
	om tors-day-en
until Friday	**indtil fredag**
	in-til fray-da
before Saturday	**før lørdag**
	fer ler-da
after Sunday	**efter søndag**
	efter sern-da
the day before yesterday	**i forgårs**
	ee for-gors
two days ago	**for to dage siden**
	for toe dayer seethen
yesterday	**i går**
	ee gor
yesterday morning	**i går morges**
	ee gor mors
yesterday afternoon	**i går eftermiddags**
	ee gor efter-meddas
last night	**i aftes**
	ee aftes
today	**i dag**
	ee day
this morning	**i formiddag**
	ee for-medda
this afternoon	**i eftermiddag**
	ee efter-medda
tonight	**i aften**
	ee aften
tomorrow	**i morgen**
	ee morn
tomorrow morning	**i morgen formiddag**
	ee morn for-medda

tomorrow afternoon	**i morgen eftermiddag**
	ee morn *efter*-medda
tomorrow evening	**i morgen aften**
	ee morn *aften*
the day after tomorrow	**i overmorgen**
	ee *o*-er-morn

MONTHS AND DATES

January	**januar**
	ya-noo-ar
February	**februar**
	fay-broo-ar
March	**marts**
	marts
April	**april**
	ah-preel
May	**maj**
	my
June	**juni**
	yoo-nee
July	**juli**
	yoo-lee
August	**august**
	ow-goost
September	**september**
	september
October	**oktober**
	oktober
November	**november**
	november
December	**december**
	december
last month	**sidste måned**
	seester maw-nethe
this month	**denne måned**
	denner maw-nethe
next month	**næste måned**
	nester maw-nethe
in spring	**om foråret**
	om for-aw-ret
in summer	**om sommeren**
	om sommer-ren

Danish

in autumn	**om efteråret**
	om *e*fter-aw-ret
in winter	**om vinteren**
	om v*i*n-ter-ren
this year	**i år**
	ee or
last year	**sidste år**
	s*ee*ster or
next year	**næste år**
	n*e*ster or
in 1985	**i nitten hundrede og femogfirs**
	ee n*i*tten-h*oo*nrer-ther o fem-o-f*ee*rs
What's the date today?	**Hvad dato er det i dag?**
	va d*a*y-toe air d*a*y ee d*a*y
It's the 6th of March	**Det er den sjette marts**
	d*a*y air den s-y*e*tter m*a*rts

Public holidays

● Shops, schools and offices are closed on the following dates:

1 January	**Nytårsdag**	New Year
. . .	**Skærtorsdag**	Maundy Thursday
. . .	**Langfredag**	Good Friday
. . .	**2. påskedag**	Easter Monday
. . .	**Store Bededag**	Common Prayer Day
. . .	**Kr. Himmelfartsdag**	Ascension Day
. . .	**2. pinsedag**	Whit Monday
. . .	**Grundlovsdag**	Constitution Day
25 December	**Juledag**	Christmas Day
26 December	**2. juledag**	Boxing Day

COUNTRIES AND NATIONALITIES

Countries

America	**Amerika**
	am*air*-ee-ka
Australia	**Australien**
	ow-str*aw*-lee-en
Austria	**Østrig**
	er-stree

Belgium	**Belgien**
	bel-ghee-en
Britain	**Storbritannien**
	stor-brittan-nee-an
Canada	**Canada**
	canada
East Germany	**Østtyskland**
	erst-toosk-lan
Eire	**Irland**
	eer-lan
England	**England**
	eng-lan
Finland	**Finland**
	fin-lan
France	**Frankrig**
	frun-kree
Greece	**Grækenland**
	gray-ken-lan
India	**Indien**
	in-dee-en
Italy	**Italien**
	ee-tay-lee-en
New Zealand	**New Zealand**
	new scaland
Norway	**Norge**
	nor-yer
Pakistan	**Pakistan**
	pakistan
Poland	**Polen**
	po-len
Portugal	**Portugal**
	por-too-gal
Scotland	**Skotland**
	skot-lan
South Africa	**Sydafrika**
	soothe-ah-freeka
Spain	**Spanien**
	spay-nee-en
Sweden	**Sverige**
	svair-ee-er
Wales	**Wales**
	wales

Danish

West Germany	**Vesttyskland**
	vest-toosk-lan
Yugoslavia	**Jugoslavien**
	you-go-slay-vee-en

Nationalities

American	**amerikaner**
	amair-ee-kayner
Australian	**australier**
	ow-straw-lee-er
British	**britte**
	britter
Canadian	**canadier**
	ca-nay-dee-er
English	**englænder**
	eng-lenner
Finnish	**finne**
	finner
Irish	**irer**
	ee-er
Norwegian	**nordmand**
	nor-man
Scottish	**skotte**
	skotter
Swedish	**svensker**
	sven-sker
Welsh	**waliser**
	va-lee-ser

Do it yourself

Some notes on the language

This section does not deal with 'grammar' as such. The purpose here is to explain some of the most obvious and elementary nuts and bolts of the language, based on the principal phrases included in the book. This information should enable you to produce numerous sentences of your own making.

There is no pronunciation guide in most of this section partly because it would get in the way of the explanations and partly because you have to do it yourself at this stage if you are serious: work out the pronunciation from earlier examples in the book.

A/An

All nouns in Danish belong to one of two genders: common or neuter, irrespective of whether they refer to living beings or inanimate objects. A/an is expressed by en with common gender nouns and by et with neuter gender nouns.

A/an	common	neuter
an address	en adresse	
an apple		et æble
a bill	en regning	
an hotel		et hotel
a key	en nøgle	
a map		et kort
a menu	en menu	
a newspaper	en avis	
a suitcase	en kuffert	
a telephone directory	en telefonbog	
a ticket	en billet	
a timetable	en køreplan	

Important things to remember

- There is no way of telling a noun's gender. Although most nouns are of common gender you have to learn and remember the gender of each noun.

- Does it matter? Not unless you want to make a serious attempt to speak correctly and scratch beneath the surface of the language. You would be understood if you said **et adresse** or **en æble**, provided your pronunciation was good.

Practise saying and writing these sentences in Danish:

Have you got an apple?	**Har De . . .?**
Have you got a menu?	
I'd like a telephone directory	**Jeg vil gerne have . . .**
I'd like a timetable	
Where can I get a ticket?	**Hvor kan jeg få . . .?**
Where can I get a map?	
Is there a key?	**Er der . . .?**
Is there a newspaper?	
Is there an address?	

THE

Where we in English say 'the newspaper', the Danish equivalent is 'newspaper the'. In other words, 'the' is added on to the end of the noun. Common gender nouns add **-en** and neuter gender nouns add **-et**. If the noun already ends in **-e**, only **n** or **t** is added.

the	common (**n**)	neuter (**t**)
the address	**adressen**	
the apple		**æblet**
the bill	**regningen**	
the hotel		**hotellet**
the key	**nøglen**	
the map		**kortet**
the menu	**menuen**	
the newspaper	**avisen**	
the suitcase	**kufferten**	
the telephone directory	**telefonbogen**	
the ticket	**billetten**	
the timetable	**køreplanen**	

PLURALS
indefinite

addresses	**adresser**
apples	**æbler**
bills	**regninger**
hotels	**hoteller**
keys	**nøgler**
maps	**kort**
menus	**menuer**
newspapers	**aviser**
suitcases	**kufferter**
telephone directories	**telefonbøger**
tickets	**billetter**
timetables	**køreplaner**

definite

the addresses	**adresserne**
the apples	**æblerne**
the bills	**regningerne**
the hotels	**hotellerne**
the keys	**nøglerne**
the maps	**kortene**
the menus	**menuerne**
the newspapers	**aviserne**
the suitcases	**kufferterne**
the telephone directories	**telefonbøgerne**
the tickets	**billetterne**
the timetables	**køreplanerne**

- There are three plural forms for Danish nouns: -(e)ne, (er)ne or no ending at all. Often the third group of nouns will have a change of vowel, for example **et barn – to børn**.
- There is no easy way of knowing which plural ending a noun takes. You have to learn this along with the noun.

Practise saying and writing these sentences in Danish:

Have you got the key?	**Har De nøglen?**
Have you got the suitcases?	**Har De . . .?**
Have you got the telephone directory?	
Have you got the menu?	

Danish

I'd like the keys	**Jeg vil gerne have nøglerne**
I'd like the bill	**Jeg vil . . .**
I'd like the suitcase	
Where is the key?	**Hvor er nøglen?**
Where is the timetable?	**Hvor er . . .?**
Where is the address?	
Where are the suitcases?	**Hvor er . . .?**
Where are the keys?	
Where are the apples?	
Where are the newspapers?	
Where can I get the address?	**Hvor kan jeg få . . .?**
Where can I get the timetables?	
Where can I get the maps?	

Now make up more sentences along the same lines.

Important things to remember

- Danish has two forms for 'you'. The informal **du** is used when talking to relatives, friends and children and between young people. **De** is used in all other cases. Throughout this book the polite form of address **De** has been used. However, the informal **du** is being used more and more and if you find yourself being addressed as **du** you may like to use this informal word yourself in your response.

- In Danish there is no general word for 'please'. When asking for something it is polite to say **Jeg vil gerne have . . . .** In other situations the tone of your voice and a pleasant way of speaking will see you through.

THIS AND THAT

	common gender	neuter gender
this	**den her**	**det her**
that	**den der**	**det der**

If you don't know the Danish word for an object you can point and say: **den her/det her** about something displayed close to you and **den der/det der** about something displayed further away from you. As you don't know the Danish word you will not know the correct gender either but you will still be understood.

Jeg vil gerne have den/det her	I'd like this
Jeg vil gerne have den/det der	I'd like that

HELPING OTHERS

You can help yourself with phrases such as:

I'd like . . . an open sandwich	**Jeg vil gerne have . . . et stykke smørrebrød**
Where can I get . . . a cup of tea?	**Hvor kan jeg få . . . en kop te?**
I'll have . . . a glass of wine	**Jeg vil have . . . et glas vin**
I need . . . a receipt	**Jeg skal bruge . . . en kvittering**

If you come across a compatriot having trouble making himself or herself understood, you should be able to speak to a Danish person on their behalf.

He'd like . . .	**Han vil gerne have . . . en kop te** han vil gair-ner ha . . . ain kop tay
She'd like . . .	**Hun vil gerne have . . . en kop te** hoon vil gair-ner ha . . . ain kop tay
Where can he get . . .?	**Hvor kan han få et stykke smørrebrød?** vor kan han faw it stookker smerrer-brerthe
Where can she get . . .?	**Hvor kan hun få et stykke smørrebrød?** vor kan hoon faw it stookker smerrer-brerthe
He'll have . . .	**Han vil have et glas vin** han vil ha it glas veen
She'll have . . .	**Hun vil have et glas vin** hoon vil ha it glas veen
He needs . . .	**Han skal bruge en kvittering** han skal broo-er ain kveettairing
She needs . . .	**Hun skal bruge en kvittering** hoon skal broo-er ain kveettairing

You can also help a couple or a group if they are having difficulties. The Danish word for *they* is **de**.

They'd like . . .	**De vil gerne have et værelse** dee vil gair-ner ha it vair-el-ser
Where can they get . . .?	**Hvor kan de få nøglen?** vor kan dee faw noy-len

Danish

They'll have . . .	**De vil have et dobbeltvaerelse** d*ee* vil h*a* it dobbelt-*vair*-el-ser
They need . . .	**De skal bruge en kvittering** dee skal br*oo*-er ain kveett*air*ing

What about the two of you? No problem. The word for *we* is **vi**.

We'd like . . .	**Vi vil gerne have et glas vin** vee vil *gair*-ner h*a* it glas v*een*
Where can we get . . .?	**Hvor kan vi få en kop te?** vor kan ee *faw* ain kop *tay*
We'll have . . .	**Vi vil have en dessert** vee vil h*a* ain dess*air*t
We need . . .	**Vi skal bruge penge** vee skal br*oo*-er peng-er

Try writing out your own checklist for these four useful phrase-starters like this:

Jeg vil gerne have . . .	**De vil gerne have . . .**
Han vil gerne have . . .	**Vi vil gerne have . . .**
Hun vil gerne have . . .	
Hvor kan jeg få . . .?	**Hvor kan de få . . .?**
Hvor kan han få . . .?	**Hvor kan vi få . . .?**
Hvor kan hun få . . .?	

MORE PRACTICE

Here are some useful Danish names of things. See how many different sentences you can make up, using the various points of information given earlier in this section.

	singular	plural
1 ashtray	**askebæger(t)**	**askebægre**
2 ball-point pen	**kuglepen(n)**	**kuglepenne**
3 bag	**taske(n)**	**tasker**
4 bottle	**flaske(n)**	**flasker**
5 car	**bil(n)**	**biler**
6 cigarette	**cigaret(n)**	**cigaretter**
7 corkscrew	**proptrækker(n)**	**proptrækkere**
8 egg	**æg(t)**	**æg**

		singular	plural
9	house	**hus(t)**	**huse**
10	knife	**kniv(n)**	**knive**
11	mountain	**bjerg(t)**	**bjerge**
12	plate	**tallerken(n)**	**tallerkener**
13	postcard	**postkort(t)**	**postkort**
14	room	**værelse(t)**	**værelser**
15	shoe	**sko(n)**	**sko**
16	stamp	**frimærke(t)**	**frimærker**
17	street	**gade(n)**	**gader**
18	ticket	**billet(n)**	**billetter**
19	train	**tog(t)**	**tog**
20	wallet	**tegnebog(n)**	**tegnebøger**

Index

Travellers' **Norwegian**

David Ellis is Director of the Somerset Language Centre and co-author of a number of language books

Margrethe Hoddevik has lived in London for a number of years and works as a freelance translator and teacher

Dr John Baldwin is Lecturer in Phonetics at University College, London

Travellers' Norwegian

D. L. Ellis, M. Hoddevik

Pronunciation **Dr J. Baldwin**

Useful address
Norwegian Tourist Board
20 Pall Mall
London SW1

Norwegian

Contents

Norwegian

Everyday expressions

[See also 'Shop talk', p. 158]

Hello ⎤ Good morning ⎬ Good day ⎦	**Morn** morn **God dag** goo dahg
Good afternoon	**God kveld** goo kvel
Good night	**God natt** goo natt
Goodbye	**Adjø** ad-yer **Ha det bra** ha-de bra
Yes	**Ja** ya
Please	**Vær så snild** var saw snil
Yes, please	**Ja, takk** ya takk
Thank you	**Takk** takk
Thank you very much	**Tusen takk** toossen takk
That's right	**Det er riktig** day ar riktee
No	**Nei** nay
No thanks	**Nei takk** nay takk
I disagree	**Jeg er ikke enig** yay ar ikker aynee
Excuse me ⎤ Sorry ⎦	**Unnskyld meg** oonshil may
That's good ⎤ I like it ⎦	**Det er bra** day ar bra
That's no good ⎤ I don't like it ⎦	**Jeg liker det ikke** yay leeker day ikker
I know	**Jeg vet det** yay vait day

It doesn't matter	**Det gjør ikke noe** day yor *i*kker n*oo*-er
Where's the toilet, please?	**Hvor er toilettet?** vor ar twa-l*e*tter
Do you speak English?	**Snakker De engelsk?** sn*a*kker dee *e*ng-elsk
I'm sorry . . .	**Unnskyld meg men . . .** *oo*nshil may men . . .
I don't speak Norwegian	**Jeg snakker ikke norsk** yay sn*a*kker *i*kker noshk
I only speak a little Norwegian	**Jeg snakker bare litt norsk** yay sn*a*kker b*a*hrer litt noshk
I don't understand	**Jeg forstår ikke** yay forst*o*r *i*kker
Please can you . . .	**Kan de . . .** kan dee . . .
repeat that?	**gjenta det?** y*e*nta day
speak more slowly?	**snakke saktere?** sn*a*kker s*u*ckter-er
write it down?	**skrive det ned?** skr*ee*ver day ned
What is this called in Norwegian? [*point*]	**Hvordan sier man det på norsk?** vordun s*ee*-er mann day paw noshk

Crossing the border

ESSENTIAL INFORMATION

- Don't waste time rehearsing what to say to border officials – the chances are you won't have to say anything at all.
- When entering Norway, have your documents ready: passport, tickets, money, travellers' cheques, insurance documents, driving licence and car registration documents.
- Look for these signs:
TOLL (customs)
GRENSE (OVERGANG) (frontier)
GRENSEPOLITI (frontier police)

Norwegian

- Random customs checks are frequent and fines for excess quantities of alcohol and tobacco high. You may be asked routine questions by customs officials [*see below*]. The other most important answer to know is 'Nothing': **Nei, ingen ting** (*nay ing-en ting*).

ROUTINE QUESTIONS

Passport?	**Pass?**
	pass
Insurance?	**Forsikring?**
	fors*i*kring
Registration document? (logbook)	**Vognkort?**
	vogn-k*o*rt
Ticket, please	**Billetten Deres, takk**
	bill*e*t-en d*a*yress, takk
Have you anything to declare?	**Har De noe å fortolle?**
	har dee n*oo*-er aw for-t*o*ller
Where are you going?	**Hvor skal De?**
	vor sk*a*hl dee
How long are you staying?	**Hvor lenge skal De være her?**
	vor l*e*ng-er sk*a*hl dee v*a*rer har
Where have you come from?	**Hvor kommer De fra?**
	vor k*o*mmer dee fra

Meeting people

[*See also 'Everyday expressions', p. 120*]

Breaking the ice

How are you?	**God dag**
	goo dahg
Pleased to meet you	**Hyggelig å hilse på Dem**
	h*i*gge-lee aw h*i*l-ser paw dem
I am here . . .	**Jeg er her . . .**
	yay ar har . . .
on holiday	**på ferie**
	paw f*a*iree-er

on business	**på forretningsreise**
	paw forretning-sraysser
Can I offer you . . .	**Vil De ha . . .**
	vil dee ha . . .
a drink?	**en drink?**
	en drink
a cigarette?	**en sigarett?**
	en sigarett
a cigar?	**en sigar?**
	en sigar
Are you staying long?	**Skal De være her lenge?**
	skahl dee varer har leng-er

Name

What is your name?	**Hva heter De?**
	va hayter dee
My name is . . .	**Jeg heter . . .**
	yay hayter . . .

Family

Are you married?	**Er De gift?**
	ar dee yift
I am . . .	**Jeg er . . .**
	yay ar . . .
married	**gift**
	yift
single	**ugift**
	oo-yift
This is . . .	**Dette er . . .**
	detter ar . . .
my wife	**min kone**
	meen koner
my husband	**min mann**
	meen mann
my son	**min sønn**
	meen sirn
my daughter	**min datter**
	meen dot-ter
my boyfriend	**min venn**
	meen venn
my girlfriend	**min venninne**
	meen venn-in-er

Norwegian

This is . . .	**Dette er . . .**
	detter ar . . .
my fiancé(e)	**min forlovede**
	meen forlaw-ved-er
my colleague	**min kollega**
	meen kolleg-ah
Do you have any children?	**Har De noen barn?**
	har dee noo-en barn
I have . . .	**Jeg har . . .**
	yay har . . .
one daughter	**en datter**
	ain dot-ter
one son	**en sønn**
	ain sirn
two daughters	**to døtre**
	too dirtrer
three sons	**tre sønner**
	tray sirnner
No, I haven't any children	**Nei, jeg har ingen barn**
	nay yay har ing-en barn

Where you live

Are you . . .	**Er De . . .**
	ar dee . . .
Norwegian?	**norsk?**
	noshk
Swedish?	**svensk?**
	svensk
I am . . .	**Jeg er . . .**
	yay ar . . .
American	**amerikansk**
	ahmerikahnsk
English	**engelsk**
	eng-elsk

[For other nationalities, see p. 211]

I live . . .	**Jeg bor . . .**
	yay boor . . .
in London	**i London**
	ee lon-don
in England	**i England**
	ee eng-lahn

in the north (of England)	**i Nord (England)**
	ee noor (eng-lahn)
in the north (of London)	**i Nord (London)**
	ee noor (lon-don)
in the south	**i Sør . . .**
	ee sir . . .
in the west	**i Vest . . .**
	ee vest . . .
in the centre (of town)	**midt i (byen)**
	mitt ee (bee-en)

For the businessman and woman

I'm from . . . (firm's name)	**Jeg er fra . . .**
	yay ar fra . . .
I have an appointment with ...	**Jeg har en avtale med . . .**
	yay har en ahv-tahler may . . .
May I speak to . . .?	**Kan jeg snakke med . . .?**
	kan yay snakker may . . .?
This is my card	**Her er kortet mitt**
	har ar korter mitt
I'm sorry I'm late	**Unnskyld at jeg kommer for sent**
	oonshil aht yay kommer for saint
Can I fix another appointment?	**Kan jeg avtale et nytt møte?**
	kan yay ahv-tahler et nitt mirter
I'm staying at the (Grand) hotel	**Jeg bor på (Grand) Hotell**
	yay boor paw (grang) hotel
I'm staying in the (Olavsgaten)	**Jeg bor i (Olavsgaten)**
	yay boor ee (olafs-gahten)

Asking the way

ESSENTIAL INFORMATION

● Keep a look out for street names, road signs, shops, cinemas etc.

Norwegian

WHAT TO SAY

Excuse me, please	**Unnskyld meg**
	*oo*nshil may
How do I get . . .	**Hvordan kommer jeg . . .**
	vordun ko*mm*er yay . . .
to Oslo?	**til Oslo?**
	til *o*shlo
to Storgata?	**til Storgata?**
	til stoor-gahta
to the airport?	**til flyplassen?**
	til fl*ee*-plahssen
to the beach?	**til stranda?**
	til stranda
to the bus station?	**til rutebilstasjonen?**
	til r*oo*ter-b*ee*l-stash*oo*nen
to the historic site?	**til det historiske området?**
	til day hist*oo*risker *o*mrawder
to the market?	**til torget?**
	til torg-er
to the police station?	**til politistasjonen?**
	til polit*ee*-stash*oo*nen
to the port?	**til havnen?**
	til havnen
to the post office?	**til postkontoret?**
	til posst-kont*oo*rer
to the railway station?	**til jernbanestasjonen?**
	til yarn-bahner-stash*oo*nen
to the sports stadium?	**til idrettsplassen?**
	til *ee*drets-plahssen
to the tourist information office?	**turistinformasjonen?**
	tourist-informa-sh*oo*nen
to the town centre?	**til sentrum?**
	til sentrum
to the town hall?	**til rådhuset?**
	til rawd-hoosser
Excuse me, please	**Unnskyld meg**
	*oo*nshil may
Is there . . . near by?	**Er det . . . i nærheten?**
	ar day . . . ee nair-hayten
an art gallery	**et kunstgalleri**
	et koonst-galler*ee*

a baker's	**en bakerforretning**
	en bahker-forretning
a bank	**en bank**
	en bank
a bar	**en bar**
	en bar
	et sjenkested
	et shenker-stayd
a botanical garden	**en botanisk hage**
	en bootahnisk hahg-er
a bus stop	**en bussholdeplass**
	en bus-holder-plahss
a butcher's	**en kjøttforretning**
	en shert-forretning
a café	**en kafé**
	en kafay
a cake shop	**et konditori**
	et konditoree
a campsite	**en kampingplass**
	en camping-plahss
a car park	**en parkeringsplass**
	en parkairingss-plahss
a change bureau	**et vekslekontor**
	et veksler-kontoor
a chemist's	**et apotek**
	et apottayk
	et parfymeri
	et parfeemer-ree
a church	**en kirke**
	en sheerker
a cinema	**en kino**
	en sheeno
a delicatessen	**en delikatesseforretning**
	en dellika-tesser-forretning
a dentist's	**en tannlege**
	en tahnn-laygher
a department store	**et stormagasin**
	et stor-magasseen
a disco	**et diskotek**
	et diskotayk
a doctor's surgery	**en lege**
	en laygher

Norwegian

Is there . . . near by?   **Er det . . . i nærheten?**
ar day . . . ee nair-hayten

a dry-cleaner's   **et renseri**
et rain-seree

a fishmonger's   **en fiskehandel**
en fisker-handel

a garage (for repairs)   **et verksted**
et vairk-sted

a greengrocer's   **en grønnsakhandel**
en grern-sahk-handel

a grocer's   **en kolonialhandel**
en kolonee-ahl-handel

a hairdresser's (ladies)   **en damefrisør**
en dahmer-free-sir

a barber-hairdresser (men)   **en barberer**
en barbairer

a hardware shop   **en jernvarehandel**
en yairn-va-rer-handel

a hospital   **et sykehus**
et seeker-hooss

a hotel   **et hotell**
et hotel

a laundry   **et selvbetjeningsvaskeri**
et sel-bet-yainingss-vaskeree

a museum   **et museum**
et moossay-oom

a newsagent's   **en avisbutikk**
en ahveess-bootick

a night club   **en nattklubb**
en natt-kloobb

a park   **en park**
en park

a petrol station   **en bensinstasjon**
en ben-seen-stashoon

a post box   **en postkasse**
en posst-kasser

a public garden   **en park**
en park

a public toilet   **et offentlig toalett**
et offentlee twa-let

a restaurant   **en restaurant**
en restoo-rung

a snack bar	**en snackbar**
	en snackbar
a sports ground	**en idrettstadion**
	en eedrets-stahdee-on
a supermarket	**et supermarked**
	et sooper-mar-ked
a sweet shop	**en godtebutikk**
	en gotter-bootikk
a swimming pool	**et svømmebasseng**
	et svermmer-basseng
a taxi stand	**en drosjeholdeplass**
	en drosher-holder-plahss
a theatre	**et teater**
	et tay-ahter
a tobacconist's	**en tobakksforretning**
	en tobaks-forretning
a travel agent's	**et reisebyrå**
	et racer-beeraw
a youth hostel	**et ungdomsherberge**
	et oong-domss-hair-bairg-er
a zoo	**en zoologisk hage**
	en soo-law-ghisk-hahg-er

DIRECTIONS

- Asking where a place is, or if a place is near by, is one thing; making sense of the answer is another.
- Here are some of the most important key directions and replies.

Left/Right	**Venstre/Høyre**
	venstrer/hay-rer
Straight on	**Rett fram**
	rett frahm
There	**Der**
	dar
First on the left/right	**Første gate til venstre/høyre**
	firster gahter til venstrer/hay-rer
Second on the left/right	**Annen gate til venstre/høyre**
	annan gahter til venstrer/hay-rer
At the crossroads	**Ved veikrysset**
	vay vay-kreesser
At the traffic lights	**Ved trafikklyset**
	vay trafeekk-leesser

At the roundabout	**Ved rundkjøringen** vay r*oo*n-shir-ing-en
At the level crossing	**Ved jernbaneovergangen** vay y*a*rn-bahner-awver-g*ah*ng-en
It's near/far	**Det er like i nærheten/langt unna** day ar l*ee*ker ee n*ai*r-hayten/ lahngt *oo*nna
One kilometre	**En kilometer** en sh*ee*lo-m*a*yter
Two kilometres	**To kilometer** too sh*ee*lo-m*a*yter
Five minutes . . .	**Fem minutter . . .** fem min*oo*ter . . .
on foot/by car	**å gå/med bil** aw gaw/may beel
Take . . .	**Ta . . .** ta . . .
the bus	**bussen** b*oo*ssen
the train	**toget** t*a*wg-er
the tram	**trikken** tr*i*kken
the underground	**undergrunden** *oo*nner-gr*oo*nnen

[*For public transport, see p. 199*]

The tourist information office

ESSENTIAL INFORMATION

- You will find a tourist information office in most major towns and resorts.
- Look for the word **TURISTINFORMASJON** or this sign
- Tourist information offices are open all the

year round in major towns and resorts. In smaller towns they open
for varying periods during the months of May, June, July, August and September.

- They will accept advance reservations for accommodation locally as well as assisting you on your arrival. They will also help you to make train, ferry, boat and bus reservations and give details on prices and road conditions.
- These offices give you free local information in the form of printed leaflets, fold-outs, brochures, lists and plans.
- For finding a tourist office, see p. 126, 130.

WHAT TO SAY

Please, have you got . . .	**Har De . . .** har dee . . .
a plan of the town?	**et kart over byen?** et kart awver bee-en
a list of events?	**en liste over begivenheter** en lister awver bay-yeeven-hayter
a list of hotels?	**en liste over hoteller** en lister awver hoteller
a list of campsites?	**en liste over campingplasser?** en lister awver camping-plahsser
a list of restaurants?	**en liste over restauranter?** en lister awver restoo-runger
a leaflet on the town?	**en brosjyre om byen?** en brush-eerei om bee-en
a leaflet on the region?	**en brosjyre om distriktet?** en brush-eerer om district-ter
a railway/bus timetable?	**en tog/buss tabell?** en tawg/bus ta-bell
In English, please	**På engelsk, takk** paw eng-elsk takk
How much do I owe you?	**Hvor mye skylder jeg Dem?** vor mee-er shiller yay dem

LIKELY ANSWERS

You need to understand when the answer is 'No'. You should be able to tell by the assistant's facial expression, tone of voice and gesture; but there are some language clues, such as:

No	**Nei** nay

I'm sorry	**Nei dessverre**
	nay dess-*vair*rer
I don't have a list of campsites	**Jeg har ingen liste over campingplasser**
	yay har *ing*-en *li*ster *aw*ver camping-*plah*sser
I haven't got any left	**Jeg har ikke flere igjen**
	yay har *ikk*er *flay*rer ee-*yen*
It's free	**Det er gratis**
	day ar *gra*-tiss

Accommodation

Hotel

ESSENTIAL INFORMATION

- If you want hotel-type accommodation, look for this sign or the following words in capital letters on name boards:
  HOTELL (usually high standard expensive establishment)
  TURISTHOTELL (high standard, expensive resort establishment with wide range of facilities)
  HØYFJELLSHOTELL (high mountain resort, expensive, high standard with wide range of facilities)
  PENSJONAT (boarding house, standard varying from relatively high and expensive to modest and inexpensive)
  GJESTGIVERI/VERTSHUS/TURISTHEIM (same as *pensjonat*)
  TURISTHYTTE (tourist lodge, usually inexpensive and modest)
  ROM (room in private house)
- A list of establishments may be obtained from the nearest Norwegian tourist office.
- Hotels are ungraded in Norway but strict legal requirements are made before establishments can use the term 'hotell'. 'Turisthotell'

and 'høfjellshotell' are of even higher standards and invariably hold a spirit licence.

- Unlisted establishments can be slightly cheaper but are probably as good as the listed ones.
- Not all boarding houses etc. provide meals apart from breakfast. Inquire about this on arrival.
- On arrival also inquire about the cost of the room before accepting it.
- The cost is per person per night. It includes VAT and service charges but not always breakfast.
- Breakfast must be ordered when booking in if not included in the price. In cities you'll be offered a choice of a cold table or an English or Continental breakfast. In the country, it'll be a cold table with the fare varying from the lavish to the simple according to the standard of the establishment.
- A cheaper full pension rate is available to guests staying at least 3–5 days. There are usually reductions of 75% for children under 3 and 50% for children 3–12(15) when sharing a room with adults.
- On arrival, you will be asked to show your passport and to fill in a special form for foreigners which usually carries an English translation.
- Leaving a tip will be appreciated but not expected.

WHAT TO SAY

I have a booking	**Jeg har reservert**
	yay har resser-va*ir*t
Have you any vacancies?	**Har De noe ledig rom?**
	har dee n*oo*-er l*ay*dee r*oo*m
Can I book a room?	**Kan jeg reservere et rom?**
	kan yay resser-v*ai*rer et r*oo*m
It's for ...	**Det er for ...**
	day ar for ...
one person	**en person**
	*ai*n pesh*oo*n
two persons	**to personer**
	too pesh*oo*ner

[*For numbers, see p. 205*]

It's for ...	**Det er for ...**
	day ar for ...
one night	**en natt**
	*ai*n natt

It's for . . .	**Det er for . . .**
	day ar for . . .
two nights	**to netter**
	too netter
one week	**en uke**
	ain ooker
two weeks	**to uker**
	too ooker
I would like . . .	**Jeg vil ha . . .**
	yay vil ha . . .
a room	**et rom**
	et room
two rooms	**to rom**
	too room
with a single bed	**et enkeltrom**
	et enkelt room
with two single beds	**med to enkelsenger**
	may too enkel-seng-er
with a double bed	**med dobbelsenger**
	may dawbel-seng-er
with a toilet	**med toilett**
	may twa-let
with a bathroom	**med bad**
	may bahd
with a shower	**med dusj**
	may doosh
with a cot	**med barneseng**
	may barner-seng
with a balcony	**med balkong**
	may bal-kong
I would like . . .	**Jeg vil ha . . .**
	yay vil ha . . .
full board	**helpensjon**
	hail-pen-shoon
half board	**halvpensjon**
	hahl-pen-shoon
bed and breakfast	**overnatting med frokost**
	awver-natting may froo-kost
Is breakfast included?	**Er frokost inkludert?**
	ar froo-kost in-kloo-dairt
Do you serve meals?	**Serverer dere middag og lunsj?**
	servay-rer dayrer middag aw lunsh

At what time is . . .   **Når serverer dere . . .**
                                   nor servay-rer dayrer . . .

  breakfast?   **frokost?**
                                   froo-kost

  lunch?   **lunsj?**
                                   lunsh

  dinner?   **middag?**
                                   middag

How much is it?   **Hvor mye koster det?**
                                   vor mee-er kost-er day

Can I look at the room?   **Kan jeg se rommet?**
                                   kan yay say roommer

I'd prefer a room . . .   **Jeg foretrekker et rom . . .**
                                   yay forer-trekker et room

  at the front/at the back   **på forsiden/baksiden**
                                   paw for-seeden/bahk-seeden

OK, I'll take it   **Det er fint, jeg tar det**
                                   day ar feent yay tar day

No thanks, I won't take it   **Nei takk, det passer ikke**
                                   nay takk day pahsser ikker

**The key to room number (10),   **Kan jeg få nøkkelen til rom
  please**   nummer (ti)?**
                                   kan yay faw nirk-ellen til room
                                   noommer (tee)

Please may I have . . .   **Kan jeg få . . .**
                                   kan yay faw . . .

  a coat hanger?   **en kleshenger?**
                                   en klaiss-heng-er

  a towel?   **et håndkle?**
                                   et hawn-kler

  a glass?   **et glass?**
                                   et glahss

  some soap?   **et såpestykke?**
                                   et sawper-sticker

  an ashtray?   **et askebeger?**
                                   et ask-er-baygher

  another pillow?   **en pute til?**
                                   en pooter til

  another blanket?   **et teppe til?**
                                   et tepper til

Come in!   **Kom inn!**
                                   kom in

Norwegian

One moment, please!	**Et øyeblikk!**
	et er-yer-blick
Please can you . . .	**Kan De . . .**
	kan dee . . .
do this laundry/dry-cleaning?	**vaske/rense dette tøyet?**
	vasker/ruinss-er detter ter-yer
call me at . . .?	**ringe meg klokken . . .?**
	ring-er may klokken . . .
help me with my luggage?	**hjelpe meg med bagasjen?**
	yelper may mer ba-ga-shen
call a taxi for . . .?	**skaffe en drosje til klokken . . .?**
[For times, see p. 207]	skaffer en drosher til klokken . . .
The bill, please	**Regningen, takk**
	raining-en takk
Is service included?	**Er service inkludert?**
	ar service inkloodairt
I think this is wrong	**Jeg tror dette er feil**
	yay troor detter ar fail
Can you give me a receipt?	**Kan De gi meg en kvittering?**
	kan dee yee may en kvittairing

At breakfast

Some more . . . please	**Kan jeg få litt mer . . .**
	kan yay faw litt mair . . .
coffee	**kaffe**
	kaffer
tea	**te**
	tay
bread	**brød**
	brer
butter	**smør**
	smer
jam	**syltetøy**
	seelter-tai
May I have a boiled egg?	**Kan jeg få et kokt egg?**
	kan yay faw et kokt egg

LIKELY REACTIONS

Have you an identity document, please?	**Har De legitimasjon?**
	har dee lay-ghee-tee-mashoon

What's your name?	**Hva er navnet?**
[*see p. 123*]	va ar na*h*vner
Sorry, we're full	**Det er dessverre fullt her**
	day ar dess-va*rr*er fu*l*lt har
I haven't any rooms left	**Jeg har ikke flere ledige rom**
	yay har *I*kker fla*yr*er laydee-yer room
Do you want to have a look?	**Vil De se rommet?**
	vil-dee say roommer
How many people is it for?	**Hvor mange personer er det for?**
	vor ma*ng*-er peshooner ar day for
From (7 o'clock) onwards	**Fra klokken (sju)**
	fra klokken (shoo)
From (midday) onwards	**Fra klokken (tolv)**
[*For times, see p. 207*]	fra klokken (ta*wl*l)
It's (80 kroner)	**Det koster (åtti kroner)**
[*For numbers, see p. 205*]	day koster (a*w*tti kroner)

Camping and youth hostelling

ESSENTIAL INFORMATION

- Look for the word: **CAMPING** or these signs

- You pay per car (if applicable), for the tent/caravan and per person. Children under 5 go free.

Norwegian

- Be prepared to provide proof of identity.
- Campsites in Norway are classified as one, two and three-star camps. Charges vary according to number of stars awarded.
- You are allowed to camp on private, unused land with the landowner's permission, as well as on state owned land. You must, however, camp away from houses and cultivated areas and leave no litter behind.
- Roads in the North and West and in the mountain regions are often too narrow for a caravan. Caravan holidays are therefore recommended around Oslo, the south-eastern part of the country and in the eastern valleys.
- Two and three-star sites have a watchman, flush toilets, shower, electric power points, laundry and ironing rooms. A notice of available amenities is posted up in each camp.
- Many sites have cabins/chalets to rent quite cheaply. These are popular and reservationws should be made early in the afternoon. They are usually fitted with 4 bunk beds, an electric heater and a hot plate for cooking. Other equipment must be provided by the camper. Chalets must be left spotlessly clean.
- Picnic area have tables and bench seats and should be left clean.

Youth hostels

- Look for this sign or **UNGDOMSHERBERGE**.
- Youth hostels are located throughout the country. The standard is usually high. Not all are open during the winter.
- There is no age limit. Most accommodate families with children in family rooms with 4–6 beds.

- Most youth hostels have cooking facilities. A hot meal and breakfast can often be purchased.
- Sheet sleeping bags are obligatory. You can bring your own or hire one at the hostel.
- Groups must make advance bookings. All are welcome, but members of **NUH** (Norwegian Youth Hostel Association) or similar associations in other countries have priority. Non-members can purchase international membership cards at most youth hostels.

WHAT TO SAY

Have you any vacancies?	**Har De noen ledig plass?** har dee noo-en laydee plahss
It's for . . .	**Det er for . . .** day ar for . . .
one adult/one person	**en voksen/en person** ain vaksen/ain peshoon
two adults/two people	**to voksne/to personer** too vaksner/too peshooner
and one child	**og et barn** aw ait barn
and two children	**og to barn** aw too barn
It's for . . .	**Det er for . . .** day ar for . . .
one night	**en natt** ain natt
one week	**en uke** ain ooker
How much is it . . .	**Hvor mye koster det . . .** vor mee-er koster day . . .
for the tent?	**for teltet?** for telter
for the caravan?	**for campingvogna?** for camping-vogna
for the car?	**for bilen?** for beelen
for the electricity?	**for strømmen?** for strermmen
per person?	**per person?** pair peshoon
per day/night?	**per dag/natt?** pair dahg/natt
Do you provide anything . . .	**Får man kjøpt noe . . .** for man shirpt noo-er . . .
to eat?	**å spise?** aw speesser
to drink?	**å drikke?** aw drikker

Norwegian

Do you have . . .	**Har dere . . .**
	har d*a*yrer . . .
a bar?	**en bar?**
	en bar
hot showers?	**varme dusjer?**
	v*a*rmer d*oo*sher
a kitchen?	**et kjøkken?**
	et sh*e*rkken
a laundry?	**vaskemaskiner?**
	vasker-mash*ee*ner
a restaurant?	**en restaurant?**
	en restoo-r*u*ng
a shop?	**en butikk?**
	en boo-t*i*ck
a swimming pool?	**et svømmebasseng?**
	et sv*e*rmmer-bass*e*ng
a takeaway?	**ferdigmat/takeaway mat?**
	f*ai*rdee-maht/tak*ea*way maht?

[*For food shopping, see p. 162 and for eating and drinking out, see p. 174*]

Where are . . .	**Hvor er . . .**
	vor ar . . .
the dustbins?	**søppelkassene?**
	s*i*rppel-k*a*hssener
the showers?	**dusjene?**
	d*oo*shener
the toilets?	**toilettene?**
	twa-lett-ener
At what time must one . . .	**Når må man . . .**
	nor maw mann . . .
go to bed?	**gå til sengs?**
	gaw til s*a*ingss
get up?	**stå opp?**
	st*a*w opp
Please, have you got. . .?	**Har dere . . .**
	har d*a*yrer
a broom?	**en feiekost?**
	en f*a*yer-k*oo*st
a corkscrew?	**en korketrekker?**
	en k*o*rker-trekker
a drying-up cloth?	**et oppvaskhåndkle?**
	et *o*ppvask-h*a*wn-kler

a fork?	**en gaffel?**
	en ga-fel
a fridge?	**et kjøleskap?**
	et shirler-skahp
a frying pan?	**en stekepanne?**
	en stayker-pahnner
an iron?	**et strykejern?**
	et streeker-yarn
a knife?	**en kniv?**
	en k-neev
a plate?	**en tallerken?**
	en tal-lairken
a saucepan?	**en kjele?**
	en shayler
a teaspoon?	**en teskje?**
	en tay-shay
a tin-opener?	**en bokseåpner?**
	en boxer-awpner
any washing powder?	**vaskepulver?**
	vasker-poolver
any washing-up liquid?	**oppvaskmiddel?**
	oppvask-middel

Problems

The toilet	**Toilettet**
	twa-letter
The shower	**Dusjen**
	dooshen
The tap	**Vannkranen**
	vahnn-krahnen
The razor point	**Stikkontakten**
	stick-kontakten
The light	**Lyset**
	leesser
. . . is not working	**. . . virker ikke**
	. . . veerker ikker
My camping gas has run out	**Gassflasken min er tom**
	gahss-flask-en meen ar tom

LIKELY REACTIONS

Have you an identity document?	**Har De legitimasjon?**
	har dee lay-ghee-tee-mashoon

Norwegian

Your membership card, please	**Kan jeg få se medlemskortet deres** kan yay faw say maid-lemss-korter dayress
What's your name? [see p. 123]	**Hva er navnet?** va ar nahvner
Sorry, we're full	**Det er dessverre fullt her** day ar dess-varrer fullt har
How many people is it for?	**Hvor mange personer er det for?** vor mang-er peshooner ar day for
How many nights is it for?	**Hvor mange netter er det for?** vor mang-er netter ar day for
It's (40) kroner . . .	**Det blir (førti) kroner . . .** day bleer (firtee) kroner . . .
per day/per night [For numbers, see p. 205]	**per dag/per natt** pair dahg/pair natt

Rented accommodation: problem solving

ESSENTIAL INFORMATION

- **For short holidays:** Arrange your accommodation before leaving. Travel agents and the Norwegian Tourist Board at home will be able to help you.
- If you want to rent accommodation when already in Norway, look for **TIL LEIE** in local newspapers or put in an advert yourself.
- For holidays the following types of accommodation are popular and readily available when booked in advance.
- **BONDEGÅRD** (farmhouse holiday). Holiday on selected working farms; guests are not expected to do any work.
- **HYTTE** (chalet holiday). Inexpensive open air holidays. Chalets situated throughout Norway, sometimes near a city. Chalets are usually comfortable and equipped for 4–6 people. Inventory complete except for linen and towels.
- **Rental apartments.** Flat or chalet with high standard of amenities.

with total or partial self-service. Accommodation often around or near cafeteria, lounges, TV rooms, grocer's shop, sauna etc.

- **RORBU** holidays. A hut on the seashore equipped with basic amenities. Mostly in the North of Norway.
- Having arranged your own accommodation and arrived with the key, check the obvious basics that you take for granted at home.
- **Electricity:** Appliances from home can be used, but may need an adaptor plug, as you will only find two-pin plugs. Electric heaters (rather like small radiators) are often attached to the wall. They get very hot and must not be covered. Fuses look like a round, white radio battery. Light bulbs screw on.
- **Gas:** Only bottled propane gas for cooking in remote chalets and *rorbus*. No gas fires. Fireplaces can be open or closed.
- **Cooker:** Always electric. Oven and plates for cooking, usually no grill. Plates sometimes slow.
- **Toilet:** Mains drainage or septic tank. Don't flush disposable nappies etc. down the toilet if you're on a septic tank.
- **Windows:** Check method of opening and shutting. Must not be left open after dark with light on because of insects.
- **Insects and snakes:** Mosquitoes bad in eastern and northern regions, particularly in June. Kept partly away by smoke spiral (**røkspiral**) which can be purchased in sports shops, general stores and 'apoteks'. In dry forest regions, look out for adders as in Norway their bites can kill. Buy antidote tablets **ormtabletter** from 'apotek' or general stores. If bitten, bleed wound and seek medical attention straightaway. Don't picnic on dry stony spots.
- **Equipment:** For buying and replacing equipment, see p. 156.
- Be clear in your mind who to contact in an emergency, even if only a Norwegian neighbour in the first instance.

WHAT TO SAY

My name is . . .	**Jeg heter . . .** yay hayter . . .
I'm staying at . . .	**Jeg bor i . . .** yay boor ee . . .
They've cut off . . .	**De har kuttet av . . .** dee har koottet ahv . . .
the electricity	**strømmen** strermmen
the water	**vannet** vahnner

Do you know of . . .   **Vet De om . . .**
                                    vait dee om . . .

  an electrician?   **en elektriker?**
                                    en el*ai*k-tricker

  a plumber?   **en rørlegger?**
                                    en rer-legger

Where is . . .   **Hvor er . . .**
                                    vor ar . . .

  the fuse box?   **sikringstavlen?**
                                    s*i*ck-ringss-t*ah*vlen

  the stopcock?   **stopperkranen?**
                                    st*o*pper-kr*ah*nen

  the boiler?   **fyren?**
                                    f*ee*ren

  the water heater?   **varmtvannsbeholderen?**
                                    varmt-v*ah*nnss-bay-h*o*lderen

Is there . . .   **Er det . . .**
                                    ar day . . .

  bottled gas?   **propangass?**
                                    prop*ah*n-gahss

  mains drainage?   **kloakkutløp?**
                                    kloo-*ah*k-ootl*e*rp

  a septic tank?   **en septiktank?**
                                    en s*e*ptik-tahnk

  central heating?   **sentralvarme?**
                                    sentr*ah*l-varmer

The cooker   **Komfyren**
                                    kom-f*ee*ren

The hairdrier   **Hårtørkeren**
                                    hor-terk-*ai*ren

The heating   **Oppvarmingen**
                                    *o*pp-varming-en

The electric heater   **Den elektriske ovnen**
                                    den el*ai*k-trissker *o*vnen

The iron   **Strykejernet**
                                    str*ee*ker-y*a*rnet

The refrigerator   **Kjøleskapet**
                                    sh*i*rler-sk*ah*per

The telephone   **Telefonen**
                                    telef*oo*nen

The toilet   **Toalettet**
                                    twa-l*e*tter

The washing machine	**Vaskemaskinen**
	vasker-mash*ee*nen
. . . is not working	**. . . virker ikke**
	. . . v*ee*rker *i*kker
Where can I get . . .	**Hvor kan jeg få . . .**
	vor kan yay faw . . .
an adaptor for this?	**en overgangskontakt til denne?**
	en *a*wver-gangss-kont*a*hkt til denner
a bottle of propane gas?	**en flaske propangass?**
	en fl*a*sk-er proop*a*hn-gahss
a fuse?	**en sikring?**
	en s*i*ck-ring
an insecticide spray?	**et insektmiddel?**
	et *i*nsekt-m*i*ddel
a light bulb?	**en lyspære?**
	en l*ee*ss-parer
The drain	**Avløpsrøret**
	*a*hv-lerps-rer-rer
The sink	**Vasken**
	v*a*hsken
. . . is blocked	**. . . er tett**
	. . . ar tett
The toilet is blocked	**Toalettet er tett**
	twa-l*e*tter ar tett
The gas is leaking	**Gassen lekker**
	g*a*hssen l*e*kker
Can you mend it straightaway?	**Kan De reparere det med en gang?**
	kan dee reppa-r*ai*rer day med ain g*a*hng
When can you mend it?	**Når kan De reparere den?**
	nor kan dee reppa-r*ai*rer den
How much do I owe you?	**Hvor mye skylder jeg Dem?**
	vor m*ee*-er sh*i*ller yay dem
When is the rubbish collected?	**Når er det søppeltømming?**
	nor ar day s*i*r-pel-termming

LIKELY REACTIONS

What's your name?	**Hva er navnet?**
	va ar n*a*hvner
What's your address?	**Hva er adressen Deres?**
	va ar ah-dr*e*ss-en d*a*yress

Norwegian

There's a shop . . .	**Det er en butikk . . .**
	day ar en boot*i*kk
in town	**i byen**
	ee b*ee*-en
I can't come . . .	**Jeg kan ikke komme . . .**
	yay kan *i*kker k*o*mmer . . .
today	**i dag**
	ee dahg
this week	**denne uken**
	denner *oo*ken
until Monday	**før mandag**
	fir m*a*hn-dahg
I can come . . .	**Jeg kan komme . . .**
	yay kan k*o*mmer . . .
on Tuesday	**på tirsdag**
	paw t*ee*sh-dahg
when you want	**når De vil**
	nor dee v*i*l
Every day	**Hver dag**
	var dahg
Every other day	**Annen hver dag**
	*a*hnen var d*a*hg
On Wednesday	**På onsdag**
	paw *oo*nss-dahg

[*For days of the week, see p. 208*]

General shopping

The chemist's

ESSENTIAL INFORMATION

- Look for the word **APOTEK** in capital letters.
- Medicines (drugs) are available only at an *apotek*.
- Some non-drugs can be bought at supermarkets and groceries.
- Toiletries are bought in small shops called **PARFYMERI** and in supermarkets, department stores and groceries, never in an *apo-*

tek. A *parfymeri* sells toiletries only not photographic equipment, baby utensils etc.

- *Apoteks* are open 9–5 Monday to Friday and 9–1 or 3 on Saturdays. They are closed on Sundays and holidays.
- All night chemists are only found in major cities.
- In emergencies ask for a doctor or the medical emergency service **LEGEVAKT**.
- Prescriptions are needed for most drugs like antibiotics etc. There is a prescription charge.
- For minor injuries and ailments *apoteks* may be able to suggest treatment that does not need prescription.
- Finding the chemist, see p. 127.
  The following articles can normally only be bought at an *apotek*. Articles marked * can also be bought at supermarkets and department stores.

I'd like . . . please	**Kunne jeg få . . .**
	k*oo*n-ner yay faw . . .
*some Alka Seltzer	**noe nyco/samarin**
	n*oo*-er n*ee*co/sama*ree*n
some antiseptic	**et antiseptisk middel**
	et *a*nti-s*e*ptisk m*i*ddel
*some bandages	**noen bandasjer**
	n*oo*-en ban-*da*-sher
some contraceptives	**et prevensjonsmiddel**
	et pray-vang-sh*oo*nss-m*i*ddel
*some cotton wool	**noe vatt**
	n*oo*-er v*a*htt
some eye drops	**noen øyendråper**
	n*oo*-en er-yen-dr*a*w-per
some inhalant	**et innåndingsmiddel**
	et *i*n-awn-dingss-m*i*ddel
*some insect repellent	**et insektmiddel**
	et *i*nsect-m*i*ddel
*some sticking plaster	**noe plaster**
	n*oo*-er pl*a*ster
*some throat pastilles	**noen halspastiller**
	n*oo*-en h*a*hlss-pa-st*i*ller
I'd like something for . . .	**Kunne jeg få noe for . . .**
	k*oo*n-ner yay faw n*oo*-er for . . .
bites/stings	**insektstikk**
	*i*nsect-st*i*ck

I'd like something for . . .	Kunne jeg få noe for . . . koon-ner yay faw noo-er for . . .
burns/scalds	**brannsår** brahn-sor
a cold	**forkjølelse** for-shirlel-ser
constipation	**forstoppelse** for-stop-el-ser
a cough	**hoste** hoosster
diarrhoea	**diarre** dee-array
earache	**øreverk** er-rer-vark
flu	**influensa** influenssa
sore gums	**sårt tannkjøtt** sort tahn-shirt
*sunburn	**solbrenthet** sool-brent-hait
*toothache	**tannverk** tahn-vark
travel sickness	**reisesyke** racer-seeker

The following articles can normally only be bought at a *parfymeri*.
Articles marked * can also be bought at supermarkets and groceries.

I need . . .	Jeg trenger . . . yay treng-er . . .
*some baby food	**noe bebymat** noo-er baby-maht
*some deodorant	**en deodorant** en day-odorant
*some disposable nappies	**papirbleier** papeer-blayer
*some hand cream	**noe håndkrem** noo-er hawn-kraim
*some lipstick	**leppestift** lepper-stift
some lip salve	**leppomade** leppom-ahder

some make-up remover	**sminkefjerner**
	sminkerf-*yair*ner
*some paper tissues	**noen papirlommetørkler**
	n*oo*-en pap*eer*-lommer-t*er*k-ler
*some razor blades	**noen barberblader**
	n*oo*-en barb*air*-bl*ah*der
*some safety pins	**noen sikkerhetsnåler**
	n*oo*-en s*i*cker-haits-n*aw*ler
*some sanitary towels	**sanitetsbind**
	sahnit*ai*ts-binn
*some shaving cream	**barberkrem**
	barb*air*-kraim
*some suntan lotion/oil	**solkrem/olje**
	s*oo*l-kraim/ol-yer
some talcum powder	**talkumpulver**
	t*ah*lkoom-p*oo*lver
*some Tampax	**tampax**
	t*ah*mpax
*some toilet paper	**noe toalettpapir**
	n*oo*-er twa-lett-pap*eer*
*some toothpaste	**noe tannkrem**
	n*oo*-er t*ah*nn-kraim
*some Vaseline	**noe Vaseline**
	n*oo*-er vasser-l*ee*n

Holiday items

ESSENTIAL INFORMATION

- Normal opening hours: 9–5 Monday–Friday and 9–1 Saturdays.
- Places to shop and signs to look for:
  BOKHANDEL (stationery-bookshop) sell stamps and postcards, not toys, records etc.
  KODAK (films)
  KOLONIAL (general store, grocery)
  KIOSK sells postcards, stamps, newspapers, often films.
  STORMARKED (department store)

Norwegian

WHAT TO SAY

I'd like . . .	Jeg vil ha . . .
	yay vil ha . . .
a bag	en bag
	en bag
a beach ball	en badeball
	en bahder-bahll
a bucket	en bøtte
	en birtter
an English newspaper	en engelsk avis
	en eng-elsk ahveess
some envelopes	noen konvolutter
	noo-en kon-vo-lutter
a guide book	en reisehåndbok
	en racer-hawn-book
a map (of the area)	et (lokal) kart
	et (lokahl)-kart
some postcards	noen prospektkort
	noo-en prospekt-kort
a spade	en spade
	en spa-der
a straw hat	en stråhatt
	en straw-hahtt
some sunglasses	et par solbriller
	et par sool-briller
an umbrella	en paraply
	en para-plee
some writing paper	skrivepapir
	skreever-papeer
I'd like . . . [show the camera]	Jeg vil ha . . .
	yay vil ha . . .
a colour film	en fargefilm
	en far-gher-film
a black and white film	en svart/hvitt film
	en svart/vitt film
for prints	for fotografier
	for footo-grafee-er
for slides	for lysbilder
	for leess-bilder
Please can you . . .	Kan De . . .
	kan dee . . .

develop/print this?	**fremkalle/kopiere denne?**
	fraim-kaller/kopee-ayrer denner
load the camera?	**sette inn filmen?**
	setter inn film-en

[*For other essential expressions, see 'Shop talk', p. 158*]

The tobacconist's

ESSENTIAL INFORMATION

- Tobacco, cigarettes etc. are sold in kiosks, sweet shops, snack bars, groceries and supermarkets.
- Most international brands are available.
- All tobacco products are exceedingly expensive in Norway.
- Rolling and pipe tobacco, cigarette paper and other rolling equipment is readily available.

WHAT TO SAY

A packet of cigarettes . . .	**En pakke sigaretter . . .**
	en pakker sigarett-er . . .
with filters	**med filter**
	may filter
without filters	**uten filter**
	ooten filter
king size	**king size**
	king size
menthol	**med mentol**
	may men-tool
Those up there . . .	**De der oppe . . .**
	dee dar opper . . .
on the right	**til høyre**
	til hay-rer
on the left	**til venstre**
	til venstrer
These [*point*]	**Disse**
	disser

Do you have . . .	**Har dere . . .**
	har dayrer . . .
English cigarettes?	**engelske sigaretter?**
	eng-elsker sigarett-er
rolling tobacco?	**rulletobakk?**
	rooller-tobakk
A packet of pipe tobacco	**En pakke pipetobakk**
	en pakker peeper-tobakk
That one [*point*]	**Den der**
	den dar
A cigar, please	**En sigar, takk**
	en sigar takk
This one [*point*]	**Denne**
	denner
Some cigars, please	**Noen sigarer, takk**
	noo-en sigar-er takk
Those [*point*]	**De der**
	dee dar
A box of matches	**En eske fyrstikker**
	en esker feer-stikker
A packet of flints [*show lighter*]	**En pakke flintesteiner**
	en pakker flinter-stainer
Lighter fuel	**Lighter bensin**
	lighter ben-seen
Lighter gas	**Lighter gass**
	lighter gahss

[*For other essential expressions, see 'Shop talk' p. 158*]

Buying clothes

ESSENTIAL INFORMATION

- Clothes are expensive but tend to be of high quality. Sales in January and August have genuine reductions and are good value for money.
- For clothes and shoes check shop windows or ask for:

DAMEKLÆR (women's clothes)
HERREKLÆR (men's clothes)
BARNEKLÆR (children's clothes)
SKOBUTIKK (shoe shop)
STORMARKED (department store)

- Most shops leave you to look around on your own and try things on.

WHAT TO SAY

I'd like . . .	**Jeg vil ha . . .**
	yay vil ha . . .
an anorak	**en anorakk**
	en ahn-oor*ah*kk
a belt	**et belte**
	et b*e*lter
a bikini	**en bikini**
	en bik*i*ni
a bra	**en B.H.**
	en b*a*y haw
a cap (swimming)	**en badehette**
	en b*ah*der-hetter
a cap (skiing)	**en skilue**
	en sh*ee*-loo-er
a cardigan	**en ulljakke**
	en *oo*ll-yakker
a coat	⎡ **en kåpe** (ladies)
	⎢ en k*aw*-per
	⎢ **en frakk** (men)
	⎣ en fr*ah*kk
a dress	**en kjole**
	en sh*o*oler
a jacket	**en jakke**
	en y*a*kker
a jumper/pullover	**en genser**
	en gh*e*n-ser
a nightdress	**en nattkjole**
	en n*a*tt-shooler
a raincoat	**en regnfrakk**
	en r*ai*n-frahkk
a shirt	**en skjorte**
	en sh*o*orter

WHAT TO SAY

I'd like . . .	**Jeg vil ha . . .**
	yay vil ha . . .
a skirt	**et skjørt**
	et sh*i*rt
a suit	**en dress**
	en dress
a swimsuit	**en badedrakt**
	en b*ah*der-drahkt
a tee-shirt	**en T-skjorte**
	en t*ay*-shoorter
I'd like a pair of . . .	**Jeg vil ha et par . . .**
	yay vil ha et par . . .
shorts	**shorts**
	shorts
stockings	**strømper**
	str*i*rm-per
tights	**strømpebukser**
	str*i*rm-per-b*oo*kser
pyjamas	**pyjamas**
	pee-sha-mass
briefs	**truser** (women)
	tr*oo*sser
	korte underbukser (men)
	k*o*rter *oo*nder-b*oo*kser
gloves	**hansker**
	han-sker
jeans	**ola-bukser**
	*oo*la-b*oo*kser
socks	**sokker**
	s*o*cker
trousers	**bukser**
	b*oo*kser
shoes	**sko**
	sk*oo*
sandals	**sandaler**
	san-d*ah*ler
skiing boots	**skistøvler**
	shee-st*i*rfler
smart shoes	**pen sko**
	p*ai*n sk*oo*
warm boots	**varme støvler**
	v*a*rmer st*i*rfler

My size is . . .	**Jeg er størrelse . . .**
[*For numbers, see p. 205*]	yay ar stir-rel-ser
Can you measure me, please?	**Kan De måle meg?**
	kan dee maw-ler may
Can I try it on?	**Kan jeg prøve den?**
	kan yay prirfer den
It's for a present	**Det er en gave**
	day ar en ga-ver
These are the measurements	**Dette er målene**
[*show written*]	detter ar maw-len-er
bust	**byste**
	beester
chest	**bryst**
	breest
hips	**hofter**
	hofter
waist	**livvidde**
	lee-vidder
Have you something . . .	**Har dere noe . . .**
	har dayrer noo-er . . .
in black?	**i svart?**
	ee svart
in white?	**i hvitt?**
	ee vitt
in grey?	**i grått?**
	ee grawt
in brown?	**i brunt?**
	ee broont
in pink?	**i rosa?**
	ee roo-sa
in green?	**i grønt?**
	ec grernt
in red?	**i rødt?**
	ee rert
in yellow?	**i gult?**
	ee goolt
in this colour? [*point*]	**i denne fargen?**
	ee denner far-ghen
in cotton?	**i bomull?**
	ee bom-ooll
in denim?	**i dongeri?**
	ee dung-ree

Norwegian

Have you something . . .	**Har dere noe . . .**
	har dayrer noo-er . . .
in leather?	**i skinn?**
	ee shinn
in nylon?	**i nylon?**
	ee neelon
in suede?	**i semsket skinn?**
	ee sem-sket shinn
in wool?	**i ull?**
	ee ooll
in this material? [*point*]	**i dette stoffet?**
	ee detter stuffer

[*For other essential expressions, see 'Shop talk', p. 158*]

Replacing equipment

ESSENTIAL INFORMATION

- Look for the signs or ask for:
  JERNVAREFORRETNING (hardware)
  GLASSMAGASIN (crockery, cutlery, ornaments etc)
  ELEKTRISKE VARER (electrical goods)
- Many groceries and general stores sell basic household equipment.
  Also ask for **kjøkken** (kitchen department) or **jernvarer** (hardware) in a department store or supermarket.
- To ask the way to the shop, see p. 127.
- At a campsite try their shop first.

WHAT TO SAY

Have you got . . .	**Har dere . . .**
	har dayrer . . .
an adaptor?	**en overgangskontakt?**
[*show appliance*]	en awver-gang-skontahkt
a bottle of propane gas?	**en flaske propangass?**
	en flasker proopahn-gahss

a bottle opener?	**en flaskeåpner?**
	en flasker *awp*ner
a corkscrew?	**en korketrekker?**
	en *kor*ker-trekker
any disinfectant?	**et desinfeksjonsmiddel?**
	et dess-infeksh*oo*nss-m*i*ddel
any disposable cups?	**papirkopper?**
	pap*ee*r-kopper
any disposable plates?	**papirtallerkner?**
	pap*ee*r-tal-*lair*k-ner
a drying-up cloth?	**et oppvaskhåndkle?**
	et *op*-vask-h*awn*-kler
any forks?	**gafler?**
	g*af*-ler
a fuse? [*show old one*]	**en sikring?**
	en *sick*-ring
an insecticide spray?	**et insektmiddel?**
	et *i*nsekt-m*i*ddel
a paper kitchen roll?	**en rull papirhandklær?**
	en rooll pap*ee*r-hawn-klair
any knives?	**kniver?**
	k-n*ee*ver
a light bulb? [*show old one*]	**en lyspære?**
	en l*ee*ss-parer
a plastic bucket?	**en plastikk-bøtte?**
	en pl*a*stikk-*bir*t-ter
a plastic can?	**en plastik-kanne?**
	en pl*a*stikk-k*ah*nner
a scouring pad?	**en gryteskrubb?**
	en gr*ee*ter-skr*oo*b
a spanner?	**en skrunøkkel?**
	en skr*oo*-nirk-el
a sponge?	**en svamp?**
	en sv*ah*mp
any string?	**hyssing?**
	h*i*ssing
any tent pegs?	**teltplugger?**
	t*e*lt-pl*oo*gger
a tin-opener?	**en bokseåpner?**
	en b*o*kser-awpner
a torch?	**en lommelykt?**
	en l*o*mmer-leekt

Have you got . . .	**Har dere . . .** har d*a*yrer . . .
any torch batteries?	**lommelykt-batterier?** lommer-leekt-b*a*hter*ee*-er
a universal plug (for the sink)?	**en universalplugg (til oppvaskkum)?** en ooniversh*a*hl-ploogg (til *o*p-vask-kum)
a washing line?	**en klesnor?** en kl*a*y-snoor
any washing powder?	**vaskepulver?** v*a*sker-p*u*ll-ver
any washing-up liquid?	**oppvaskmiddel?** *o*pvask-m*i*ddel
a washing-up brush?	**en oppvaskbørste?** en *o*pvask-b*u*rster

[*For other essential information, see 'Shop talk' below*]

Shop talk

ESSENTIAL INFORMATION

- The illustrated coins are in wide circulation.
  Notes 10, 50, 100, 500, 1000 kroner (kr).
- Know how to say the important weights and measures.

50 grams	**en halv hekto** en hahl h*e*ktoo
100 grams	**en hekto** en h*e*ktoo
250 grams	**en kvart kilo** en kvart sh*ee*lo
500 grams	**en halv kilo** en hahl sh*ee*lo
1000 grams	**en kilo** en sh*ee*lo
2000 grams	**to kilo** too sh*ee*lo

¼ litre	**en kvart liter**
	en kvart leeter
½ litre	**en halv liter**
	en hahl leeter
1 litre	**en liter**
	en leeter
2 litres	**to liter**
[For numbers see p. 205]	too leeter

CUSTOMER

I'm just looking	**Jeg bare ser**
	yay bar-er sair
Excuse me	**Unnskyld**
	oonshil
How much is this/that?	**Hvor mye koster denne/den?**
	vor mee-er koster denner/den
What is that? ⎤	**Hva er det?**
What are those? ⎦	va ar day
Is there a discount?	**Er det noen rabatt?**
	ar day noo-en rabaht
I'd like that, please	**Takk, jeg tar den**
	takk yay tar den
Not that	**Ikke den**
	ikker den
Like that	**Sånn**
	sonn
That's enough, thank you	**Takk, det er nok**
	takk day ar nok
More, please	**Litt mer takk**
	litt mair takk
Less	**Litt mindre**
	litt meendrer
That's fine	**Det er fint**
	day ar feent
O.K.	**O.K.**
	O.K.
I won't take it, thank you	**Nei takk, jeg tar den ikke**
	nay takk yay tar den ikker
It's not right	**Den passer ikke**
	den pahsser ikker
Have you got something . . .	**Har De noe . . .**
	har dee noo-er . . .
better?	**bedre?**
	bedrer

cheaper?	**billigere?**
	billi-rer
different?	**annet?**
	ahnet
larger?	**større?**
	stir-rer
smaller?	**mindre?**
	meendrer
At what time do you . . .	**Når . . . dere?**
	nor . . . dayrer
open?	**åpner**
	awpner
close?	**stenger**
	steng-er
Can I have a bag, please?	**Kan jeg få en pose?**
	kan yay faw en poosser
Can I have a receipt?	**Kan jeg få en kvittering?**
	kan yay faw en kvittairing
Do you take . . .	**Tar dere . . .**
	tar dayrer . . .
English/American money?	**engelske/amerikanske penger?**
	eng-elsker/ahmerikahnsker peng-er
travellers' cheques?	**reisesjekker?**
	racer-shecker?
credit cards?	**kreditt kort?**
	kreditt kort
I'd like . . .	**Jeg vil ha . . .**
	yay vil ha . . .
one like that	**en sånn en**
	en sonn en

SHOP ASSISTANT

Can I help you?	**Vær så god?**
	var saw goo
What would you like?	**Hva skal det være?**
	va skahl day varer
Will that be all?	**Er det det hele?**
	ar day day hailer
Is that all?	**Er det alt?**
	ar day ahlt
Anything else?	**Var det noe annet?**
	var day noo-er ahnet
Would you like it wrapped?	**Skal jeg pakke den inn?**
	skahl yay pahkker den inn

Norwegian

Is it a present?	**Skal det værer en gave?**
	skal day varer en gahver
Sorry, none left	**Vi er dessverre utsolgt?**
	vee ar dess-varrer oot-salt
I haven't got any	**Jeg har ikke noen**
	yay har ikker noo-en
I haven't got any left	**Jeg har ikke flere igjen**
	yay har ikker flayrer ee-yen
How many do you want?	**Hvor mange vil De ha?**
	vor mahng-er vil dee ha
How much do you want?	**Hvor mye vil De ha?**
	vor mee-er vil dee ha
Is that enough?	**Er det nok?**
	ar day nok

Shopping for food

Bread

ESSENTIAL INFORMATION

- Finding a baker's, see p. 127.
- Key words to look for:
  BAKERI (baker's), sells cakes as well
  BRØD (bread)
  CONDITORI (baker's with cake shop attached)
- Supermarkets, groceries and general stores always sell ready packed, unsliced bread.
- Opening hours as for other shops.
- Most characteristic are the following loaves of bread: **kneipbrød and vitabrød**, a whitish wheatgerm bread; **vanlig brød**, a large, greyish plain bread and **loff**, a finer white bread.
- You can also simply say **et brød** and point.

WHAT TO SAY

A loaf (like that)	**Et (sånt) brød**
	et (sont) brer

A homemade loaf	**Et hjemmebakt brød**
	et yemmer-bahkt brer
A French loaf	**Et franskbrød**
	et fransk-brer
A large one	**Et stort et**
	et stoort et
A small one	**Et lite et**
	et leeter et
A bread roll	**Et rundstykke**
	et roon-sticker
A crescent roll	**Et horn**
	et hoorn
Two loaves	**To brød**
	too brer
Two homemade loaves	**To hjemmebakte brød**
	too yemmer-bahkter brer
Four bread rolls	**Fire rundstykker**
	feerer roon-sticker
A sliced loaf	**Et oppskåret brød**
	et op-skaw-ret brer
A wholemeal loaf	**Et helkornbrød**
	et hail-koorn-brer

[*For other essential expressions, see 'Shop talk' p. 158*]

Cakes

ESSENTIAL INFORMATION

- Key words to look for:
  BAKERI (baker's) sells cakes and bread
  KONDITORI (cake shop) sells cakes to take away or to be eaten on the premises. Coffee, tea and various soft drinks are also served.
  KAFÉ, KAFETERIA both sell a limited selection of cakes.
- Supermarkets, groceries and some kiosks sell prepacked cakes.
- To find a cake shop see p. 127.

Norwegian

WHAT TO SAY

The types of cakes you find in shops vary from region to region but the following are the most common.

berlinerbolle	doughnut
berl*ee*ner-b*o*ller	
bolle	bun
b*o*ller	
bløtkake	cream gateau
bl*e*rt-k*a*hker	
honningkake	a heavy, brown spicy honey cake
h*o*nning-k*a*hker	sold in thick slices
lefse	a large, round, flat, soft and sweet
l*e*f-ser	bread. Served, folded up like a
	sandwich with butter, sugar and
	cinnamòn
Napoleonskake	custard slice
nap*oo*leonss-k*a*hker	
skolebrød	large, flattish wheat bun with coconut
sk*oo*ler-brer	icing and egg custard on top
vafler	waffles
v*a*hf-ler	
vannbakkels	cream éclairs
v*a*hn-b*a*kkelss	
wienerbrød	Danish pastry
veener-brer	
smultring	doughnut ring
sm*oo*lt-ring	

[*For other essential expressions,
see 'Shop talk' p. 158*]

Ice-cream and sweets

ESSENTIAL INFORMATION

- Prepacked ice-cream is sold in kiosks, groceries, sweet shops, snack bars and some petrol stations. Look for **IS** (ice-cream).
- There is always a poster with pictures of the various kinds of ice-cream on offer.

- Many varieties come on sticks like ice lollies, but are in fact ice-cream. There are also prepacked cones, sandwiches, etc.
- Point to what you would like.
- Soft ice-cream and scoop ice-cream are available from machines – usually in snack bars and cafeterias.
- Prepacked sweets are available in groceries, supermarkets, kiosks and sweet shops.

WHAT TO SAY

A . . . ice, please	**En . . . is** en . . . eess
chocolate	**sjokolade** shooko-*lah*der
roasted nuts	**krokan** kruck-*ah*n
strawberry	**jordbær** y*oo*r-bar
vanilla	**vanilje** va-*neel*-yer
An ice-cream cone, please	**En kuleis** en k*oo*ler-eess
An ice-cream stick, please	**En pinneis** en p*i*nner-eess
A soft ice, please	**En soft is** en soft-eess
An ice-cream like that	**En sånn is** en sonn eess
A lollipop, please	**En kjærlighet på pinne** en sharlee-hait paw p*i*nner
A packet of . . .	**En pakke . . .** en p*a*kker . . .
chewing gum	**tyggegummi** t*i*gger-g*oo*mmi
mints	**peppermynte** pepper-m*i*nter
Five/ten/twenty . . .	**Fem/ti/tjue . . .** fem/tee/sh*oo*-er . .
toffees	**karameller** kara-m*e*ller
chocolates	**små-sjokolader** sm*aw*-shooko-l*ah*der
A box of chocolates	**En eske konfekt** en *e*sker kon-fekt

[*For other essential expressions, see 'Shop talk', p. 158*]

Norwegian

Picnic food

ESSENTIAL INFORMATION

- Look for **DELIKATESSEN** or the cold meat counter in supermarkets.
- Supermarkets and groceries always sell a wide range of prepacked foods.

WHAT TO SAY

Two slices of . . .	**To skiver . . .** too sheever . . .
ham	**kokt skinke** cookt shinker
roast pork	**stekt skinke** staykt shinker
spam	**skinkerull** shinker-rool
salami	**salami** salamee
(parma) ham	**kokt svinekam** cookt sveener-kahm
tongue	**tunge** toong-er

You might also like to try some of these:

roastbiff roast-biff	finely sliced, rare roast beef
reker rayker	fresh cooked shrimps/prawns, often bought and eaten at the harbour
rekesalat rayker-salaht	salad with shrimps, sliced cabbage and mayonnaise
italiensk salat eetalee-ainsk salaht	salad with sliced ham, cabbage, onion and mayonnaise
kalverull kahlver-rooll	boiled, finely sliced veal
okserull okser-rooll	salty, boiled, finely sliced beef

sursild
s*oo*r-sill

pieces of salted herring, pepper and onions in water

kryddersild
kr*i*dder-sill

pieces of salted herring, pepper and bayleaves in tomato sauce

røkt makrell
rerkt ma-kr*e*ll

smoked mackerel

røkelaks
r*e*rker-lahks

smoked salmon

gravlaks
gr*ah*v-lahks

cured salmon with dill

røkt ørret
rerkt *e*r-ret

smoked trout

leverpostei
l*a*yver-pust*ay*

paté

flatbrød
fl*a*tt-brer

crispy, unleavened paper-thin bread

multesyltetøy
m*oo*lter-silter-t*ay*

cloudberry jam, yellow, sweet and tasty

brunost
br*oo*n-ost

brown sweet cheese, of which there are numerous varieties some with goat's milk

nøkkelost
n*e*rk-kel-ost

hard cheese with cloves and caraway seeds

Try some of these cured foods – salty, dry meat, eaten uncooked and finely sliced:

spekeskinke
sp*ay*ker-sh*i*nker

cured ham

spekepølse
sp*ay*ker-p*e*rl-ser

cured sausage, eaten in sandwiches

fenalår
f*ay*na-lor

cured leg of lamb

fårepølse
f*o*rer-p*e*rl-ser

cured mutton sausage

spekesild
sp*ay*ker-sill

cured herring

Fruit and vegetables

ESSENTIAL INFORMATION

- Fruit (**FRUKT**) is bought in sweet shops, some kiosks, groceries and supermarkets, and at the market place (**TORG**).
- Vegetables (**GRØNNSAKER**) are bought at supermarkets and groceries, some butchers and at the market place (**TORG**).
- Fruit and vegetables tend to be expensive in Norway and the selection is often limited.

WHAT TO SAY

1 kilo (2 lbs) of . . .	**En kilo . . . .**
	ain sh*ee*lo . . .
apples	**epler**
	*e*pler
apricots	**aprikoser**
	ahpree-k*oo*-ser
bananas	**bananer**
	ba-n*a*-ner
cherries (sweet)	**moreller**
	mor*e*ller
cherries (slightly bitter)	**kirsebær**
	k*i*sher-b*a*r
grapes	**druer**
	dr*oo*-er
oranges	**appelsiner**
	appel-s*ee*ner
peaches	**ferskner**
	f*a*shk-ner
pears	**pærer**
	p*a*rer
plums	**plommer**
	pl*o*mmer
strawberries	**jordbær**
	y*oo*r-bar
A pineapple, please	**En ananas**
	en *a*nna-nass
A grapefruit	**En grapefrukt**
	en gr*a*pe-fr*oo*kt

A melon	**En melon**
	en mel*oon*
A water melon	**En vannmelon**
	en v*ah*n-mel*oon*
½ kilo of . . .	**En halv kilo . . .**
	en hahl sh*ee*lo . . .
carrots	**gulrøtter**
	g*oo*l-rert-ter
green beans	**franske bønner (haricots verts)**
	fr*a*nsker b*u*rner (arrikaw v*a*r)
leeks	**purre**
	p*oo*r-rer
mushrooms	**sjampinjonger**
	sh*a*mping-y*o*ng-er
onions	**løk**
	lerk
potatoes	**poteter**
	pot-*a*yter
spinach	**spinat**
	spin-*ah*t
tomatoes	**tomater**
	tom-*ah*ter
A bunch of . . .	**En bunt . . .**
	en b*oo*nt
parsley	**persille**
	pash*i*ller
radishes	**redikker**
	red-ikker
A head of garlic	**En hvitløk**
	en v*ee*t-lerk
A lettuce	**Et salathode**
	et sal*ah*t-hooder
A cauliflower	**Et blomkålhode**
	et blom-kawl-hooder
A cucumber	**En slangeagurk**
	en shlang-er-ag*oo*rk
Like that, please	**En sånn en**
	en sonn en

[*For other essential expressions, see 'Shop talk' p. 158*]

Meat

ESSENTIAL INFORMATION

- Key word to look for:
  KJØTTVARER (butcher's)
- Norwegian butchers never exhibit fresh meat in the window, only salami, cured sausages, cured hams etc. As meat is very expensive, the selection inside may be limited.
- Most supermarkets sell ready cut, prepacked meat. A shop with a wide selection of unpacked, uncut meat is hard to find. Few supermarkets and groceries and even fewer butchers sell chicken and other poultry.
- Kidneys are seldom eaten, hearts and brains never.
- The diagrams on p. 171 will help you to get the cuts you want. Point to the appropriate word on the diagram and the butcher will understand.

WHAT TO SAY

For a joint, choose the type of meat and then say how many people it is for:

Some beef, please	**Jeg skal ha litt oksekjøtt**
	yay skahl ha litt *okser-shirtt*
Some lamb	**Litt lammekjøtt**
	litt *lahmmer-shirtt*
Some mutton	**Litt fårekjøtt**
	litt *forer-shirtt*
Some pork	**Litt svinekjøtt**
	litt *sveener-shirtt*
Some veal	**Litt kalvekjøtt**
	litt *kalver-shirtt*
A joint of lamb/mutton	**En lamme/fårestek**
	en *lammer/forer-stayk*
for two people	**til to personer**
	til too *peshooner*
for four people	**til fire personer**
	til *feerer peshooner*
for six people	**til seks personer**
	til *seks peshooner*

Beef Okse

1. Høyrygg
2. Entrekotkam
3. Oksekam (kotelett)
4. T. Benkam
5. Mørbrand
6. Lår
7. Bryst
8. Bog
9. Bibringe
10. Buklist (rulleskinn)
11. Skank

Veal Kalv

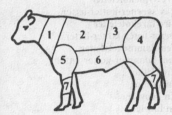

1. Høyrygg
2. Kotelettkam
3. T. Benkam
4. Lår
5. Bog
6. Rulleskinn
7. Kalveknoke

Pork Svin

1. Skinke
2. Kotelettkam
3. Nakkekotelett
4. Ribbe (buklist)
5. Bog
6. Labber

Lamp/Mutton Lam/Får

1. Lår (stek)
2. Rygg (sadel)
3. Nakke
4. Rulleskinn (ribbe)
5. Bog

Norwegian

For steak and liver do as above:

Some steak, please	**Jeg skal ha litt biff**
	yay skahl ha litt b_iff_
Some liver	**Litt lever**
	litt _lay_ver
Some sausages	**Noen pølser**
	n_oo_-en _perl_-ser
for three people	**til tre personer**
	til tr_ay_ _pe_shooner
Two veal escalopes, please	**To skiver kalvekjøtt**
	too sh_ee_ver _kah_lver-shirtt
Three pork chops	**Tre svinekoteletter**
	tray sv_ee_ner-kotter-l_e_tter
Four mutton chops	**Fire fårekoteletter**
	f_ee_rer f_o_rer-kotter-l_e_tter
Five lamb chops	**Fem lammekoteletter**
	fem l_ah_mmer-kotter-l_e_tter
A small chicken	**En kylling**
	en sh_i_lling
A large chicken	**En broyler**
	en br_oi_ler
Please can you . . .	**Kan De . . .**
	kan dee . . .
mince it?	**male det?**
	m_ah_ler day
dice it?	**skjære det i småbiter?**
	sh_a_rer day ee sm_aw_-beeter
trim the fat?	**skjære bort flesket?**
	sh_a_rer bort fl_e_sker

Fish

ESSENTIAL INFORMATION

- Sign to look for: **FISK** (fish).
- Fresh fish can be bought at fishmongers all over the country, and

in some open air markets particularly in Bergen where the fish is kept live.

- Supermarkets and groceries sell frozen fish much the same as at home. **Findus** and **Frionor** are well-known marks.
- Shrimps and prawns (**reker**) can often be purchased freshly caught and cooked at the harbour.

WHAT TO SAY

Purchase large fish and small shellfish by weight:

½ kilo of . . .	**En halv kilo . . .**
	en hahl sh*ee*lo . . .
cod	**torsk**
	toshk
whiting	**hvitting**
	v*i*tting
dover sole	**sjøtunge**
	sh*e*r-tung-er
shrimps	**små reker**
	smaw r*a*yker
prawns	**store reker**
	st*oo*rer r*a*yker
mussels	**blåskjell**
	bl*a*w-shell
sardines	**sardiner**
	sard*ee*ner
haddock	**kolje**
	k*o*l-yer
salmon	**laks**
	lahks
halibut	**hellefisk**
	h*e*ller-fisk

For some shellfish and 'frying pan' fish, specify the numbers:

A crab, please	**En krabbe**
	en kr*a*hbber
A lobster	**En hummer**
	en h*u*mmer
A female crab	**En hunkrabbe**
	en h*oo*n-krahbber
A big lobster	**En stor hummer**
	en st*oo*r h*u*mmer

Norwegian

A trout	**En ørret**
	en *er*-ret
A sole	**En flyndre**
	en fl*i*ndrer
A mackerel	**En makrell**
	en ma-kr*e*ll
A hake	**En lysing**
	en l*ee*-sing

Other essential expressions [*see also p. 159*]

Please can you . . .	**Kan De . . .**
	kan dee . . .
take the heads off?	**skjære av hodene?**
	sh*a*rer ahv h*oo*dener
clean them?	**rense dem?**
	r*a*ynsser dem
fillet them?	**skjære bort bena?**
	sh*a*rer bort b*a*yna

Eating and drinking out

Ordering a drink

ESSENTIAL INFORMATION

- Places to ask for: **HOTELL, RESTAURANT, BAR** and **VERTSHUS.**
- Alcoholic beverages are expensive, so make full use of your duty free quota.
- Some Norwegian towns and counties, particularly in the West and South are 'dry'. However, big hotels in these counties often sell alcohol by special licence.
- Beer and wine can be enjoyed all day. Spirits are only available between 3 and 11 p.m. and never on Sundays or public holidays. At 11 p.m. an establishment may therefore stop selling spirits but continue to sell beer and wine, unless of course they hold a special licence.

- Many establishments enforce a **spiseplikt** (duty to eat) – that is to say you cannot buy an alcoholic beverage without ordering food.
- Beer **øl** can be bought in most supermarkets unless you are in a 'dry' town; wine and spirits only in the state wine monopoly shops **Vinmonopolet**. These are found in towns with more than 4000 inhabitants. However there is only one shop to each minor town and no **Vinmonopol** in dry counties.
- Coffee is the most popular hot drink. Served black, accompanied by sugar and cream.
- Tea is less popular, served on demand with sugar and a slice of lemon. White tea is unknown, you will have to ask for milk and no lemon.
- In winter, try hot beefstock, hot blackcurrant juice or hot chocolate with whipped cream.
- BE WARNED! Driving and drinking is a serious offence. Random checks are frequent. More than a very small amount could mean the loss of your licence and prison for 21 days.

WHAT TO SAY

I'll have . . . please	**Kan jeg få . . .**
	kan yay f*aw* . . .
a tea	**en te**
	en t*ay*
with milk	**med melk**
	may m*e*lk
with lemon	**med sitron**
	may sitr*oo*n
a glass of milk	**et glass melk**
	et glahss melk
a hot chocolate	**en kopp sjokolade**
	en kopp shooko-l*ah*der
with/without cream	**med/uten krem**
	may/*oo*ten kraim
a glass of water	**et glass vann**
	et glahss vahnn
a lemonade (fizzy)	**en sitronbrus**
	en sitr*oo*n-brooss
a Coca-Cola	**en coca cola**
	en coca-c*oo*la
an orangeade (fizzy)	**en appelsinbrus**
	en appel-s*ee*n-brooss

an orange juice	**et glass appelsinsaft**
	et glahss appel-s*een*-saft
an apple juice	**et glass eplesaft**
	et glahss *e*ppler-saft
a blackcurrant juice	**et glass solbærsaft**
	et glahss s*oo*l-bar-saft
a milkshake	**en milk shake**
	en milk shake
Do you serve beer or wine?	**Serverer dere øl eller vin?**
	serv*ay*-rer d*ay*rer erl *e*ller veen
A lager	**En pils**
	en pilss
A glass of draught lager	**Et glass fatøl**
	et glahss f*a*-terl
A pint of draught lager	**Et stort glass fatøl**
	et st*oo*rt glahss f*a*-terl
A brown ale	**En bukkøl**
	en b*oo*kk-erl
A glass of . . .	**Et glass . . .**
	et glahss . . .
red wine	**rødvin**
	r*er*-veen
white wine	**hvitvin**
	v*ee*t-veen
rosé wine	**rosévin**
	ross*ay*-veen
dry/sweet wine	**tørr/søt vin**
	terr/s*i*rt veen
A bottle of . . .	**En flaske . . .**
	en fl*a*sker . . .
sparkling wine	**sprudlende vin**
	spr*oo*dlen-er veen
champagne	**champagne**
	shamp*ah*g-ner
A whisky	**En whisky**
	en wh*i*sky
with water	**med vann**
	may v*a*hnn
with ice	**med isbiter**
	may *ee*ss-beeter
with soda	**med soda**
	may s*oo*da

A gin	**En gin**
	en gin
and tonic	**og tonic**
	aw tonic
with lemon	**med sitron**
	may sitroon
A brandy/cognac	**En brandy/cognac**
	en brandy/conyac

These are drinks you may like to try:

Lagerøl/Brigg	non alcoholic lager
lager-erl/brigg	
Vørterøl	a sweet, heavy, non alcoholic ale –
virter-erl	good for the stomach
Pils	Norwegian lager
pilss	
Export	a stronger kind of lager
export	
Bayer	strong dark ale
ba-yer	
Bokkøl	a stronger, darker version of Bayer
bokk-erl	
Akevitt	Norwegian firewater (40%
ahk-ker-vitt	alcohol), served chilled with
	heavy dishes and often chased
	down with beer
Solo	a fizzy, not too sweet orangeade
soolo	
Selters	a kind of soda water
seltesh.	
Buljong	hot beefstock
bull-yong	

Other essential expressions:

The bill, please	**Kan jeg få regningen**
	kan yay faw raining-en
How much does that come to?	**Hvor mye kommer det på?**
	vor mee-er kommer day paw
Is the service included?	**Er service inkludert?**
	ar service inkloo-dairt
Where is the toilet, please?	**Hvor er toalettet?**
	vor ar twa-letter

Norwegian

Ordering a snack

ESSENTIAL INFORMATION

- Look for **KIOSK, SNACKBAR, KONDITORI, KAFÉ, KAFETERIA, KRO** and **VEIKRO** (the last four sell complete meals as well).
- Kiosks and snack bars throughout Norway are good places for inexpensive snacks. They all sell tasty hot dogs and crisps, and many sell chicken, cakes and pizza.
- For cakes see p. 163.
- For ice-cream see p. 164.
- For picnic-type snacks see p. 166.

WHAT TO SAY

I'll have . . . please	**Jeg vil ha . . .**
	yay vil ha . . .
a cheese sandwich	**et ostesmørbrød**
	et *oo*ster-sm*i*r-brer
a ham sandwich	**et skinkesmørbrød**
	et sh*i*nker-sm*i*r-brer
an egg and tomato sandwich	**et egg og tomat smørbrød**
	et *egg* aw tom*ah*t sm*i*r-brer

These are some other snacks you may like to try

en pølse med lompe/brød	a steamed frankfurter sausage with
en per*l*-sør may l*u*mper/brer	potato cake/soft roll
en grillpølse med sennep og ketchup	a thick, grilled frankfurter with mustard and ketchup
en gr*i*ll-per*l*-ser may sennep aw ketchup	
en pose potetgull	a bag of crisps
en p*oo*sser pot*ai*t-gooll	
en pizza	a pizza
en pizza	
et rekesmørbrød	an open prawn sandwich
et r*ay*ker-sm*i*r-brer	
et roastbiffsmørbrød	an open sandwich with slightly
et r*oa*st-biff-sm*i*r-brer	underdone roast beef

et rundstykke med gaudaost/ brunost	half a largish roll with gouda or brown cheese on top
et r*oo*n-sticker may g*ou*da-ost/ br*oo*n-ost	
et smørbrød med eggerøre	open sandwich with scrambled egg
et sm*i*r-brer may *egg*er-r*i*r-er	
pommes frites	chips
pom frit	

In a restaurant

ESSENTIAL INFORMATION

- The place to ask for:
  EN RESTAURANT [*see p. 128*]
- You can eat in these places or where you see this sign
  RESTAURANT
  CAFÉ
  KAFETERIA
  SNACK BAR
  KRO (reasonable self-service establishments)
  VEIKRO (reasonable self-service establishments)
  GRILLRESTAURANT (various grilled foods)
- The menus are not always displayed in the window. The look of a restaurant is therefore the best indication you'll have of whether it will suit you. Norwegian restaurants tend to be expensive.
- Service charges are often included. Tipping is at your discretion: small change after a snack and maybe 5% after a good meal.
- You can choose between large and small portions, a large portion often being very large.
- In self-service establishments, snacks can be purchased all day and hot dinner type meals from midday onwards.
- Expensive restaurants often serve buffets and open sandwiches for lunch and dinner from 7 p.m.
- A starter is by no means universal. Norwegians tend to be satisfied

by a main course and a dessert followed by coffee. Soup is the most frequent form of starter.
- And remember no alcohol with your meal if you are driving!

WHAT TO SAY

May I book a table?	**Kan jeg bestille et bord?**
	kan yay bes*ti*ller et b*oor*
I've booked a table	**Jeg har bestilt et bord**
	yay har bes*ti*lt et b*oor*
A table . . .	**Et bord . . .**
	et b*oor* . . .
for one	**for en person**
	for ain pesh*oon*
for three	**for tre personer**
	for tray pesh*oon*er
The à la carte menu, please	**Kan jeg få à la carte menyen**
	kan yay f*aw* ah la c*a*rt men-*ee*-en
Today's special menu	**Dagens meny**
	d*a*hg-enss men*ee*
What is this, please?	**Hva er det?**
[point to the menu]	va ar d*a*y
Do you serve beer and wine?	**Serverer dere øl og vin?**
	serv*ay*-rer d*a*yrer erl aw v*ee*n
The wine list, please	**Kan jeg få vinkartet**
	kan yay faw v*ee*n-karter
A carafe of wine, please	**En karaffel vin**
	en kar*a*ffel v*ee*n
A half carafe	**En halv karaffel**
	en hahl kar*a*ffel
A bottle	**En flaske**
	en fl*a*sker
A half bottle	**En halv flaske**
	en hahl fl*a*sker
A litre	**En liter**
	en l*ee*ter
Red/white/rosé/house wine	**Rød/hvit/rosé/husets vin**
	rer/veet/rossay/h*oo*ss-ess v*ee*n
Some more bread, please	**Kan jeg få litt mer brød**
	kan yay faw litt mair brer
Some more wine	**Litt mer vin**
	litt mair v*ee*n

Some oil	**Litt olje** litt *o*l-yer
Some vinegar	**Litt eddik** litt *e*ddik
Some salt	**Litt salt** litt s*ah*lt
Some pepper	**Litt pepper** litt p*e*pper
Some water	**Litt vann** litt v*ah*nn
How much does that come to?	**Hvor mye kommer det på?** vor m*ee*-er kommer day paw
Is service included?	**Er service inkludert?** ar service inkloo-d*ai*rt
The bill, please	**Regningen takk** r*ai*ning-en takk
Can you give me a receipt?	**Kan jeg få en kvittering?** kan yay faw en kvitt*ai*ring

Key words for courses as seen on some menus: [*Only ask the question if you want the waiter to remind you of the choice*]

What have you got in the way of . . .	**Hva slags . . . har dere?** va shl*ah*gss . . . har d*a*yrer
STARTERS?	**FORRETTER?** for-retter
SOUP?	**SUPPE?** s*oo*pper
EGG DISHES?	**EGGRETTER?** egg-retter
MEAT?	**KJØTTRETTER?** shirtt-retter
GAME?	**VILTRETTER?** vilt-retter
FOWL?	**FUGLERETTER?** f*oo*gler-retter
VEGETABLES?	**GRØNNSAKER?** gr*er*n-sahker
CHEESE?	**OST?** ost
FRUIT?	**FRUKT?** frookt

Norwegian

ICE-CREAM?	**ISKREM?**
	*ee*ss-kra*im*
DESSERT?	**DESSERT?**
	dess*ar*

UNDERSTANDING THE MENU

- You will find the names of the principal ingredients of most dishes on these pages:

Starters p. 167	Fruit p. 168
Meat p. 170	Dessert p. 163–164
Fish p. 172	Cheese p. 167
Vegetables p. 169	Ice-cream p. 164

- Used together with the following lists of cooking and menu terms, they should help you to decode the menu.
- The following cooking and menu terms are for understanding only – not for speaking aloud.

Cooking and menu terms

blandet	mixed
blodig	rare
brunet i smør	sautéed
dampet	steamed
fløte	unwhipped cream
forlorent	poached
frityrstekt	deep fried in breadcrumbs
fyllt	stuffed
godt stekt	well done
griljert/grillet	grilled
grytestekt	braised
hermetisk	canned
kokt	boiled
krem	whipped cream
marinert	marinated
medium	medium
med/uten løk	with/without fried onion
ovnstekt	baked/roasted
revet	grated
ristet	toasted
røkt	smoked
rå	raw/rare

saft	juice
salted/speket	cured
saus	sauce/gravy
hvit saus	white, creamy sauce
remulade saus	mayonnaise sauce with diced pickled gherkins
rød/bringebær saus	red/raspberry sauce
vaniljesaus	custard (cold)
sur	bitter
søt	sweet

Further words to help you understand the menu

asparges	asparagus
bayonskinke	cooked ham (for dinner)
betasuppe	soup consisting of chunks of meat, marrow bones and vegetables
blandet kjøttgryte	different meats roasted together
blomkålsuppe	cream of cauliflower soup
dyrestek/reinsdyrstek	roast reindeer
eggerøre	scrambled egg
elgstek	roast moose
erter	peas
ertesuppe	thick yellow pea soup with ham
fenalår	cured leg of mutton
fersk suppe	hearty meat and vegetable soup
fiskegrateng	fish in thick, creamy, white sauce
fiskesuppe	fish soup
fjellørret	mountain trout
franske poteter/pommes frites	chips
gravlaks	cured salmon with dill
gås	goose
gåselever	goose liver
hønsefrikassé	chicken stew
kalvefrikassé	veal stew
karamellpudding	cream caramel
karbonade	beefburger
kjøttkaker (med surkål)	meat balls (with sweet and sour cabbage)
klippfisk	boiled, dried, salty fish
klubb	potato dumpling with bacon
kålrabi	swede

Norwegian

kålruletter	stuffed cabbage leaves
kålstuing	creamed cabbage
lapskaus	beef stew
lever	liver
lutefisk	cod soaked in lye, then boiled; jelly like when served
mandelpudding	vanilla blancmange with almonds
medisterkaker	pork meat balls
medisterpølser	thick pork sausages
middagspølser	thick, smoked sausages
multer	arctic cloudberries
oksehalesuppe	oxtail soup
potetstappe	mashed potato
rakørret	semi fermented salmon/trout (mostly for daring nationals)
ribbe	roast pork rib
risgrøt	hot rice pudding, served with butter, sugar and cinnamon
riskrem	cold rice pudding, made with whipped cream
rosenkål	brussels sprouts
ryper	roast grouse/ptarmigan
rødbeter	beetroot
rødkål	red cabbage
røkelaks	smoked salmon
rømmegrøt	porridge made with sour cream, semolina or wheat flour
seifillet	fried fillet of coalfish, often served with fried onions
semulepudding	semolina pudding
sjokoladepudding	chocolate blancmange
smørgrøt	cream´porridge made with wheat flour
spinatsuppe	cream of spinach soup
surkål	sweet and sour cabbage
syltelabber	pigs trotters
tomatsuppe	tomato soup
torskerogn	cod roe
tyttebær	cranberry
wienerschnitzel	fillet of pork, fried in breadcrumbs with anchovy and capers

Health

ESSENTIAL INFORMATION

- There is a reciprocal British–Norwegian health agreement giving Britons the same rights to medical treatment as Norwegians. Other nationals are advised to take out a travel insurance. A travel agent will help.
- Norwegians stay free of charge in hospitals. But doctors do charge a consultation fee, be it in a doctor's surgery, your own abode or the casualty unit at a hospital. Apply to the local social insurance office in Norway (**trygdekasse**) for a refund. You will need to produce your passport.
- In remote areas doctors may be few and far between.
- In towns doctors are on duty day and night Ask for **LEGEVAKT**.
- There is no one common telephone num   for medical emergencies throughout Norway. Look under **LEGER** (doctors) in the classified directory or ask a Norwegian.
- Also look for **SYKEBIL/AMBULANSE** (ambulance) on the inside of the front cover of the telephone directory.
- Take your own first aid kit with you.
- A chemist **apotek** will suggest treatment for minor disorders.
- For asking your way to a doctor, dentist or chemist, see p. 127.

What's the matter?

I have a pain . . .	**Jeg har vondt . . .**
	yay har voont . . .
in my abdomen	**i underlivet**
	ee oonner-leever
in my ankle	**i ankelen**
	ee ankel-en
in my arm	**i armen**
	ee arm-en
in my back	**i ryggen**
	ee riggen
in my bladder	**i urinblæren**
	ee ooreen-blaren
in my bowels	**i tarmene**
	ee tarmen-er

I have a pain . . .	Jeg har vondt . . .
	yay har voont . . .
in my breast	i et bryst
	ee et brist
in my chest	i brystet
	ee brister
in my ear	i øret
	ee er-rer
in my eye	i øyet
	ee erer
in my foot	i foten
	ee footen
in my head	i hodet
	ee hooder
in my heel	i hælen
	ee hailen
in my kidney	i nyret
	ee neerer
in my leg	i benet
	ee bainer
in my lung	i en lunge
	ee en lung-er
in my neck	i nakken
	ee nahkken
in my penis	i penis
	ee painiss
in my shoulder	i skulderen
	ee skoolderen
in my stomach	i maven
	ee mahven
in my testicle	i testikelen
	ee testick-el-en
in my throat	i halsen
	ee hahl-sen
in my vagina	i skjeden
	ee shay-den
in my wrist	i håndleddet
	ee hawn-ledder
I have a pain here [*point*]	Jeg har vondt her
	yay har voont har
I have a toothache	Jeg har tannverk
	yay har tahnn-vark
I have broken . . .	Jeg har ødelagt . . .
	yay har er-derlagt

my dentures	**gebisset mitt**
	gheb*i*sser mitt
my glasses	**brillene mine**
	br*i*ll-en-er m*ee*ner
I have lost . . .	**Jeg har mistet . . .**
	yay har m*i*ss-tet . . .
my contact lenses	**kontaktlinsene mine**
	kont*a*hkt-lin-sen-er m*ee*ner
a filling	**en plumbe**
	en pl*oo*m-ber
My child is ill	**Barnet mitt er sykt**
	b*a*rn-er mitt ar seekt
He/she has a pain in his/her . . .	**Han/hun har vondt i . . .**
	han/hun har v*oo*nt ee . . .
ankle [*see list above*]	**ankelen**
	*a*nkel-en

How bad is it?

I'm ill	**Jeg er syk**
	yay ar s*ee*k
It's serious	**Det er alvorlig**
	day ar ahl-v*o*rlee
It's not serious	**Det er ikke alvorlig**
	day ar *i*kker ahl-v*o*rlee
It hurts (a lot)	**Det gjør (veldig) vondt**
	day yer (v*e*ldee) v*oo*nt
I've had it for . . .	**Jeg har hatt det i . . .**
	yay har h*a*tt day ee . . .
one hour/one day	**en time/en dag**
	en t*ee*mer/en d*a*hg
It's a . . .	**Det er en . . .**
	day ar ain . . .
sharp pain	**skarp smerte**
	skarp sm*a*rter
dull ache	**dump smerte**
	domp sm*a*rter
nagging pain	**nagende smerte**
	n*a*hg-en-er sm*a*rter
I feel . . .	**Jeg føler meg . . .**
	yay f*e*rler may . . .
dizzy	**svimmel**
	sv*i*mmel
sick/weak	**kvalm/svak**
	kvalm/svahk

Norwegian

I think I have a fever	**Jeg tror jeg har feber**
	yay troor yay har f*a*yber

Already under treatment for something else?

I take . . . regularly [*show*]	**Jeg tar . . . regelmessig**
	yay tar . . . r*a*y-ghel-m*e*ssy
this medicine	**denne medisinen**
	d*e*nner medic*ee*nen
these pills	**disse pillene**
	d*i*sser p*i*ll-en-er
I have . . .	**Jeg har . . .**
	yay har . . .
a heart condition	**hjertefeil**
	y*a*rter-fail
haemorrhoids	**hemorroider**
	hem-orr*ee*der
rheumatism	**gikt**
	yeekt
I am . . .	**Jeg er . . .**
	yay ar . . .
diabetic	**diabetiker**
	dee-ah-b*a*yticker
asthmatic	**astmahtiker**
	ahst-m*a*-ticker
allergic to penicillin	**allergisk mot penicillin**
	all*a*rghisk moot penicil*ee*n
pregnant	**gravid**
	gra-v*ee*d

Other essential expressions

Please can you help?	**Kan De hjelpe meg?**
	kan dee y*e*lper may
A doctor, please	**Jeg trenger en lege**
	yay tr*e*ng-er en l*a*ygher
I need a dentist	**Jeg trenger en tannlege**
	yay tr*e*ng-er en t*ah*nn-laygher
I don't speak Norwegian	**Jeg snakker ikke norsk**
	yay sn*a*kker *i*kker noshk

From the doctor: key sentences to understand

Take this . . .	**Ta dette . . .**
	ta detter . . .
every day/hour	**hver dag/time**
	var dahg/teemer
twice/three times a day	**to/tre ganger om dagen**
	too/tray gang-er um dahg-en
Stay in bed	**Hold sengen**
	hawl seng-en
Don't travel , , ,	**Ikke reis . . .**
	ikker race . .
for . . . days/weeks	**før om . . . dager/uker**
	fir om . . . dahg-er/ooker
You must go to hospital	**De må legges inn på sykehus**
	dee maw legg-ess in paw seeker-hooss

Problems: complaints, loss, theft

ESSENTIAL INFORMATION

- Problems with:
  camping facilities, see p. 140
  household appliances, see p. 156
  health, see p. 185
  the car, see p. 156
- If the worst comes to the worst, find the police station. To ask the way, see p. 126
- Look for **POLITI**
- If you lose your passport, report the loss to the police and contact your country's Consulate.
- There is no one common telephone number for fire and police covering all Norway. Therefore, look for **BRANN** (fire) and **POLITI** (police) inside the front cover of telephone directory.
- If you have lost something on the bus or train, go to the station of the appropriate service and ask for **HITTEGODS** (lost property) or go to the police.

Norwegian

COMPLAINTS

I bought this . . .	**Jeg kjøpte denne . . .**
	yay shirp-ter denner . . .
today	**i dag**
	ee dahg
yesterday	**i går**
	ee gor
on Monday [see p. 208]	**på mandag**
	paw mahn-dahg
It's no good	**Den er ikke riktig**
	den ar ikker riktee
Look	**Se**
	say
Here [point]	**Her**
	har
Can you . . .	**Kan De . . .**
	kan dee . . .
change it?	**bytte den?**
	bitter den
mend it?	**reparere den?**
	repar-rairer den
give me a refund?	**gi meg pengene tilbake?**
	yee may peng-en-er til-bahker
Here is the receipt	**Her er kvitteringen**
	har ar kvittairing-en

LOSS

[See also 'Theft' below: the lists are interchangeable]

I have lost . . .	**Jeg har mistet . . .**
	yay har miss-tet . . .
my bag	**vesken min**
	vess-ken meen
my bracelet	**armbåndtet mitt**
	arm-bonner mitt
my car keys	**bilnøklene mine**
	beel-nerk-len-er meener
my car logbook	**vognkortet mitt**
	vogn-korter mitt
my driving licence	**sertifikatet mitt**
	sartifik-ahter mitt
my insurance certificate	**forsikringsattesten min**
	for-sick-ringss-attest-en meen

THEFT
[*See 'Loss' above: the lists are interchangeable*]

Someone has stolen . . .	**Noen har stjålet . . .**
	noo-en har st-yaw-let . . . .
my car	**bilen min**
	beelen meen
my luggage	**bagasjen min**
	ba-gashen meen
my money	**pengene mine**
	peng-en-er meener
my purse	**pungen min**
	poong-en meen
my tickets	**billettene mine**
	bill-aitten-er meener
my travellers' cheques	**reisesjekkene mine**
	racer-shecken-er meener
my wallet	**lommeboken min**
	lommer-booken meen
my watch	**klokken min**
	klokken meen

LIKELY REACTIONS: key words to understand

Wait	**Vent**
	vent
When?	**Når**
	nor
Name?	**Navn?**
	nahvn
Address?	**Adresse?**
	ah-dresser
I can't help you	**Jeg kan ikke hjelpe Dem**
	yay kan ikker yelper dem
Nothing to do with me	**Jeg har ikke noe med det**
	yay har ikker noo-er may day

Norwegian

The post office

ESSENTIAL INFORMATION

- Look for the word **POST** and this sign
- Stamps can also be purchased in kiosks, bookshops and stationers.
  Ask for **FRIMERKER** (stamps).
- Telegrams can be sent from the post office or by dialling 013 on the telephone.
- Telexes can be sent from major post offices only.
- Letterboxes are red.

WHAT TO SAY

To England, please | **Til England**
til *eng*-lahn

[*Hand letters, cards or parcels over the counter*]

To Australia | **Til Australia**
til owst*ra*-lee-ah

To the United States | **Til De Forente Stater/USA**
til dee for*ay*nter st*ah*ter/oo-ess-ah

[*For other countries, see p. 211*]

Airmail | **Luftpost**
*loo*ft-posst

Surface mail | **Ikke luftpost**
*i*kker *loo*ft-posst

Telephoning

ESSENTIAL INFORMATION

- Unless you read or speak Norwegian well, it's best not to make the call yourself. Go to a post office or snack bar, write the town and number you want on a piece of paper and add **PERSONLIG SAMTALE** if you want a person to person call or **NOTERINGS-OVERFØRING** if you want to reverse the charges.
- Telephone boxes are grey or red. Put the appropriate coins in the slot on top of the telephone, they will fall in automatically when the call is answered. Put more coins in the slot, and they will fall through automatically when needed.
- For dialling direct to the U.K. dial 095 then 44 then the code of your town etc. For the U.S.A. dial 095 and then check the rest of the codes in the telephone directory under *De Forente Stater*.
- Alternatively look in the telephone directory for the heading 'How to telephone in Norway' or dial 093 for an English speaking operator.
- To ask the way to public telephone or post office, see p. 126.

WHAT TO SAY

I'd like this number . . .	**Jeg trenger dette nummeret . . .**
[show number]	yay treng-er detter noommerer ....
in England	**i England**
	ee eng-lahn
in Canada	**i Kanada**
	ee ka-na-da
Can you dial it for me, please?	**Kan De slå det for meg?**
	kan dee slaw day for may
May I speak to . . .?	**Kan jeg få snakke med . . .?**
	kan yay faw snakker may . . .
Extension . . .	**Linje . . .**
	lin-yer
Do you speak English?	**Snakker De engelsk?**
	snakker dee eng-elsk
Thank you, I'll phone back	**Takk, jeg ringer igjen siden**
	takk yay ring-er ee-yen seeden

Norwegian

LIKELY REACTIONS

That's . . .	**Det er . . .**
	day ar . . .
Cabin number (3)	**Avlukke nummer (tre)**
[*For numbers, see p. 205*]	*ahv*-lookker noommer (tray)
Don't hang up	**Ikke legg på'**
	ikker legg paw
I'm trying to connect you	**Jeg skal sette Dem over**
	yay skahl setter dem *awv*ver
You're through	**Vær så god**
	var saw goo
There's a delay	**Han er opptatt**
	han ar *o*pp-tahtt
I'll try again	**Jeg kan forsøke igjen**
	yay kan for-s*i*rker ee-yen

Changing cheques and money

ESSENTIAL INFORMATION

- Finding your way to a bank or change bureau, see p. 127.
- Look for these words on buildings: **BANK, VEKSLEKONTOR, EXCHANGE**.
- International credit cards are not as widely used as in other countries. Only major department stores, shops and restaurants are likely to be familiar with them. Traveller's cheques are easier to cash. In towns most shops will accept them. In the countryside and off the beaten track, use cash.
- Banks are open from Monday to Friday. Opening hours vary from town to country and from one city to another. The safest is to seek a bank between 8.30 a.m. and 3 p.m.
- Always have your passport handy for identification.

WHAT TO SAY

I'd like to cash . . .	**Jeg vil løse inn . . .**
	yay vil l*i*r-ser inn . . .

this travellers' cheque	**denne reisesjekken** denner racer-shecken
this cheque	**denne sjekken** denner shecken
I'd like to change this into Norwegian crowns	**Jeg vil veksle disse i norske kroner** yay vil veksler disser ee noshker krooner

For excursions into neighbouring countries

I'd like to change this . . . [*show bank notes*] into Swedish/Danish crowns	**Jeg vil veksle disse . . .** yay vil veksler disser . . . **i svenske/danske kroner** ee svensker/dahn-sker krooner
into Finnish marks/Russian rubles	**i finske mark/russiske rubler** ee finsker mark/rooss-isker roobler

LIKELY REACTIONS

Your passport, please	**Kan jeg få se passet Deres** kan yay faw say passer dayress
Sign here	**Vil De skrive under her** vil dee skreever oonner har
Your banker's card, please	**Kan jeg få se bankkortet Deres** kan yay faw say bank-korter dayress
Go to the cash desk	**Gå til kassen** gaw til kahssen

Car travel

ESSENTIAL INFORMATION

- Finding a filling station or garage, see p. 128.
- Grades of petrol:
  SUPER (98 octan) **NORMAL** (96 octan) **REGULÆR** (93 octan)
- 1 gallon is about 4½ litres (accurate enough up to 6 gallons).

- Types of garages: for filling station **BENSINSTASJON** look for the names of oil companies like, **BP**, **MOBIL, SHELL, TEXACO** etc. Filling stations are helpful with minor problems but do not handle major repairs, for that you need a garage **VERKSTED**, look for this sign

- Filling stations are open from 7 a.m. to 8 p.m. on weekdays and from 8 a.m. to 8 p.m. on Sundays and most holidays. Most filling stations have self-service, look for **SELVBETJENING, SELVTANK**.
- When driving through the vast, thinly populated areas, be sure to start out with a full tank.

WHAT TO SAY
[*for numbers, see p. 205*]

(9) litres of . . .	**(Ni) liter . . .**
	(nee) leeter . . .
(100) crowns of . . .	**. . . for (hundre) kroner**
	. . . for (hoondrer) krooner
four star	**super/98 octan**
	sooper/nitti awtter octahn
two star	**regulær/93 octan**
	regular/nitti tray octahn
diesel	**diesel**
	deessel
Fill it up, please	**Fyll opp tanken**
	fill opp tahnken
Will you check . . .	**Kan De sjekke . . .**
	kan dee shecker . . .
the oil?	**oljen?**
	ol-yen
the battery?	**batteriet?**
	bahtteree-er
the radiator?	**radiatoren?**
	rahdee-ahtooren
the tyres?	**dekkene?**
	dekken-er

I've run out of petrol | **Jeg har kjørt tom for bensin**
yay har shirt tom for ben-*seen*

Can I borrow a can, please? | **Kan jeg få låne en kanne?**
kan yay faw *lawner* en *kanner*

My car has broken down | **Bilen min har fått motorstopp**
beelen meen har fott *mootor*-stop

Can you help me, please? | **Kan De hjelpe meg?**
kan dee *yelper* may

Do you do repairs? | **Foretar dere reparasjoner?**
forer-tar *dayrer* rep-ahra-*shooner*

I have a puncture | **Jeg har punktert**
yay har poong-*tairt*

I have a broken windscreen | **Jeg har knust frontruten**
yay har k-*noosst* front-rooten

I think the problem is here . . . [*point*] | **Jeg tror feilen er her . . .**
yay troor *failen* ar har . . .

Can you . . . | **Kan De . . .**
kan dee . . .

repair the fault? | **reparere feilen?**
rep-ahray-rer *failen*

come and look? | **komme og se?**
kommer aw say

estimate the cost? | **gi et overslag over kostnadene?**
yee et *awver*-shlahg *awver* kost-*nahden*-er

write it down? | **skrive det ned?**
skreever day naid

How long will the repair take? | **Hvor lang tid tar reparasjonen?**
vor lang *tee* tar rep-ahra-*shooen*

This is my insurance document | **Dette er forikringspapirene mine**
detter ar for-sick-ringss-*papeerener* *meener*

HIRING A CAR

Can I hire a car? | **Kan jeg leie en bil?**
kan yay *layer* en *beel*

I need a car . . . | **Jeg trenger en bil . . .**
yay *treng*-er en *beel* . . .

for five people | **for fem personer**
for fem pesh*ooner*

for a week | **for en uke**
for en *ooker*

Can you write down . . .	**Kan De skrive ned . . .**
	kan dee skr*ee*ver na*i*d . . .
the deposit to pay?	**depositum?**
	dep*o*ssit-um
the charge per kilometre?	**prisen per kilometer?**
	pr*ee*-sen pair sh*ee*lo-maiter
the daily charge?	**prisen per dag?**
	pr*ee*-sen pair d*ah*g
the cost of insurance?	**prisen på forsikringen?**
	pr*ee*-sen paw for-s*i*ck-ring-en
Can I leave it in (Oslo)?	**Kan jeg levere den i (Oslo)?**
	kan yay lev*a*yrer den ee (*o*shlo)
What documents do I need?	**Hva slags papierer trenger jeg?**
	va shlahgss pap*ee*rer treng-er yay

LIKELY REACTIONS

We don't do repairs	**Vi foretar ikke reparasjoner**
	vee forer-tar *i*kker rep-ahra-sh*oo*ner
Where is your car?	**Hvor er bilen Deres?**
	vor ar b*ee*len d*a*yress
What make is it?	**Hva slags merke er den?**
	va shlahgss m*a*rker ar den
Come back tomorrow/on Monday	**Kom igjen i morgen/på mandag**
	kom ee-yen ee m*o*ren/paw m*ah*ndahg

[*For days of the week see p. 208*]

We don't hire cars	**Vi leier ikke ut biler**
	vee l*a*yer *i*kker oot b*ee*ler
Your driving licence, please	**Kan jeg få se sertifikatet Deres**
	kan yay faw say sertifi-k*ah*ter d*a*yress
The mileage is unlimited	**De kan kjøre så mye De vil**
	dee kan shir-er saw m*ee*-er dee v*i*l

Public transport

ESSENTIAL INFORMATION

- Finding the way to a bus station, a bus stop, a tram stop, a railway station and a taxi rank, see p. 129.
- People usually queue for buses, particularly in towns.
- Most towns and cities have taxi ranks. Taxis rarely cruise for passengers. Find a taxi rank or look under **DROSJER** (taxis) in the telephone directory. You can hail a taxi with the 'taxi free' sign up. All taxis are metered and expensive.
- There is a national train network called **NSB** (Norwegian State Railways). From Oslo trains run to all parts of Norway with connections to local lines. There are also trains going to Sweden with connections to the Continent.
- Buses and coach services between neighbouring towns and tourist centres in populated parts of the country are good and frequent. In sparsely populated parts, less frequent.
- Oslo is serviced by trams, buses and two small underground networks. In Oslo's trams and buses there is a single fare system. A ticket allows you to interchange once within the hour. Tram, bus and underground tickets are bought as you enter, or from a roving conductor. Train tickets are bought at the railway station.
- In Oslo there is a **'universalkort'** (special ticket) which gives unlimited travel within city limits for either two weeks or a month. In Bergen there is a 48 hour tourist ticket for buses and trolley buses available from the Tourist Information Office and most hotels.
- Many smaller towns have their own airport, and local flights are becoming increasingly popular.
- Key words and signs to look for:

BILLETTER (tickets)	**TOGTABELL** (train timetable)
INNGANG (entrance)	**RUTETABELL** (bus timetable)
UTGANG (exit)	
ADGANG FORBUDT (no entry)	
PLATTFORM/SPOR (platform)	
TURISTINFORMASJON (tourist information)	
VEKSLEKONTOR (exchange)	
OPPBEVARING (left luggage)	
BUSSHOLDEPLASS (regular bus stop)	
STOPPER PÅ SIGNAL (stops on request)	

Norwegian

WHAT TO SAY

Where does the train for (Oslo) leave from?
Hvor går toget til (Oslo) fra?
vor gor tawg-er til (oshlo) fra

At what time does the train leave for (Oslo)?
Når går toget til (Oslo)?
nor gor tawg-cr til (oshlo)

At what time does the train arrive in (Oslo)?
Når kommer toget til (Oslo)?
nor kommer tawg-er til (oshlo)

Is this the train for (Oslo)?
Er dette toget til (Oslo)?
ar detter tawg-er til (oshlo)

Where does the bus for (Hønefoss) leave from?
Hvor går (Hønefoss) bussen fra?
vor gor (hern-erfoss) boossen fra

Is this the bus for (Hønefoss)?
Er dette (Hønefoss) bussen?
ar detter (hern-erfoss) boossen

Do I have to change?
Må jeg bytte?
maw yay bit-ter

Where can I get a taxi?
Hvor kan jeg finne en drosje?
vor kan yay finner en drosher

Can you put me off at the right stop, please?
Kan De si fra når jeg må gå av?
kan dee see fra nor yay maw gaw ahv

Can I book a seat?
Kan jeg bestille en plass?
kan yay best-iller en plahss

A single
Én vei
ain vay

A return
Tur-retur
toor-ret-toor

First class
Første klasse
firster klahsser

Second class
Annen klasse
annen klahsser

One adult
En voksen
ain vaksen

Two adults
To voksne
too vaksner

and one child
og et barn
aw et barn

and two children
og to barn
aw too barn

How much is it?
Hvor mye koster det?
vor mee-er koster day

LIKELY REACTIONS

Over there	**Der borte**
	dar borter
Here	**Her**
	har
Platform (1)	**Plattform/spor (en)**
[For times, see p. 207]	platform/spoor (ain)
Change at (Dombås)	**Bytt på (Dombås)**
	bitt paw (dombawss)
Change at (the town hall)	**Bytt ved (rådhuset)**
	bitt vaid (rawd-hoosser)
There is only tourist class	**Det er bare turistklasse**
	day ar bahrer toorist-klahsser
There is a supplement	**Det er et tillegg**
	day ar et till-egg

Leisure

ESSENTIAL INFORMATION

- Finding your way to a place of entertainment, see p. 127, 129.
- For times of day, see p. 207.
- Smoking is not permitted in cinemas, theatres, etc. during performances. You may, however, smoke during intervals, away from the seating area.
- Foreign films have subtitles and are not dubbed.
- No usherettes in cinemas as lights are on when you enter.
- In theatres it is customary to leave one's coat in the cloakroom.

WHAT TO SAY

At what time does . . . open?	**Når åpner . . .?**
	nor awpner . . .
the museum	**museet**
	moossay-er

At what time does . . . close?	**Når stenger . . .?**
	nor steng-er . . .
the art gallery	**kunstmuseet/galleriet**
	koonst-mooss*ay*-er/galler*ee*-er
At what time does . . . start?	**Når begynner . . .?**
	nor be-y*i*nr . . .
the concert	**konserten**
	konsert-en
the film	**filmen**
	f*i*lmen
the match	**kampen**
	k*a*hmpen
the performance/play	**forestillingen**
	forer-st*i*lling-en
How much is it . . .	**Hvor mye koster det . . .**
	vor m*ee*-er koster day . . .
for an adult?	**for en voksen?**
	for en v*a*ksen
for a child?	**for et barn?**
[*state the price, if there's a choice*]	for et barn
Stalls/circle/upper circle/sun/ shade	**Parkett/losje/balkong/sol/skygge**
	par-k*et*/l*oo*sher/balk*o*ng/sool/ sh*i*hgg-er
Do you have . . .	**Har De . . .**
	har dee . . .
a programme/guide book?	**et program?**
	et pru-gr*a*hm
I would like lessons in . . .	**Jeg vil ha . . . timer**
	yay vil ha . . . t*ee*mer
skiing	**ski**
	shee
sailing	**seile**
	s*ai*ler
water skiing	**vannski**
	v*a*hnn-shee
Can I hire . . .	**Kan jeg leie . . .**
	kan yay l*ay*-er . . .
some skis?	**ski?**
	shee
some ski boots?	**skistøvler?**
	sh*ee*-stirfler

a boat?	**en båt?** en b*aw*t
a fishing rod?	**en fiskestang?** en f*i*sker-stahng
a sun lounger?	**en solseng?** en s*oo*l-seng
a beach chair?	**en fluktstol?** en fl*oo*kt-stool
a sun umbrella?	**en solparasoll?** en s*oo*l-para-soll
the necessary equipment?	**nødvendig utstyr?** nird-vendee *oo*t-steer
How much is it . . .	**Hvor mye koster det . . .** vor m*ee*-er k*o*st-er day . . .
per day/per hour?	**per dag/per time?** pair d*ah*g/pair t*ee*mer
Do I need a licence?	**Trenger jeg tillatelse?** treng-er yay till-*ah*tel-ser

Asking if things are allowed

ESSENTIAL INFORMATION

- May one smoke here?
  May we smoke here?   **Kan man røke her?**
  May I smoke here?   kan man r*i*rk-er har
  Can one smoke here?
  Can I smoke here?
- All these English variations can be expressed in one way in Norwegian. To save space, only the first English version (May one . . .?) is shown below.

WHAT TO SAY

Excuse me, please	**Unnskyld meg** *oo*nshil may

May one . . .	Kan man . . .
	kan man . . .
camp here?	**sette opp telt her?**
	setter opp telt har
come in?	**gå inn?**
	gaw inn
dance here?	**danse her?**
	dancer har
fish here?	**fiske her?**
	fisker har
get a drink here?	**få en drink her?**
	faw en drink har
get out this way?	**gå ut denne veien?**
	gaw oot denner vay-en
get something to eat here?	**få noe å spise her?**
	faw noo-er aw speesser har
eat something here?	**spise her?**
	speesser har
leave one's things here?	**legge igjen sakene sine her?**
	legger ee-yen sahkener seener har
look around?	**se seg om?**
	say say um
park here?	**parkere her?**
	park-airer har
picnic here?	**sette seg og spise her?**
	setter say aw speesser har
sit here?	**sitte her?**
	sitter har
smoke here?	**røke her?**
	rirker har
swim here?	**bade her?**
	bahder har
telephone here?	**låne telefonen?**
	lawner telefoonen
take photos here?	**ta bilder her?**
	ta bilder har
wait here?	**vente her?**
	venter har

LIKELY REACTIONS

Yes, certainly	**Ja, selvfølgelig**
	ya sell-firl-gaylee

Help yourself	**Ja, vær så god**	
	ya var saw goo	
I think so	**Ja, jeg tror det**	
	ya yay troor day	
Of course	**Selvfølgelig**	
	sell-firl-gaylee	
Yes, but be careful	**Ja, men vær forsiktig**	
	ya men var for-siktee	
No, certainly not	**Nei, det er ikke tillatt**	
	nay day ar ikker till-att	
I don't think so	**Nei, jeg tror ikke det**	
	nay yay troor ikker day	
Not normally	**Nei, ikke vanligvis**	
	nay, ikker vahnlee-veess	
Sorry	**Beklager**	
	bay-klahg-er	

Reference

NUMBERS
Cardinal numbers

0	**null**	nooll
1	**en**	ain
2	**to**	too
3	**tre**	tray
4	**fire**	feerer
5	**fem**	fem
6	**seks**	seks
7	**sju**	shoo
8	**åtte**	awtter
9	**ni**	nee
10	**ti**	tee
11	**elleve**	elver
12	**tolv**	tawl
13	**tretten**	tretten
14	**fjorten**	f-yorten

15	**femten**	femten
16	**seksten**	saysten
17	**søtten**	sirtten
18	**atten**	ahtten
19	**nitten**	nitten
20	**tjue**	shoo-er
21	**tjueen**	shoo-er-ain
22	**tjueto**	shoo-er-too
23	**tjuetre**	shoo-er-tray
24	**tjuefire**	shoo-er-feerer
25	**tjuefem**	shoo-er-fem
26	**tjueseks**	shoo-er-seks
27	**tjuesju**	shoo-er-shoo
28	**tjueåtte**	shoo-er-awtter
29	**tjueni**	shoo-er-nee
30	**tretti**	tretti
31	**trettien**	tretti-ain
32	**trettito**	tretti-too
33	**trettitre**	tretti-tray
34	**trettifire**	tretti-feerer
35	**trettifem**	tretti-fem
40	**førti**	firty
45	**førtifem**	firty-fem
50	**femti**	femti
55	**femtifem**	femti-fem
60	**seksti**	seksti
66	**sekstiseks**	seksti-seks
70	**søtti**	sirtti
77	**søttisju**	sirtti-shoo
80	**åtti**	awtti
88	**åttiåtte**	awtti-awtter
90	**nitti**	nitti
99	**nittini**	nitti-nee
100	**hundre**	hoondrer
101	**hundreogen**	hoondrer-aw-ain
102	**hundreogto**	hoondrer-aw-too
125	**hundreogtjuefem**	hoondrer-aw-shoo-er-fem
150	**hundreogfemti**	hoondrer-aw-femti
175	**hundreogsøttifem**	hoondrer-aw-sirtti-fem
200	**to hundre**	too-hoondrer
300	**tre hundre**	tray-hoondrer
400	**fire hundre**	feerer hoondrer
500	**fem hundre**	fem hoondrer

1000	**tusen**	*too*-sen
2000	**to tusen**	too *too*-sen
10,000	**ti tusen**	tee *too*-sen
100,000	**hundre tusen**	h*oo*ndrer *too*-sen
1,000,000	**en million**	ain milli-*oo*n

Ordinal numbers

1st	**første (1.)**	*fir*ster
2nd	**andre (2.)**	*ah*ndrer
3rd	**tredje (3.)**	tr*ai*d-yer
4th	**fjerde (4.)**	f-*y*arder
5th	**femte (5.)**	*fem*ter
6th	**sjette (6.)**	*shet*ter
7th	**sjuende (7.)**	sh*oo*-en-er
8th	**åttende (8.)**	*awt*tener
9th	**niende (9.)**	*nee*-en-er
10th	**tiende (10.)**	*tee*-en-er
11th	**ellevte (11.)**	*el*lefter
12th	**tolvte (12.)**	*tawlf*-ter

TIME

What time is it?	**Hvor mange er klokken?**
	vor m*ah*ng-er ar kl*o*kken
It's . . .	**Klokken er . . .**
	kl*o*kken ar . . .
one o'clock	**ett**
	*ai*tt
two o'clock	**to**
	t*oo*
three o'clock	**tre**
	tr*ay*
It's noon	**Den er tolv**
	den ar t*aw*l
It's midnight	**Det er midnatt**
	day ar m*i*d-natt
It's . . .	**Den er . . .**
	den ar . . .
five past five	**fem over fem**
	fem *aw*ver fem
twenty to six	**tjue på seks**
	sh*oo*-er paw seks
ten to six	**ti på seks**
	t*ee* paw seks

Norwegian

At what time . . . (does the train leave)?	Når . . . (går toget)?
	nor . . . (gor tawg-er)
At . . .	Klokken . . .
	klokken . . .
13.00	tretten
	tretten
22.45	tjueto førtifem
	shoo-er-too firty-fem
0.55	null femtifem
	nooll femti-fem

DAYS

Sunday	søndag
	sirn-dahg
Monday	mandag
	mahn-dahg
Tuesday	tirsdag
	teesh-dahg
Wednesday	onsdag
	onss-dahg
Thursday	torsdag
	toosh-dahg
Friday	fredag
	fray-dahg
Saturday	lørdag
	ler-dahg
last Monday	forrige mandag
	forree-er mahn-dahg
next Tuesday	neste tirsdag
	nester teesh-dahg
on Wednesday	på onsdag
	paw onss-dahg
on Thursdays	på torsdagene
	paw toosh-dahg-en-er
until Friday	til fredag
	til fray-dahg
before Saturday	før lørdag
	fir ler-dahg
after Sunday	etter søndag
	etter sirn-dahg
the day before yesterday	i forgårs
	ee for-gorss
two days ago	for to dager siden
	for too dahg-er seeden

yesterday	**i går**
	ee gor
yesterday morning	**i går morges**
	ee gor mor-res
yesterday afternoon	**i går ettermiddag**
	ee gor ettermiddag
last night	**i natt**
	ee natt
today	**i dag**
	ee dahg
this morning	**i dag morges**
	ee dahg mor-res
this afternoon	**i ettermiddag**
	ee ettermiddag
tonight	**i natt**
	ee natt
tomorrow	**i morgen**
	ee moren
tomorrow morning	**i morgen tidlig**
	ee moren teelee
tomorrow afternoon	**i morgen ettermiddag**
	ee moren ettermiddag
tomorrow evening	**i morgen kveld**
	ee moren kvel
tomorrow night	**i morgen natt**
	ee moren natt
the day after tomorrow	**overimorgen**
	awver-ee-moren

MONTHS AND DATES

January	**januar**
	yan-oo-ar
February	**februar**
	febroo-ar
March	**mars**
	marsh
April	**april**
	ahpreel
May	**mai**
	my
June	**juni**
	yoonee

Norwegian

July	**juli**
	yoolee
August	**august**
	owgoost
September	**september**
	september
October	**oktober**
	oktoober
November	**november**
	november
December	**desember**
	december
last month	**forrige måned**
	forree-er mawner
in spring	**om våren**
	om voren
in summer	**om sommeren**
	om sommer-en
in autumn	**om høsten**
	om herssten
in winter	**om vinteren**
	om vinter-en
this year	**i år**
	ee or
last year	**i fjor**
	ee f-yoor
next year	**neste år**
	nester or
in 1985	**i nitten åttifem**
	ee nitten awtti-fem
What's the date today?	**Hvilken dato er det i dag?**
	vilken dahtoo ar day ee dahg
It's the 6th of March	**Det er den sjette mars**
	day ar den shetter marsh

Public holidays

● Offices, shops and schools are all closed on the following days

(NB Christmas eve and the day before Easter have half day closing.)

1 January	**Nyttårsdag**	New Year's Day
. . .	**Skjærtorsdag**	Maundy Thursday
. . .	**Langfredag**	Good Friday
. . .	**Annen påskedag**	Easter Monday

1 May	**Arbeidets dag**	Labour Day
17 May	**Nasjonaldagen**	Constitution Day
. . .	**Kristi Himmelfartsdag**	Ascension Day
. . .	**Annen pinsedag**	Whit Monday
25 December	**Første Juledag**	Christmas Day
26 December	**Annen Juledag**	Boxing Day

COUNTRIES AND NATIONALITIES
Countries

Australia	**Australia** owstra-lee-ah
Austria	**Østerrike** erster-reeker
Belgium	**Belgia** bel-ghee-ah
Britain	**Storbritannia** stoor-britannia
Canada	**Kanada** ka-na-da
East Africa	**Øst-Afrika** erst ahfreeka
Eire	**Eire** eye-ray
England	**England** eng-lahn
France	**Frankrike** frahnk-reeker
Greece	**Hellas** hell-ahss
India	**India** india
Italy	**Italia** eeta-lee-ah
Luxembourg	**Luksemburg** looks-emburg
Netherlands	**Nederland/Holland** naider-lahn/holl-ahn
New Zealand	**New Zealand** new sealahn
Northern Ireland	**Nord-Irland** noor-eer-lahn
Pakistan	**Pakistan** pakee-stahn

Portugal	**Portugal**
	portoo-gahl
Scotland	**Skotland**
	skot-lahn
South Africa	**Sør-Afrika**
	sir-ahfreeka
Spain	**Spania**
	spahn-ee-ah
Switzerland	**Sveits**
	svaits
United States	**De Forente Stater/USA**
	dee forainter stahter/oo-ess-ah
Wales	**Wales**
	wales
West Germany	**Vest-Tyskland**
	vest-tisk-lahn

Nationalities

American	**amerikansk**
	ahmeri-kahnsk
Australian	**australiensk**
	owstra-lee-ainsk
British	**britisk**
	brittisk
Canadian	**kanadisk**
	ka-na-disk
East African	**øst-afrikansk**
	erst-ahfree-kahnsk
English	**engelsk**
	eng-elsk
Indian	**indisk**
	in-disk
Irish	**irsk**
	eeshk
New Zealander	**new zealandsk**
	new sea-lahnsk
Pakistani	**pakistansk**
	pa-kistahnsk
Scottish	**skotsk**
	skotsk
South African	**sør-afrikansk**
	sir-ahfree-kahnsk
Welsh	**walesisk**
	va-lay-sisk

Do it yourself

Some notes on the language

This section does not deal with 'grammar' as such. The purpose here is to explain some of the most obvious and elementary nuts and bolts of the language, based on the principal phrases included in the book. This information should enable you to produce numerous sentences of your own making.

There is no pronunciation guide in the first part of this section partly because it would get in the way of the explanations and partly because you have to do it yourself at this stage, if you are serious: work out the pronunciation from all the earlier examples in the book.

THE

All nouns in Norwegian belong to one of three genders: masculine, feminine or neuter, irrespective of whether they refer to living beings or inanimate objects. Most feminine words can also be used as masculine words, but never the other way round.

The in Norwegian is tagged on to the end of the word, so that instead of *the boy* they say *boy the*. That is *boy* – **gutt**, *the boy* – **gutten**. *The* is **-en** after a masculine noun, **-a** after a feminine noun and **-et** after a neuter noun.

The	masculine	feminine	neuter
the address	adressen		
the apple			eplet
the bill	regningen		
the cup of tea	tekoppen		
the glass of beer			ølglasset
the key	nøkkelen		
the luggage	bagasjen		
the menu	menyen		
the newspaper		avisa	
the receipt	kvitteringen		
the ham sandwich			skinke-smørbrødet
the suitcase	kofferten		
the telephone directory	telefon-katalogen		
the train timetable	togtabellen		

Norwegian

Important things to remember

- There is no easy way of predicting if a noun is masculine, feminine or neuter. You just have to learn and remember its gender. But it may help you to know that most words are masculine, and that you can, if you like, eliminate the feminine gender altogether.
- Does it matter? Not unless you want to make a serious attempt to speak correctly and scratch beneath the surface of the language. You would be understood if you said **eplen** or **nøkkelet** provided your pronunciation was good.

Plural

the addresses	**adressene**
the apples	**eplene**
the bills	**regningene**
the bus timetables	**rutetabellene**
the cups of tea	**tekoppene**
the glasses of beer	**ølglassene**
the keys	**nøklene**
the menus	**menyene**
the newspapers	**avisene**
the receipts	**kvitteringene**
the ham sandwiches	**skinkesmørbrødene**
the suitcases	**koffertene**
the telephone directories	**telefonkatalogene**

Important things to remember

- In plural most words end in **-ene** irrespective of gender.
- However, some Norwegian nouns do not follow the above rule. Their endings may be slightly different and their vowels may change in the singular and plural like 'ox' and 'goose' in English. In Norwegian we have *the daughter – the daughters* = **datteren – døtrene**. The rules for these exceptions are too many and too complicated to be explained here. Besides, there is no great harm done if you should happen to say **datterene** instead of **døtrene**. You will be understood provided your pronunciation is good.

Practice saying and writing these sentences in Norwegian. Notice that the verb remains unchanged from singular to plural.

Where is the key?	**Hvor er nøkkelen?**
Where is the receipt?	**Hvor er . . .?**

Where is the address?
Where is the luggage?
Where are the keys?   **Hvor er nøklene?**
Where are the ham sandwiches?   **Hvor er . . .?**
Where are the newspapers?
Where are the apples?

Now make up more sentences along these lines.

Practise saying and writing these sentences in Norwegian:

Have you got the key?   **Har De nøkkelen?**
Have you got the suitcase?   **Har De . . .?**
Have you got the luggage?
Have you got the telephone directory?
Have you got the menu?
I'd like the key   **Kan jeg få nøkkelen?**
I'd like the train timetable
I'd like the receipt
I'd like the keys
Where can I get the key?   **Hvor kan man få nøkkelen?**
Where can I get the address?
Where can I get the bus timetables?

Now make up more sentences along these lines.

A/AN

A/an	masculine	feminine	neuter
an address	en adresse		
an apple			et eple
a bill	en regning		
a cup of tea	en kopp te		
a glass of beer			et glass øl
a key	en nøkkel		
a menu	en meny		
a newspaper		ei avis	
a receipt	en kvittering		
a ham sandwich			et skinke-smørbrød
a suitcase	en koffert		
a telephone directory	en telefon-katalog		
a train timetable	en togtabbell		

Norwegian

Important things to remember

- *A* or *an* is **en** before masculine nouns, **ei** before feminine nouns and **et** before neuter nouns.
- The plural for *some* or *any* is **noen** irrespective of gender when referring to an indefinite number of a certain thing, and **noe** irrespective of gender, when referring to an unknown quantity.
- The plural ending is **-er**, irrespective of gender, except for one syllable neuter words (**et brød** – **noen brød**) which don't get any ending at all.
- You may have noticed that in the restaurant and shopping sections, **noen** and **noe** have on occasions been omitted, sometimes substituted with **en** or **et** and sometimes with **litt** (a little). The rules that dictate these irregularities are many and complicated and to give a full description of them here would only lead to confusion. When looking up a given phrase in this book, use the given phrase. When making your own phrase, use **noen** and **noe** according to the above rules. Your phrase will then be basically if not absolutely correct, and you will be understood.

some/any (plural) indefinite number

some addresses	**noen adresser**
some apples	**noen epler**
some bills	**noen regninger**
some bus timetables	**noen rutetabeller**
some cups of tea	**noen kopper te**
some glasses of wine	**noen glass vin**
some keys	**noen nøkler**
some menus	**noen menyer**
some receipts	**noen kvitteringer**
some sandwiches	**noen smørbrød**
some suitcases	**noen kofferter**
some telephone directories	**noen telefonkataloger**

some/any part of a larger quantity

some butter	**noe smør**
some meat	**noe kjøtt**
some paper	**noe papir**
some toothpaste	**noe tannkrem**

Practise writing and saying these sentences in Norwegian:

Have you got a receipt?	**Har De en kvittering?**
Have you got a menu?	
I'd like a telephone directory	**Kan jeg få en telefonkatalog?**
I'd like some sandwiches	**Kan jeg få noen smørbrød?**
Where can I get some newspapers?	**Hvor kan jeg få noen aviser?**
Where can I get a cup of tea?	
Is there a key?	**Er det en nøkkel?**
Is there a train timetable?	
Are there any keys?	**Er det noen nøkler?**
Are there any newspapers?	

Now make up more sentences along these lines.

THIS AND THAT

There are two different sets of words for *this* and *that* in Norwegian according to the gender of the word they are referring to.

Masculine/feminine	*Neuter*
denne this	**dette** this
den that	**det** that

- If you don't know the gender of the object that you are referring to or even its name, it does not really matter. You will be understood even if you use the wrong gender. Just point and say:

Jeg vil ha denne/dette	I'd like this
Jeg vil ha den/det	I'd like that
Jeg trenger denne/dette	I need this

HELPING OTHERS

There is really no adequate and easy way in which to say *I'd like* in Norwegian. There is a rather long phrase which is somewhat daunting for the inexperienced speaker of the language and the phrase **jeg vil ha . . .** (I'll have) which in some cases may seem a little abrupt. What Norwegians often do is to say **kan jeg få . . .?** (may I have?) when what they really mean is *I'd like*. This is why *I'd like* in this book is sometimes translated by **jeg vil ha . . .** and sometimes by **kan jeg få . . .?**

You can help yourself with phrases such as:

I'd like . . . a sandwich	**Jeg vil ha . . . et smørbrød**
Where can I get . . . a cup of tea?	**Hvor kan jeg få . . . en kopp te?**
I'll have . . . a glass of wine	**Jeg vil ha et glass vin**
I need . . . a receipt	**Jeg trenger . . . en kvittering**

If you come across a compatriot having trouble making himself or herself understood, you should be able to speak to the Norwegian on their behalf.

He'd like . . .	**Han vil ha et skinkesmørbrød**
	han vil ha et shinker-smir-brer
She'd like . . .	**Hun vil ha et skinkesmørbrød**
	hun vil ha et shinker-smir-brer

Strictly speaking, **kan man . . .?** means *can one . . .?* and normally serves instead of *can I . . .?* (**kan jeg . . .?**), *can he . . .?*, *can she . . .?*, *can they . . .?* and *can we . . .?* However, all the above-mentioned variations in Norwegian are included in the remainder of this section because of their potential usefulness.

Where can he get . . .?	**Hvor kan han få en kopp te?**
	vor kan han faw en kopp tay
Where can she get . . .?	**Hvor kan hun få en kopp te?**
	vor kan hun faw en kopp tay
He'll have . . .	**Han vil ha et glass øl**
	han vil ha et glahss erl
She'll have . . .	**Hun vil ha et glass øl**
	hun vil ha et glahss erl
He needs . . .	**Han trenger en kvittering**
	han treng-er en kvittairing
She needs . . .	**Hun trenger en kvittering**
	hun treng-er en kvittairing

You can also help a couple or a group if *they* are having difficulties. The Norwegian word for *they* is **de**. Note that **De** written with a capital is also the polite form of *you*.

They'd like . . .	**De vil ha ost**
	dee vil ha ost
Where can they get . . .?	**Hvor kan de få noe smør?**
	vor kan dee faw noo-er smir

They'll have . . .   **De vil ha vin**
                            dee vil ha *veen*

They need . . .   **De trenger vann**
                            dee treng-er *vahnn*

What about the two of you? No problem the word for *we* is **vi**.

We'd like . . .   **Vi vil ha vin**
                            vee vil ha *veen*

Where can we get . . .?   **Hvor kan vi få vann?**
                            vor kan vee faw *vahnn*

We'll have . . .   **Vi vil ha noe smør**
                            vee vil ha noo-er smir

We need . . .   **Vi trenger sukker**
                            vee treng-er sookker

Try writing out your own checklist for these four useful phrase-starters, like this:

Jeg vil ha . . .   **Vi vil ha . . .**
Han vil ha . . .   **De vil ha . . .**
Hun vil ha . . .
Hvor kan jeg . . . få? **Hvor . . . vi . . .?**
Hvor kan han . . . få? **Hvor . . . hun . . .?**
Hvor . . . hun . . . få?

You may have noticed that the verb never changes from one person to another: **jeg vil, han vil, hun vil, vi vil** etc.

MORE PRACTICE

Here are some Norwegian names of things. See how many different sentences you can make up, using the various points of information given earlier in this section.

		singular	plural
1	ashtray	**askebeger** (*m*)	**askebegrene**
2	ballpen	**kulepenn** (*m*)	**kulepennene**
3	bag	**veske** (*f*)	**veskene**
4	bottle	**flaske** (*f*)	**flaskene**
5	car	**bil** (*m*)	**bilene**
6	cigarette	**sigarett** (*m*)	**sigarettene**
7	corkscrew	**korketrekker** (*m*)	**korketrekkerne**
8	egg	**egg** (*n*)	**eggene**
9	house	**hus** (*n*)	**husene**

		singular	plural
10	knife	kniv (*m*)	knivene
11	mountain	fjell (*n*)	fjellene
12	plate	tallerken (*m*)	tallerknene
13	postcard	prospektkort (*n*)	prospektkortene
14	room	rom (*n*)	rommene
15	shoe	sko (*m*)	skoene
16	stamp	frimerke (*n*)	frimerkene
17	street	gate (*f*)	gatene
18	ticket	billett (*m*)	billettene
19	train	tog (*n*)	togene
20	wallet	lommebok (*f*)	lommebøkene

Index

Travellers' **Swedish**

David Ellis is Director of the Somerset Language Centre
and co-author of a number of language books

Lotta Bernadotte works in advertising and publicity
and has recently returned to Stockholm after living in London

Dr John Baldwin is Lecturer in Phonetics at
University College, London

Travellers' Swedish

D. L. Ellis,

Pronunciation **Dr J. Baldwin**

Useful address

Swedish National Tourist Office
3 Cork Street
London W1

Swedish

Contents

Swedish

Everyday expressions

[See also 'Shop talk', p. 266]
- There is no word that corresponds exactly with 'please' in Swedish. **Tack** (thank you) is used instead. When handing over something, the phrase 'please' is **var så god**.

Hello (informal)	**Hej** hay
Good bye (informal)	**Hej då** hay daw
Good bye (formal)	**Adjö** ah-yer
Good morning	**God morgon** goo morron
Good afternoon	**God middag** goo mid-da
Good day (formal)	**God dag** goo da
Good evening	**God afton** goo af-ton
Good night	**God natt** goo naht
Yes	**Ja** ya
Please [see above]	**Var så god/tack** var saw goo/tak
Thank you	**Tack** tak
Thank you very much	**Tack så mycket** tak saw mee-ket
That's right	**Det är riktigt** det air rik-tit
No	**Nej** nay
No, thank you	**Nej tack** nay tak
I disagree	**Jag håller inte med** ya holler inter med
Excuse me	**Ursäkta mig** yoo-shek-ta may

That's good	**Det är bra**
	det air bra
That's no good	**Det är inte bra**
	det air *i*nter bra
I know	**Jag vet**
	ya vet
It doesn't matter	**Det gör ingenting**
	det yer *i*ng-en-ting
Where's the toilet, please?	**Var är toaletten?**
	var air toh-ah-*le*t-ten
Do you speak English?	**Talar ni engelska?**
	ta-lar nee *e*ng-el-ska
I'm sorry . . .	**Tyvärr . . .**
	tee-*va*ir . . .
I don't speak Swedish	**jag talar inte svenska**
	ya *ta*-lar *i*nter sven-ska
I don't understand	**jag förstår inte**
	ya fer-*sto*r *i*nter
Please can you . . .	**Kan ni . . . tack**
	kan nee . . . tak
repeat that?	**säga om det?**
	*sa*y-ah om det
speak more slowly?	**tala långsammare?**
	ta-la *lo*ng-sam-ah-rer
write it down?	**skriva ner det?**
	skr*ee*va nair det?
What is this called in Swedish?	**Vad heter det här på svenska?**
[*point*]	vad h*ai*ter det hair paw sven-ska

Crossing the border

ESSENTIAL INFORMATION

- Don't waste time just before you leave rehearsing what you are going to say to the border officials – the chances are that you won't have to say anything at all, especially if you travel by air.
- It's more useful to check that you have your documents handy for

the journey: passports, tickets, money, travellers' cheques, insurance documents, driving licence and car registration documents.
● Look out for these signs:
TULL (customs)
GRÄNS (border)
GRÄNSPOLIS (frontier police)
● You may be asked routine questions by the customs officials [*see below*]. If you have to give personal details, see 'Meeting people' p. 233. The other important answer to know is 'Nothing':
Ingenting (ing-en-ting).

ROUTINE QUESTIONS

Passport?	**Pass?**
	pass
Insurance?	**Försäkring?**
	fer-*saik*-ring
Registration document? (logbook)	**Registreringsbevis?**
	reg-ee-strair-ings-bay-vees
Ticket, please	**Biljetten, tack**
	bil-*yet*-ten tak
Have you anything to declare?	**Har ni något att deklarera?**
	har nee n*aw*-got aht deklah-r*ai*ra
Where are you going?	**Vart är ni på väg?**
	vart air nee paw v*ai*g
How long are you staying?	**Hur länge stannar ni?**
	hoor l*ai*ng-er st*a*n-nar nee
Where have you come from?	**Var kommer ni ifrån?**
	var k*o*m-mer nee *ee*-frawn

Meeting people

[*See also 'Everyday expressions', p. 230*]

Breaking the ice

How are you?	**Hur mår ni?**
	hoor mor nee
I am here . . .	**Jag är här . . .**
	ya air hair . . .
on holiday	**på semester**
	paw se-mes-ter
on business	**i affärer**
	ee af-fairer
Can I offer you . . .	**Kan jag få bjuda . . .**
	kan ya faw b-yoo-da . . .
a drink?	**på en drink?**
	paw en drink
a cigarette?	**på en cigarrett?**
	paw en cigarett
a cigar?	**på en cigarr?**
	paw en cigar
Are you staying long?	**Stannar ni länge?**
	stan-nar nee laing-er

Name

What's your name?	**Vad heter ni?**
	vad haiter nee
My name is . . .	**Mitt namn är . . .**
	mitt namn air . . .

Family

Are you married?	**Är ni gift?**
	air nee yeeft
I am . . .	**Jag är . . .**
	ya air . . .
married	**gift**
	yeeft
single	**ogift**
	o-yeeft

This is . . .	Det här är . . .
	det hair air . . .
my wife	min fru
	min froo
my husband	min man
	min man
my son	min son
	min sawn
my daughter	min dotter
	min dot-ter
my boyfriend	min pojkvän
	min poyk-ven
my girlfriend	min flickvän
	min flick-ven
my colleague (male or female)	min kollega
	min kol-lai-ga
Do you have any children?	Har ni några barn?
	har nee nora barn
I have . . .	Jag har . . .
	ya har . . .
one daughter	en dotter
	en dot-ter
one son	en son
	en sawn
two daughters	två döttrar
	tvaw dert-rar
three sons	tre söner
	tray sern-er
No, I haven't any children	Nej, jag har inga barn
	nay ya har inga barn

Where you live

Are you . . .	Är ni . . .
	air nee . . .
Swedish?	svensk/svenska?*
	svensk/sven-ska
Norwegian?	norsk/norska?*
	norsk/nor-ska
Danish?	dansk/danska?*
	dansk/dan-ska

*Use the first alternative for men, the second for women

I am . . .	**Jag är . . .**
	ya air . . .
American	**amerikan/amerikanska***
	am-ree-*kahn*/am-ree-*kahn*-ska
English	**engelsman/engelska***
	eng-els-man/*eng*-el-ska

[*For other nationalities, see p. 320*]

I live . . .	**Jag bor . . .**
	ya boor . . .
in London	**i London**
	ee *l*on-don
in England	**i England**
	ee *eng*-land
in the north (of Sweden)	**i norra (Sverige)**
	ee n*or*-ra (sv*air*-yer)
in the south	**i södra**
	ee *serd*-ra
in the west	**i västra**
	ee v*ais*t-ra
in the east	**i östra**
	ee *erst*-ra
in the centre (of Stockholm)	**i centrum (av Stockholm)**
	ee c*e*ntrum (ahv st*o*ck-holm)

For the businessman and woman

I'm from . . . (firm's name)	**Jag kommer från . . .**
	ya k*o*m-mer frawn . . .
I have an appointment with . . .	**Jag har ett möte med . . .**
	ya har ett m*e*rter med . . .
May I speak to . . .?	**Kan jag få tala med . . .?**
	kan ya faw ta-la med . . .
This is my card	**Här är mitt kort**
	hair air mitt kort
I'm sorry, I'm late	**Jag är ledsen, att jag är sen**
	ya air l*e*d-sen aht ya air sain
Can I fix another appointment?	**Kan jag bestämma ett nytt möte**
	kan ya be-st*e*m-ma ett neet m*e*rter
I am staying at the hotel . . .	**Jag bor på hotell . . .**
	ya boor paw hot*e*ll . . .

*First alternative for men, second for women

Swedish

Asking the way

ESSENTIAL INFORMATION

- Keep a look out for all these place names as you will find them on shops, maps and notices.

WHAT TO SAY

Excuse me, please	**Ursäkta mig** yoo-shek-ta may
How do I get . . .	**Hur kommer jag . . .** hoor kom-mer ya . . .
to the airport?	**till flygplatsen?** till fleeg-platsen
to the beach?	**till stranden?** till stran-den
to the bus station?	**till busshållplatsen?** till booss-holl-platsen
to Gothenburg?	**till Göteborg?** till yerter-bory
to the market?	**till torget?** till tor-yet
to the police station?	**till polisstationen?** till police-sta-shonen
to the post office?	**till posten?** till pos-ten
to the railway station?	**till tågstationen?** til tawg-sta-shonen
to the sports stadium?	**till sportstadion?** till sport-stad-ee-on
to the Stora Hotel?	**till Stora hotellet?** till stoora hotellet
to the tourist information office?	**till turist informationen?** till toorist-informa-shonen
to the town centre?	**till centrum?** till centrum
to the town hall?	**till rådhuset?** till rawd-hoos-et
Excuse me, please	**Ursäkta mig** yoo-shek-ta may

Is there . . . near by?	Finns det . . . i närheten?
	finss det . . . ee nair-haiten
an art gallery	**ett konstgalleri**
	ett konst-galler*ee*
a baker's	**ett bageri**
	ett bahg-er-ree
a bank	**en bank**
	en bank
a bar	**en bar**
	en bar
a botanical garden	**en botanisk trädgård**
	et bot-*a*hn-eesk tr*ai*d-gord
a bus stop	**en busshållplats**
	en b*oo*ss-holl-platss
a butcher's	**en slaktare**
	en sl*a*kta-rer
a café	**ett kafé**
	ett café
a cake shop	**ett konditori**
	ett k*o*ndit-oree
a campsite	**en campingplats**
	en kamping-plats
a car park	**en parkeringsplats**
	en park-*ai*rings-plats
a change bureau	**ett växelkontor**
	ett v*ai*k-sel-kont*o*r
a chemist's	**ett apotek**
	ett ap-o-ta*i*k
a church	**en kyrka**
	en sh*ee*r-ka
a cinema	**en biograf**
	en b*ee*-oo-graf
a delicatessen	**en delikatessaffär**
	en delee-ka-*te*ss-af-fair
a dentist's	**en tandläkare**
	en t*a*nd-laik-arer
a department store	**ett varuhus**
	ett v*a*-roo-hoos
a disco	**ett diskotek**
	ett disko-t*e*k
a doctor's surgery	**en läkarmottagning**
	en l*ai*k-ar-mot-tag-ning

Swedish

Is there . . . near by?	Finns det . . . i närheten?
	finss det . . . ee n*air*-haiten
a dry cleaner's	**en kemtvätt**
	en sh*ai*m-tvet
a fishmonger's	**en fiskaffär**
	en f*i*sk-af-fair
a garage	**en bilverkstad**
	en b*ee*l-vairk-stad
a greengrocer's	**en grönsaksaffär**
	en gr*er*n-saks-af-fair
a hairdresser	**en hårfrisör**
	en hor-free-ser
a hardware shop	**en järnaffär**
	en y*ai*rn-af-fair
a Health and Social Security office	**en försäkringskassa**
	en fer-s*ai*k-rings-kas-sa
a hospital	**ett sjukhus**
	ett sh*oo*k-hoos
a hotel	**ett hotell**
	ett hot*e*ll
an ice-cream parlour	**en glassbar**
	en gl*a*ss-bar
a laundry	**en tvätt**
	en tvet
a museum	**ett museum**
	ett m*oo*-say-um
a night club	**en nattklubb**
	en n*a*ht-klubb
a park	**en park**
	en park
a petrol station	**en bensinstation**
	en b*e*n-seen-sta-shon
a post box	**en brevlåda**
	en br*ai*v-law-da
a restaurant	**en restaurang**
	en resto-r*a*ng
a (snack) bar	**en (grill)-bar**
	en (gr*i*ll)-bar
a sports ground	**en idrottsplats**
	en *ee*drots-plats
a supermarket	**ett snabbköp**
	ett sn*a*hb-kerp

a sweet shop	**en godisaffär**
	en go-dees-af-fair
a swimming pool	**en swimming pool**
	en swimming pool
a telephone (booth)	**en telefon (kiosk)**
	en telefon (shee-osk)
a theatre	**en teater**
	en tay-ah-ter
a tobacconist's	**en tobaksaffär**
	en toh-baks-af-fair
a toilet	**en toalett**
	en toh-ah-let
a travel agent's	**en resebyrå**
	en raiser-bee-raw
a youth hostel	**ett vandrarhem**
	ett vand-rar-hem
a zoo	**en djurpark**
	en yoor-park

DIRECTIONS

- Asking where a place is, or if a place is near by, is one thing; making sense of the answer is another.
- Here are some of the most important key directions and replies.

Left	**Vänster**
	venster
Right	**Höger**
	herg-er
Straight on	**Rakt fram**
	rakt fram
There	**Där**
	dair
First left/right	**Första vänster/höger**
	fer-sta ven-ster/herg-er
Second left/right	**Andra vänster/höger**
	andra venster/herg-er
At the crossroads	**I korsningen**
	ee korsning-en
At the traffic lights	**Vid trafikljusen**
	veed tra-feek-yoos-en
At the roundabout	**Vid rondellen**
	veed rond-ellen

Swedish

At the level crossing	**Vid järnvägsövergången**
	veed yairn-vaigs-erver-gawng-en
It's near/far	**Det är nära/långt**
	det air naira/lawngt
One kilometre	**En kilometer**
	en kilo-maiter
Two kilometres	**Två kilometer**
	tvaw kilo-maiter
Five minutes . . .	**Fem minuter . . .**
	fem min-ooter . . .
on foot/by car	**till fots/med bil**
	till foots/med beel
Take . . .	**Ta . . .**
	ta . . .
the bus	**bussen**
	boossen
the train	**tåget**
	taw-get
the underground	**tunnelbanan**
	toon-nel-ba-nan
the tram	**spårvagnen**
	spor-vang-nen

[For public transport, see p. 306]

The tourist information office

ESSENTIAL INFORMATION

- There are tourist information offices in over 200 locations throughout Sweden.
- Look out for this sign or the following words:
  TURISTBYRÅ
  TURIST INFORMATION
- Tourist offices offer you free information in the form of maps and brochures.

- You may have to pay for some types of documents, but this is not usual.
- There is usually a hotel booking service, **RUMSFÖRMEDLING** or **HOTELLCENTRAL** attached to the tourist office where you can get help finding overnight accommodation in a hotel, in a private home, or where you can rent a chalet **STUGA**.
- For finding a tourist office, see p. 236.

WHAT TO SAY

Please, have you got . . .	**Har ni . . .**
	har nee . . .
a plan of the town?	**en karta över staden?**
	en karta erver sta-den?
a list of hotels?	**en lista på hotell?**
	en leesta paw hotell
a list of campsites?	**en lista på campingplatser?**
	en leesta paw kamping-plats-er
a list of restaurants?	**en lista på restauranger?**
	en leesta paw resto-rang-er
a list of events?	**en lista på evenemang?**
	en leesta paw ev-en-emang
a leaflet of the town?	**en broschyr om staden?**
	en bro-sheer om sta-den
a leaflet on the region?	**en broschyr om regionen?**
	en bro-sheer om reg-ee-onen
a railway/bus timetable?	**en tåg/busstidtabell?**
	en tawg/booss-tecd-tah-bell
In English, please	**På engelska, tack**
	paw eng-el-ska tak
How much do I owe you?	**Hur mycket är jag skyldig?**
	hoor mee-ket air ya sheel-dig

LIKELY ANSWERS

You need to understand when the answer is 'No'. You should be able to tell by the assistant's facial expression, tone of voice and gesture; but there are some language clues, such as:

No	**Nej**
	nay
I'm sorry	**Tyvärr**
	tee-vair

I don't have a list of hotels	**Jag har ingen lista på hotell**
	ya har *i*ng-en l*ee*sta paw hot*e*ll
I haven't got any left	**Jag har inga kvar**
	ya har *i*nga kvar
It's free	**Det är gratis**
	det air gr*a*tis

Accommodation

Hotel

ESSENTIAL INFORMATION

- If you want hotel-type accommodation, all the following words in capital letters are worth looking for on name boards:
  HOTELL
  MOTELL
  PENSIONAT (boarding house)
  VÄRDSHUS (type of inn with a limited number of rooms)
  RUM (room to let in a private house, bed and breakfast) or look for this sign
- A list including all types of accommodation except **RUM** in the town or district can be obtained at the local tourist information office [see p. 236].
- Not all hotels and boarding houses provide meals apart from breakfast; inquire about this on arrival.
- The cost of the room is per night and not per person. It includes service charges, VAT and usually breakfast.
- Almost all hotels provide a substantial Swedish breakfast where you help yourself to a wide choice of cereals, yoghurts, eggs, cheese and cold meats, bread, jam and fruit juices.
- On arrival you will be asked to complete a registration document and the receptionist will want to see your passport.
- It is customary to tip the porter.
- Finding a hotel, [see p. 238].

WHAT TO SAY

I have a booking	**Jag har beställt**
	ya har be-stellt
Have you any vacancies, please?	**Har ni några lediga rum?**
	har nee nora laid-eega room
Can I book a room?	**Kan jag beställa ett rum?**
	kan ya bestel-la ett room
It's for . . .	**Det är för . . .**
	det air fer . . .
one person	**en person**
	en per-soon
two people	**två personer**
[For numbers, see p. 313]	tvaw per-soon-er
It's for . . .	**Det är för . . .**
	det air fer . . .
two nights	**två nätter**
	tvaw nait-ter
one week	**en vecka**
	en vaika
two weeks	**två veckor**
	tvaw vaik-or
I would like . . .	**Jag ska be att få . . .**
	ya ska bay aht faw . . .
a room	**ett rum**
	ett room
two rooms	**två rum**
	tvaw room
a room with a single bed	**ett enkelrum**
	ett en-kel-room
a room with two single beds	**ett dubbelrum**
	ett doob-bel-room
with toilet	**med toalett**
	med toh-ah-let
with bathroom	**med badrum**
	med bad-room
with shower	**med dusch**
	med doosh
with cot	**med barnsäng**
	med barn-seng
with balcony	**med balkong**
	med bal-kong

Swedish

I would like . . .	**Jag ska be att få . . .**
	ya ska bay aht faw . . .
full board	**helpension**
	h*ail*-pan-shoon
half board	**halvpension**
	h*alv*-pan-shoon
bed and breakfast	**övernattning med frukost**
	erver-nattning med fr*oo*-kost
Do you serve meals?	**Serverar ni mat?**
	serv*air*-ar nee mat
At what time is . . .	**När serveras . . .**
	nair serv*air*-as . . .
breakfast?	**frukost?**
	fr*oo*-kost
lunch?	**lunch?**
	lunch
dinner?	**middag?**
	m*id*-da
How much is it?	**Hur mycket kostar det?**
	hoor m*ee*-ket kostar det
Can I look at the room?	**Kan jag få titta på rummet?**
	kan ya faw t*it*-ta paw r*oo*m-et
I'd prefer a room . . .	**Jag föredrar ett rum . . .**
	ya f*erer*-drar ett room . . .
at the front/the back	**på framsidan/baksidan**
	paw fr*am*-seed-an/b*ak*-seed-an
OK, I'll take it	**Tack, jag tar det**
	tak ya tar det
No thanks, I won't take it	**Nej tack, jag tar det inte**
	nay tak ya tar det *int*er
The key to number (10), please	**Nyckeln till nummer (10), tack**
	n*eek*-eln till n*oo*m-mer (t*ee*-oo) tak
Please, may I have . . .	**Kan jag få . . .? Tack**
	kan ya faw . . . tak
a coat hanger?	**en klädhängare?**
	en kl*aid*-heng-arer
a towel?	**en handduk?**
	en h*and*-dook
a glass?	**ett glas?**
	ett glass
some soap?	**lite tvål?**
	l*eet*er tvawl

an ashtray?	**ett askfat?** ett *ask*-fat
another pillow?	**en kudde till?** en k*oo*d-der till
another blanket?	**en filt till?** en filt till
Come in!	**Kom in!** kom in
One moment, please!	**Ett ögonblick!** ett *e*rgon-blick
Please can you . . .	**Kan ni . . .** kan nee . . .
do this laundry/dry- cleaning?	**ta hand om min tvätt/kemtvätt?** ta hand om min tvet/sh*ai*m-tvet
call me at . . .?	**väcka mig klockan . . .?** v*ai*ka may klock-an . . .
help me with my luggage?	**hjälpa mig med bagaget?** y*e*lpa may med ba-*ga*-shet
call me a taxi for . . .?	**ringa efter en taxi till . . .?** r*i*nga *e*fter en t*a*xi till . . .
The bill, please	**Notan, tack** n*o*-tan tak
Is service included?	**Ingår dricks?** *in*-gor dricks
I think it is wrong	**Jag tror att den är fel** ya troor aht den air fel
May I have a receipt?	**Kan jag få ett kvitto?** kan ya faw ett kv*i*t-to

At breakfast

Some more . . . please	**Lite till . . . tack** l*ee*ter till . . . tak
coffee	**kaffe** k*a*f-fer
tea	**te** tay
bread/butter	**bröd/smör** brerd/smer
jam	**marmelad** mar-mer-l*a*d
May I have a boiled egg?	**Kan jag få ett kokt ägg?** kan ya faw ett kookt egg

LIKELY REACTIONS

Have you an identity document, please?	**Har ni ett pass eller någon annan identitetshandling?** har nee ett pass el-ler naw-gon an-an eedent-eetaits-handling
What's your name? [see p. 233]	**Vad heter ni?** vad haiter nee
Sorry, we're full	**Tyvärr, vi har fullt** tee-vair vee har fullt
I haven't any rooms left	**Jag har inga rum kvar** ya har inga room kvar
Do you want to have a look?	**Vill ni titta på det?** vill nee tit-ta paw det
How many people is it for?	**För hur många personer är det?** fer hoor monga per-sooner air det
From (7 o'clock) onwards	**Från och med (klockan sju)** frawn ock med (klock-an shoo)
From (midday) onwards [For times, see p. 314]	**Från och med (klockan tolv)** frawn ock med (klock-an tolv)
It's (350) crowns	**Det blir (350) kronor** det bleer (tray-hoondra-fem-tee-oo) kroon-or

---

Camping and youth hostelling

ESSENTIAL INFORMATION
Camping

- There are some 600 campsites in Sweden, all approved and classified by the Swedish Tourist Board.
- Look out for this sign or the word:
  CAMPINGPLATS
- Be prepared to have to pay:
  per person

for the car (if applicable)
for the tent or caravan plot   for electricity
At some places there are small charges for showers, laundry etc.

- You must provide proof of identity, such as your passport.
- A camping carnet is required at most camping sites. It is issued at the first camping site you visit and is then valid throughout the whole season. Holders of the 'Camping International' card do not need the Swedish camping carnet.
- Sites are classified from one to three stars; a third of Sweden's campsites are three star establishments.
- **LPG** (liquid petroleum gas) is called **GASOL** in Sweden. Butane gas is not available, only propane gas. When refilling your **LPG** bottle in Sweden, please make sure that propane gas is not filled into a butane gas bottle as this is dangerous. Try to bring enough gas with you or buy an expendable **LPG** bottle for attachment to your camping equipment.
- A number of campsites also have camping cabins for hire. These usually have 2–6 beds, a cooking range and kitchen utensils. You must, however, provide your own bedclothes. It is advisable to book these cabins in advance.

Youth hostels

- Look for the word **VANDRARHEM** or the sign on pages 31 and 138.
- There are some 200 youth hostels run by the Swedish Touring Club in Sweden.
- Membership cards of youth hostel organizations affiliated to the **IYHF** (International Youth Hostel Federation) are valid in all the Swedish youth hostels. Otherwise you have to buy an international guest card (season ticket) or a 'one night' guest card.
- The youth hostels are open to anyone irrespective of age. Rates vary according to standards.
- Bring your own linen (or it can be rented). Sleeping bags are not allowed.
- All youth hostels have facilities for cooking your own meals, a few offer full meal service.
- Cleaning up is compulsory in the bedrooms, washrooms and kitchen.
- Most youth hostels are open only during the summer season (mid June – mid August). You are advised to book in advance.
- The maximum length of stay is 5 nights in each location but this can be extended according to availability.
- For buying or replacing equipment, see p. 264.

Swedish

WHAT TO SAY

Have you any vacancies?	**Har ni något ledigt?** har nee naw-got laid-it
It's for . . .	**Det är för . . .** det air fer . . .
one adult/person	**en vuxen/person** en vooksen/per-soon
two adults/people	**två vuxna/personer** tvaw vooks-na/per-sooner
and one child	**och ett barn** ock ett barn
and two children	**och två barn** ock tvaw barn
It's for . . .	**Det är för . . .** det air fer . . .
one night	**en natt** en naht
one week	**en vecka** en vaika
How much is it . . .	**Hur mycket kostar det . . .** hoor mee-ket kostar det . . .
for the tent?	**för tältet?** fer telt-et
for the caravan?	**för husvagnen?** fer hoos-vang-nen
for the car?	**för bilen?** fer beelen
for the electricity?	**för elektriciteten?** fer elek-tree-see-taiten
per person?	**per person?** per per-soon
per day/night?	**per dag/natt?** per da/naht
May I look around?	**Kan jag se mig omkring?** kan ya say may om-kring
Do you provide anything . . .	**Serverar ni något . . .** servair-ar nee naw-got . . .
to eat?	**att äta?** aht aita
to drink?	**att dricka?** aht dricka

Do you have . . .	**Har ni . . .**
	har nee . . .
a bar?	**en bar?**
	en bar
hot showers?	**dusch med varmt vatten?**
	doosh med varmt vat-ten
a kitchen?	**ett kök?**
	ett sherk
a laundry?	**en tvättinrättning**
	en tvet-in-ret-tning
a restaurant?	**en restaurang?**
	en resto-rang
a shop?	**en butik?**
	en boot-eek
a swimming pool?	**en swimming pool?**
	en swimming pool

[*For food shopping, see p. 270,*
and for eating and drinking out,
see p. 283]

Where are . . .	**Var är . . .**
	var air . . .
the dustbins?	**soptunnorna?**
	soop-toon-or-na
the showers?	**duscharna?**
	doosh-ar-na
the toilets?	**toaletterna?**
	toh-ah-let-ter-na
At what time must one . . .	**När måste man . . .**
	nair mos-ter man . . .
go to bed?	**gå och lägga sig?**
	gaw ock leg-ga sig
get up?	**gå upp?**
	gaw oop
Please, have you got . . .	**Har ni . . .**
	har nee . . .
a broom?	**en sopborste?**
	en soop-borster
a corkscrew?	**en korkskruv?**
	en kork-skroov
a drying-up cloth?	**en trasa?**
	en tra-sa
a fork?	**en gaffel?**
	en gaffel

Swedish

Please, have you got . . .	**Har ni . . .**
	har nee . . .
a fridge?	**en kyl?**
	en sheel
a frying pan?	**en stekpanna?**
	en staik-pan-na
an iron?	**ett strykjärn?**
	ett streek-yairn
a knife?	**en kniv?**
	en k-neev
a plate?	**en tallrik?**
	en tal-rick
a saucepan?	**en kastrull?**
	en ka-strool
a teaspoon?	**en tesked?**
	en tay-shaid
a tin-opener?	**en konservöppnare?**
	en kon-sairv-erpna-rer
any washing-up liquid?	**något tvättmedel?**
	naw-got tvet-maid-el

Problems

The toilet	**Toaletten**
	toh-ah-let-ten
The shower	**Duschen**
	doosh-en
The razor point	**Uttaget för rakapparaten**
	oot-ta-get fèr rak-ap-parah-ten
The light	**Ljuset**
	yoos-et
. . . is not working	**. . . fungerar inte**
	foong-airar inter
My camping gas has run out	**Min gas har tagit slut**
	min gas har ta-geet sloot

LIKELY REACTIONS

• Have you an identity document?	**Har ni någon identitets-handling?**
	har nee naw-gon eedent-eetaits-handling
Your membership card, please	**Ert medlemskort, tack**
	airt maid-lems-kort tak

What's your name? [*see p. 233*]	**Vad heter ni?** vad h*ai*ter nee
How many people is it for?	**För hur många personer är det?** fer hoor m*o*nga per-s*oo*n-er air det
How many nights is it for?	**För hur många nätter är det?** fer hoor m*o*nga n*ai*ter air det
It's (80) crowns . . .	**Det blir (åttio) kronor . . .** det bleer (ot-tee-oo) kr*oo*n-or . . .
per day/night [*For numbers, see p. 313*]	**per dag/natt** per da/naht

---

Rented accommodation: problem solving

ESSENTIAL INFORMATION

- If you are looking for accommodation to rent, look out for:
  STUGA (cottage)
  STUGBY (cottage village)
  VÅNING (flat)
  ATT HYRA (to let)
  RUM (rooms)
- For arranging details of your let, see 'Hotel' p. 000.
- Key words you will meet if renting on the spot:
  deposition (deposit)
  deposee-sh*oo*n
  nyckel (key)
  n*ee*-kel
- Having arranged your own accommodation and arrived with the key, check the obvious basics that you take for granted at home.
  Electricity: Voltage? Razors and small appliances brought from home may need adjusting. You may need an adaptor.
  Cooker: Don't be surprised to find the grill inside the oven, or no grill at all.
  Toilet: Mains drainage or septic tank? Don't flush disposable napkins or anything else down the toilet if you are on a septic tank.

Water: Find the stopcock. Check taps and plugs – they may not operate in the way you are used to. Check how to turn on the hot water.

Windows: Check the method of opening and closing windows and shutters.

Insects: Is an insecticide spray provided? If not, get one locally.

Equipment: See p. 00 for buying or replacing equipment.

- You will probably have an official agent, but be clear in your own mind who to contact in an emergency, even if it is only a neighbour in the first instance.

WHAT TO SAY

My name is . . .	**Mitt namn är . . .** mitt namn air . . .
I'm staying at . . .	**Jag bor på . . .** ya boor paw . . .
They've cut off . . .	**De har stängt av . . .** day har stengt ahv . . .
the electricity	**elektriciteten** elek-tree-see-*tait*en
the gas	**gasen** g*a*s-en
the water	**vattnet** vat-net
Is there . . . in the area?	**Finns det . . . i närheten?** finss det . . . ee n*a*ir-haiten
an electrician	**en elektriker** en el*e*k-tree-ker
a plumber	**en rörmokare** en r*e*r-mok-arer
Where is . . .	**Var är . . .** var air . . .
the fuse box?	**proppskåpet?** pr*o*p-skawpet
the stopcock?	**huvudkranen?** h*oo*v-od-kra-nen
the boiler?	**oljepannan?** *o*l-yer-pan-nan
the geiser?	**varmvattensberedaren?** varm-vat-tens-bay-r*ai*da-ren
Is there . . .	**Finns det . . .** finss det . . .

a septic tank?	**en septisk tank?**
	en septisk tank
central heating?	**centralvärme?**
	central-vairmer
The cooker	**Spisen**
	speesen
The hairdrier	**Hårtorken**
	hor-tor-ken
The heating	**Värmen**
	vairmen
The iron	**Strykjärnet**
	streek-yairnet
The pilot light	**Kontroll-lampan**
	kon-trol-lampa
The refrigerator	**Kylskåpet**
	sheel-skawpet
The telephone	**Telefonen**
	tele-fonen
The toilet	**Toaletten**
	toh-ah-let-ten
The washing machine	**Tvättmaskinen**
	tvet-masheenen
. . . is not working	**. . . fungerar inte**
	. . . fong-airar inter
Where can I get . . .	**Var kan jag få tag på . . .**
	var kan ya faw tag paw . . .
an adaptor for this?	**en adaptor till den här?**
	en ah-dap-tor till den hair
a fuse?	**en propp?**
	en prop
an insecticide spray?	**en insektsspray?**
	en insekts-spray
a light bulb?	**en glödlampa?**
	en glerd-lampa
The drains	**Rören**
	rer-ren
The sink	**Diskhon**
	disk-hoon
The toilet	**Toaletten**
	toh-ah-let-ten
. . . is blocked	**Det är stopp i . . .**
	det air stop ee . . .

Swedish

The gas is leaking	**Gasen läcker**
	gas-en laiker
Can you mend it straightaway?	**Kan ni laga det meddetsamma?**
	kan nee la-ga det med-det-samma
When can you mend it?	**När kan ni laga det?**
	nair kan nee la-ga det
How much do I owe you?	**Hur mycket blir jag skyldig?**
	hoor mee-ket bleer ya sheel-dig
When is the rubbish collected?	**När hämtas soporna?**
	nair hem-tas soop-orna

LIKELY REACTIONS

What's your name?	**Vad heter ni?**
	vad haiter nee
What's your address?	**Vad har ni för adress?**
	vad har nee fer ah-dress
There's a shop . . .	**Det finns en affär . . .**
	det fins en af-fair . . .
in town	**i staden**
	ee sta-den
in the village	**i byn**
	ee been
I can't come . . .	**Jag kan inte komma . . .**
	ya kan inter kom-ma . . .
today	**idag**
	ee-da
this week	**den här veckan**
	den hair vaikan
until Monday	**förrän på måndag**
	fer-ren paw mon-da
I can come . . .	**Jag kan komma . . .**
	ya kan kom-ma . . .
on Tuesday	**på tisdag**
	paw tees-da
when you want	**när ni vill**
	nair nee vill
Every day	**Varje dag**
	var-yer da
Every other day	**Varannan dag**
	var-an-an da
On Wednesdays	**På onsdagar**
	paw oons-dahg-ar

[*For days of the week, see p. 315*]

General shopping

The chemist's

ESSENTIAL INFORMATION

- Look out for the word **APOTEK** or this sign
- Medicines are available only at the *apotek*.
- Toiletries can also be bought at department stores, supermarkets and perfumeries.
- **Apotek** are open weekdays 9.00 a.m. to 6.00 p.m. and Saturdays 9.00 a.m. to 1.00 p.m.
- Try the chemist before going to the doctor's as they are usually qualified to treat minor ailments.
- Finding a chemist, see p. 237.

WHAT TO SAY

I'd like . . .	**Jag ska be att få . . .** ya ska bay aht faw . . .
some Alka Seltzer	**lite Alka Seltzer** leeter alka seltzer
some antiseptic	**lite antiseptiskt** leeter anti-sep-tiskt
some aspirin	**lite aspirin** leeter aspi-reen
some bandage	**lite bandage** leeter band-*ash*
some cotton wool	**lite bomull** leeter bom-ool
some eye drops	**lite ögondroppar** leeter *ergon*-droppar
some inhalant	**lite näsdroppar** leeter n*ais*-droppar
some insect repellent	**lite myggspray** leeter m*ee*g-spray
some lip salve	**lite läppsalva** leeter lep-sal-va
some sticking plaster	**lite plåster** leeter pl*aws*-ter
some throat pastilles	**lite halstabletter** leeter h*a*ls-tab-let-ter
some Vaseline	**lite vaselin** leeter-va-ser-leen

Swedish

I'd like something for . . .	Jag ska be att få något för . . . ya ska bay aht faw naw-got fer . . .
bites/stings	**bett** bett
burns	**brännsår** bren-sor
a cold	**förkylning** fer-sheel-ning
constipation	**förstoppning** fer-stop-ning
a cough	**hosta** hos-ta
diarrhoea	**diarré** dee-ah-rer
ear-ache	**örsprång** er-sprong
flu	**influensa** in-floo-en-sa
sore gums	**ömt tandkött** ermt tand-shert
sunburn	**solbränna** sool-bren-na
travel sickness	**ressjuka** rais-shooka

I need . . .	Jag behöver . . . ya bay-herver . . .
some baby food	**lite barnmat** leeter barn-mat
some contraceptives	**lite preventivmedel** leeter preven-teev-maidel
a deodorant	**en deodorant** en deo-der-rant
some disposable nappies	**lite engångsblöjor** leeter en-gongs-bler-yor
some hand cream	**lite handkräm** leeter hand-kraim
some lipstick	**lite läppstift** leeter lep-stift
some make-up remover	**lite rengöringskräm** leeter rain-yer-ings-kraim
some paper tissues	**lite ansiktsservietter** leeter an-sikts-servietter

some razor blades	**lite rakblad**
	leeter rak-blad
some safety pins	**lite säkerhetsnålar**
	leeter saiker-haits-naw-la
some sanitary towels	**lite dambindor**
	leeter dahm-beend-or
some shaving cream	**lite rakkräm**
	leeter rak-kraim
some soap	**lite tvål**
	leeter tvawl
some suntan oil/lotion	**lite sololja/solkräm**
	leeter sool-ol-ya/sool-kraim
some talcum powder	**lite talk**
	leeter talk
some Tampax	**lite Tampax**
	leeter tam-pax
some (soft) toilet paper	**lite (mjukt) toalettpapper**
	leeter (m-yookt) toh-ah-let-pap-per
some toothpaste	**lite tandkräm**
	leeter tand-kraim

[*For other essential expressions, see 'Shop talk', p. 266*]

Holiday items

ESSENTIAL INFORMATION

- Places to shop at and signs to look for:
  BOKHANDEL (bookshop, stationery)
  PAPPERSHANDEL (stationery)
  FOTOHANDEL (films)
  and of course department stores such as:
  DOMUS
  NK
  TEMPO
  ÅHLENS
- In the countryside look out for **HEMSLÖJD**, handicraft centres
  which sell local crafts.

WHAT TO SAY

I'd like . . .	**Jag ska be att få . . .** ya ska bay aht faw . . .
a bag	**en väska** en vaiska
a beach ball	**en strandboll** en strand-bol
a bucket	**en hink** en hink
an English newspaper	**en engelsk tidning** en eng-elsk tee-ning
some envelopes	**några kuvert** nora koo-vair
a guide book	**en guidebok** en guide-book
a map (of the area)	**en karta (över området)** en kar-ta (erver om-raw-det)
some postcards	**några vykort** nora vee-kort
a spade	**en spade** en spa-der
a straw hat	**en stråhatt** en straw-hat
some sunglasses	**ett par solglasögon** ett par sool-glas-ergon
an umbrella	**ett paraply** ett para-plee
some writing paper	**lite skrivpapper** leeter skreev-pap-per
I'd like . . . [show camera]	**Jag ska be att få . . .** ya ska bay aht faw . . .
a colour film	**en färgfilm** en fairy-film
a black and white film	**en svart/vit film** en svart/veet film
for prints	**för papperskopior** fer pap-pers-kopee-or
for slides	**för dia** fer dee-ah
Please can you . . .	**Kan ni . . .** kan nee . . .

develop/print this?	**framkalla/kopiera?**
	fram-kal-la/kopee-aira
load the camera for me?	**sätta in filmen åt mig, tack?**
	set-ta in film-en awt may tak

[For other essential expressions, see 'Shop talk' p. 266]

The tobacconist's

ESSENTIAL INFORMATION

- Tobacco is sold where you see these signs:
  TOBAK   TOBAKSHANDEL
- To ask if there is one near by, see p. 239.
- Most usual brands of tobacco, cigars and cigarettes may be bought at supermarkets and at **PRESSBYRÅN**, a chain of kiosks which also sell newspapers, magazines, sweets and fruit.

WHAT TO SAY

A packet of cigarettes . . .	**Ett paket cigarretter . . .**
	ett pa-kait cigaret-ter . . .
with filters	**med filter**
	med filter
without filters	**utan filter**
	ootahn filter
king size	**king size**
	king size
menthol	**mentol**
	ment-ol
Those up there . . .	**De där uppe . . .**
	day dair ooper . . .
on the right	**till höger**
	till herg-er
on the left	**till vänster**
	till venster
These [*point*]	**De här**
	day hair

Have you got . . .	**Har ni . . .**
	har nee . . .
English cigarettes?	**engelska cigarretter**
	eng-elska cigaret-ter
rolling tobacco?	**rulltobak?**
	rool-toh-bak
A packet of pipe tobacco	**Ett paket piptobak**
	ett pa-kait peep-toh-bak
This one [*point*]	**Den här**
	den hair
A cigar, please	**En cigarr, tack**
	en cigar tak
Some cigars, please	**Några cigarrer, tack**
	nora cigar-rer tak
A box of matches	**En ask tändstickor**
	en ask tend-stick-or
A packet of pipe cleaners	**Ett paket piprensare**
	ett pa-kait peep-rensa-rer
A packet of flints	**Ett paket stift till tändare**
[*show lighter*]	ett pa-kait stift till tenda-rer
Lighter fuel	**Bensin till tändare**
	ben-seen til tenda-rer
Lighter gas, please	**Gas till tändare, tack**
	gas till tenda-rer tak

[*For essential expressions, see 'Shop talk', p. 266*]

Buying clothes

ESSENTIAL INFORMATION

* Look for:
  DAMKLÄDER (women's clothes)
  HERRKLÄDER (men's clothes)
  BARNKLÄDER (children's clothes)
  SKOAFFÄR (shoe shop)
* Don't buy without being measured first or without trying things on.
* If you are buying for someone else, take their measurements with you.

WHAT TO SAY

I'd like . . .	**Jag ska be att få . . .**
	ya ska bay aht faw . . .
an anorak	**en anorak**
	en *an*-no-rak
a belt	**ett bälte**
	ett b*e*ll-ter
a bikini	**en bikini**
	en bik*i*ni
a bra	**en behå**
	en bay-haw
a cap (swimming)	**en badmössa**
	en b*a*d-mers-sa
a cap (skiing)	**en skidmössa**
	en sh*ee*d-mers-sa
a cardigan	**en kofta**
	en k*o*fta
a coat	**en kappa**
	en k*a*p-pa
a dress	**en klänning**
	en kl*e*n-ning
a hat	**en hatt**
	cn hat
a jacket	**en jacka**
	en *ya*cka
a jumper	**en jumper**
	en y*oo*mper
a nightdress	**ett nattlinne**
	ett n*a*ht-linner
a pullover	**en tröja**
	en tr*er*-ya
a pair of pyjamas	**en pyjamas**
	en pee-*ya*-mas
a raincoat	**en regnrock**
	en r*ai*ng-n-rock
a shirt	**en skjorta**
	en sh*oo*rta
a suit	**en kostym**
	en kos-t*ee*m
a swimsuit	**en baddräkt**
	en b*a*hd-drekt
a tee-shirt	**en T-shirt**
	en t*ee*-shirt

Swedish

I'd like a pair of . . .   **Jag ska be att få ett par . . .**
                                   ya ska bay aht faw ett par . . .

gloves   **handskar**
                              hand-skar

socks (short/long)   **sockor (korta/långa)**
                              sock-or (korta/longa)

stockings   **strumpor**
                              stroom-por

tights   **trikåbyxor**
                              trickaw-beek-sor

trousers   **långbyxor**
                              long-beek-sor

underpants   **kalsonger**
                              kal-song-er

shoes   **skor**
                              skoor

canvas shoes   **tygskor**
                              teeg-skoor

sandals   **sandaler**
                            san-da-ler

beach shoes   **strandskor**
                              strand-skoor

smart shoes   **finskor**
                              feen-skoor

boots   **stövlar**
                            sterv-lar

moccasins   **moccasiner**
                            mocca-seener

My size is . . .   **Min storlek är . . .**
[For numbers see p. 313]   min stoor-laik air . . .

Can you measure me, please? **Kan ni se vad jag har för storlek?**
                              kan nee say vad ya har fer
                                stoorlaik

Can I try it on?   **Kan jag få prova?**
                              kan ya faw proova

It's for a present   **Det är en present**
                              det air en pres-ent

These are the measurements **Det här är måtten . . .**
. . . [show written]   det hair air mawt-ten . . .

bust/chest   **byst/bröst**
                              beest/brerst

collar   **krage**
                              krahg-er

hip	**höft**
	herft
leg	**ben**
	bain
waist	**midja**
	meed-ya
Have you something . . .	**Har ni något . . .**
	har nee naw-got . . .
in black?	**i svart?**
	ee svart
in white?	**i vitt?**
	ee veett
in grey?	**i grått?**
	ee grawtt
in blue?	**i blått?**
	ee blawtt
in brown?	**i brunt?**
	ee broont
in pink?	**i rosa?**
	ee rawsa
in green?	**i grönt?**
	ee grernt
in red?	**i rött?**
	ec rert
in yellow?	**i gult?**
	ee goolt
In this colour? [*point*]	**i den här färgen?**
	ee den hair fairr-yen
in cotton?	**i bomull?**
	ee bom-ool
in denim?	**i denim?**
	ee denim
in leather?	**i läder?**
	ee laider
in nylon	**i nylon?**
	ee neel-awn
in suede?	**i mocka?**
	ee mokka
in wool?	**i ull?**
	ee ool
in this material?	**i det här materialet?**
	ee det hair mat-ree-ah-let

[*For other essential expressions, see 'Shop Talk', p. 266*]

Swedish

Replacing equipment

ESSENTIAL INFORMATION

- Look out for these shops and signs:
  JÄRNHANDEL/JÄRNAFFÄR (hardware)
  ELAFFÄR (electrical shop)
  ELARTIKLAR (electrical goods)
  HUSHÅLLSARTIKLAR (household articles)
  KEMISKA ARTIKLAR (household cleaning materials)
- To ask the way to the shop, see p. 236.
- At a campsite try their shop first.

WHAT TO SAY

Have you got . . .	**Har ni . . .**
	har nee . . .
an adaptor?	**en adaptor?**
[show appliance]	en adap-tor
a bottle of propane gas?	**en flaska propangas?**
	en flaska prop-ahn-gahs
a bottle opener?	**en flasköppnare?**
	en flask-erpna-rer
a corkscrew?	**en korkskruv?**
	en kork-skroov
any disinfectant?	**något desinficeringsmedel?**
	naw-got des-infee-sairings-maidel
any disposable cups?	**några engångskoppar?**
	nora en-gongs-kop-par
a drying-up cloth?	**en trasa?**
	en tra-sa
any forks?	**några gafflar?**
	nora gafflar
a fuse? [show old one]	**en propp?**
	en prop
an insecticide spray?	**en insektsspray?**
	en insekts-spray
a paper kitchen roll?	**en hushållspappersrulle?**
	en hoos-hols-pap-pers-rooler
any knives?	**några knivar?**
	nora k-nee-var

a light bulb? [*show old one*]	**en glödlampa?**
	en glerd-l*a*mpa
a plastic bucket?	**en plasthink?**
	en pl*a*st-hink
a plastic can?	**en plastburk?**
	en pl*a*st-boork
a scouring pad?	**en skurtrasa?**
	en sk*oo*r-tra-sa
a spanner?	**en skruvnyckel?**
	en skr*oo*v-neekel
a sponge?	**en tvättsvamp?**
	en tv*e*t-svamp
any string?	**något snöre?**
	n*aw*-got sn*e*r-rer
any tent pegs?	**några tältpinnar?**
	n*o*ra telt-pin-nar
a tin-opener?	**en konservöppnare?**
	en kon-s*ai*rv-erpna-rer
a torch?	**en ficklampa?**
	en f*i*ck-lampa
any torch batteries?	**några ficklampsbatterier?**
	n*o*ra fick-lamps-bat-ter-r*ee*-er
a washing line?	**en tvättlina?**
	en tv*e*t-leena
any washing powder?	**något tvättmedel?**
	n*aw*-gut tv*e*t-maidel
a washing-up brush?	**en diskborste?**
	en d*i*sk-burster
any washing-up liquid?	**något diskmedel?**
	n*aw*-got d*i*sk-maidel

[*For other essential expressions, see 'Shop talk', p. 266*]

Shop talk

ESSENTIAL INFORMATION

- Coins: see illustration. The crown is divided into 100 ören.
  Notes: 10, 50, 100, 1000, 10 000 kronor (crowns).
- Know how to say the important weights and measures. You will
  hear **grams**, **kilos** and **hektos** being used in shops and supermarkets. **Ett hekto (1 hg) = 100 grams.**

50 grams	**femtio gram/ett halvt hekto**
	fem-tee-oo gram/ett halvt hek-to
100 grams	**hundra gram/ett hekto**
	hoon-dra gram/ett hek-to
200 grams	**tvåhundra gram**
	tvaw-hoon-dra gram
250 grams	**tvåhundrafemtio gram**
	tvaw-hoon-dra-fem-tee-oo gram
½ kilo	**ett halvt kilo**
	ett halvt kilo
1 kilo	**ett kilo**
	ett kilo
2 kilos	**två kilo**
	tvaw kilo
½ litre	**en halv liter**
	en halv lee-tair
1 litre	**en liter**
	en lee-tair
2 litres	**två liter**
[For numbers, see p. 313]	tvaw lee-tair

CUSTOMER

I'm just looking	**Jag tittar bara**
	ya tit-tar ba-ra
Excuse me	**Ursäkta mig**
	yoo-shek-ta may
How much is that/this?	**Hur mycket kostar den där/den här**
	hoor mee-ket kostar den dair/den hair
What's that?	**Vad är det?**
	vad air det

What are those?	**Vad är de här?**
	vad air day hair
Is there a discount?	**Har ni någon rabatt?**
	har nee naw-gon ra-bat
I'd like that, please	**Jag ska be att få det, tack**
	ya ska bay aht faw det tak
Not that	**Inte det**
	inter det
Like that	**Som det**
	som det
That's enough, thank you	**Det räcker, tack**
	det raiker tak
More, please	**Mer, tack**
	mair tak
Less, please	**Mindre, tack**
	min-drer tak
That's fine	**Det är bra**
	det air bra
OK	**OK**
	okay
I won't take it, thank you	**Jag tar det inte, tack**
	ya tar det inter tak
It's not right	**Det är inte rätt**
	det air inter raitt
Have you something . . .	**Har ni något . . .**
	har nee naw-got . . .
better?	**bättre?**
	bet-rer
cheaper?	**billigare?**
	bil-lee-ga-rer
different?	**annorlunda?**
	an-nor-loonda
larger?	**större?**
	ster-rer
smaller?	**mindre?**
	min-drer
At what time do you . . .	**När . . . ni?**
	nair . . . nee
open?	**öppnar**
	erp-nar
close?	**stänger**
	steng-er

Can I have a bag, please	**Kan jag få en påse, tack**
	kan ya faw en pawser tak
Can I have a receipt?	**Kan jag få ett kvitto**
	kan ya faw ett kvit-to
Do you take . . .	**Tar ni . . .**
	tar nee . . .
English/American money?	**engelska/amerikanska pengar**
	eng-el-ska/am-ree-kahn-ska pengar
travellers' cheques?	**resecheckar?**
	raiser-checkar
credit cards?	**kreditkort?**
	kred-eet-koort
I'd like . . .	**Jag ska be att få . . .**
	ya ska bay aht faw . . .
one like that	**en sån där**
	en sawn dair

SHOP ASSISTANT

Can I help you?	**Kan jag hjälpa er?**
	kan ya yelpa ehr
What would you like?	**Vad önskar ni?**
	vad ern-skar nee
Will that be all?	**Är det allt?**
	air det allt
Anything else?	**Något annat?**
	naw-got an-nat
Would you like it wrapped?	**Vill ni ha det inslaget?**
	vill nee ha det in-sla-get
Sorry, none left	**Tyvärr, inga kvar**
	tee-vair inga kvar
I haven't got any	**Jag har inga**
	ya har inga
I haven't got any more	**Jag har inga fler**
	ya har inga flair
How many do you want?	**Hur många vill ni ha?**
	hoor monga vill nee ha
How much do you want?	**Hur mycket vill ni ha?**
	hoor mee-ket vill nee ha
Is this enough?	**Räcker det här?**
	raiker det hair

Swedish

Shopping for food

Bread

ESSENTIAL INFORMATION

- Finding a baker's, see p. 237.
- Key words to look for:
  BAGERI (baker's)
  BAGARE (baker)
  BRÖD (bread)
- Supermarkets of any size and general stores nearly always sell bread.
- Opening times are usually 9.00 a.m. to 6.00 p.m. weekdays and 9.00 a.m. to 1.00 or 2.00 p.m. on Saturdays.
- The most characteristic loaves are **limpa**, a type of rye bread, and **hårt bröd**, hard bread.
- Most bread is sold unsliced in bakeries but can sometimes be sliced on request. Supermarkets normally sell both sliced and unsliced bread.

WHAT TO SAY

A loaf (like that)	**(Ett sådant) bröd**
	(ett sawnt) brerd
A French loaf	**En långfranska**
	en long-fran-ska
A tin loaf	**Ett formbröd**
	ett form-brerd
A rye bread loaf	**En limpa**
	en lim-pa
A wholemeal loaf	**Ett fullkornsbröd**
	ett full-korns-brerd
A packet of hard bread	**Ett paket hårt bröd**
	ett pa-kait hort brerd
A packet of pumpernickel	**Ett paket pumpernickel**
	ett pa-kait poomper-nickel
A bread roll	**En småfranska**
	en smaw-fran-ska
Two packets of rusks	**Två paket skorpor**
	tvaw pa-kait skor-por

A bun (plain)	**En vetebulle**
	en v*ai*ter-bool-ler
A bun (spiced with cinnamon)	**En kanelbulle**
	en kan-*ai*l-bool-ler
Wheat bread (spiced with saffron and raisins)	**Ett saffransbröd**
	ett saf-rans-brerd
Wheat bread (spiced with cardamon)	**Ett kardemummabröd**
	ett karder-m*oo*ma-brerd

[*For other essential expressions, see 'Shop talk' p. 266*]

Cakes

ESSENTIAL INFORMATION

- Key words to look for:
  BAGERI (bread and cake shop)
  KONDITORI (cake shop, often with a tea room in the back)
  KAKOR (cakes)
  BAKELSER (pastries)
- To find a cake shop, see p. 237.

WHAT TO SAY

The following are the most common cakes and pastries. Cakes are sold per **hekto** (1 hekto = 100 grams, see also p. 266) and pastries are bought per slice or piece.

småkakor	small butter cakes, many different
sm*aw*-ka-kor	types available
pepparkakor	gingerbread
p*e*p-par-ka-kor	
mazarin	'mazarin', small tart with sweet
ma-za-r*ee*n	pastry base and hard sugar topping
chokladbiskvi	almond cake topped with chocolate
shok-l*a*-bee-skvee	cream
sockerkaka	sponge cake
soccer-k*a*-ka	

jordgubbstårta	strawberry cake
yoord-goobs-torta	
prinsesstårta	vanilla/cream/marzipan gateau
princess-torta	
toscatårta	gateau with caramel glaze
tosca-torta	
wienerbröd	'Danish' pastry
veener-brerd	
gräddtårta	cream gateau
graid-torta	

Ice-cream and sweets

ESSENTIAL INFORMATION

- Key words to look for:
  GLASS (ice-cream)
  GLASSKIOSK (ice-cream stand)
  GLASSBAR (ice-cream parlour)
  KONDITORI (cake/pastry shop)
  GODIS (sweets)
  GODISAFFÄR (sweet shop)
- Best known ice-cream brand-name is: **GB**
- When buying ice-cream, specify what price cone or tub you want.
- Prepacked sweets and ice-cream are available in general stores, supermarkets and at **PRESSBYRÅN** (see p. 259).

WHAT TO SAY

A cone with . . . ice, please	**En strut med . . . glass, tack**
	en stroot med . . . glass tak
A waffle/tub with . . . ice, please	**En våffla/bägare med . . . glass, tack**
	en voff-la/baig-arer med . . . glass tak
banana	**banan**
	ba-nahn

chocolate	**choklad**
	shok-la
mocha	**mokka**
	mokka
pistachio	**pistasch**
	pist-ahsh
strawberry	**jordgubbs**
	yoord-goobs
vanilla	**vanilj**
	van-il-ee
One (4 crown) cone	**En (fyra kronors) strut**
	en (feera kroon-ors) stroot
Two (5 crown) waffles	**Två (fem kronors) våfflor**
	tvaw (fem kroon-ors) voff-lor
A lollipop	**En klubba**
	en kloob-ba
A packet of . . .	**Ett paket . . .**
	ett pa-kait . . .
100 grams of . . .	**Hundra gram . . .**
	hoon-dra gram . . .

[*For further details of Swedish weights, see 'Shop talk' p. 266*]

chewing gum	**tuggummi**
	toog-goom-mee
chocolates	**chokladbitar**
	shok-la-beetar
liquorice (sweet/salt)	**lakrits (söt/salt)**
	lak-rits (sert/salt)
mints	**mintkarameller**
	mint-ka-ra-mel-ler
sweets	**karameller**
	ka-ra-mel-ler
toffees	**kola**
	kawla

[*For other essential expressions, see 'Shop talk' p. 266*]

Picnic food

ESSENTIAL INFORMATION

- Key words to look for:
  DELIKATESSER (delicatessen)
  MATAFFÄR (supermarket)
- Prepared picnic food can be found in every supermarket. Major supermarkets usually have a special delicatessen counter.

WHAT TO SAY

Two slices of . . .	**Två skivor . . .**
	tvaw sk*ee*vor . . .
roast beef	**rostbiff**
	r*o*st-biff
smoked ham	**rökt skinka**
	r*e*rkt shinka
boiled ham	**kokt skinka**
	k*oo*kt shinka
tongue	**tunga**
	t*oo*nga
salami	**salami**
	sal-l*a*-mee
liver paste	**leverpastej**
	l*ai*ver-pastay
150 grams of . . .	**Hundrafemtio gram . . .**
	h*oo*n-dra fem-tee-oo gram . . .

[*For further details of Swedish weights, see 'Shop talk', p. 266*]

potato salad	**potatissallad**
	po-ta-tis-sal-lad
herring salad	**sillsallad**
	s*i*ll-sal-lad
green salad	**grönsallad**
	gr*e*rn-sal-lad
coleslaw	**kålsallad**
	k*a*wl-sal-lad
olives	**oliver**
	ool*ee*-ver

You might also like to try some of these:

lite kaviar	'Swedish caviar' smoked cod roe
leeter kav-y*a*r	
lite löjrom	black roe
leeter ler-y-rom	
en strömming	a type of herring
en strerm-ming	
lite sill	some herring
leeter sill	
lite böckling	some smoked herring
leeter berk-ling	
lite rökt makrill	some smoked mackerel
leeter rerkt m*a*k-rill	
lite sardiner	some sardines
leeter sar-d*ee*ner	
lite rökt ål	some smoked eel
leeter rerkt awl	
lite rökt lax	some smoked salmon
leeter rerkt laks	
lite rökt renkött	some smoked venison
leeter rerkt r*ai*n-shert	
lite köttbullar	some meatballs
leeter shert-bool-lar	
lite västkustsallad	some shrimp/mussel/mushroom
leeter v*ø*st-k*oo*st-sal-lad	salad
lite kycklingsallad	some chicken salad
leeter sh*ee*k-ling-sal-lad	
lite ost-och skinksallad	some cheese and ham salad
leeter *oo*st-ock sh*i*nk-sal-lad	
Herrgårdsost	semi-hard cheese with a mild to
herr-gords-oost	medium strength flavour
Grevéost	Grevé cheese
graiver-oost	
Västerbottenost	pungent cheese from Northern
v*e*ster-bot-ten-oost	Sweden
Sveciaost	Svecia cheese – semi-hard with
svay-see-ah-oost	strong flavour
mjukost	soft white cheese
m-y*ee*k-oost	

Fruit and vegetables

ESSENTIAL INFORMATION

● Key words to look for:
  FRUKT (fruit)
  FRUKTHANDEL (fruiterer)
  GRÖNSAKER (vegetables)
  GRÖNSAKSHANDEL (greengrocer)
[*For further details of Swedish weights, see 'Shop talk'. p. 266*]

WHAT TO SAY

1 kilo (2 lbs) of . . .	**Ett kilo . . .**
	ett kilo . . .
apples	**äpplen**
	epp-len
apricots	**aprikoser**
	apree-*koo*ser
bananas	**bananer**
	ba-*nah*-ner
bilberries	**blåbär**
	b*law*-bair
cherries	**körsbär**
	she*rs*-bair
cloudberries	**hjortron**
	yort-ron
grapes (black/white)	**vindruvor (blå/gröna)**
	veen-droovor (blaw/*grerna*)
oranges	**apelsiner**
	ap-pel-*see*ner
peaches	**persikor**
	per-*see*-kor
pears	**päron**
	pair-on
plums	**plommon**
	plom-mon
raspberries	**hallon**
	hal-lon
strawberries	**jordgubbar**
	yord-goob-bar
wild strawberries	**smultron**
	sm*ool*t-ron

A pineapple, please	**En ananas, tack**
	en *a*n-na-nas tak
A grapefruit	**En grapefrukt**
	en *g*rape-frookt
A melon	**En melon**
	en mer-l*oo*n
A water melon	**En vattenmelon**
	en v*a*t-ten-mer-loon
½ kilo of . . .	**Ett halvt kilo . . .**
	ett halvt kilo . . .
artichokes	**kronärtskocka**
	kr*oo*n-airts-kocka
asparagus	**sparris**
	sp*a*r-ris
aubergines	**auberginer**
	*o*ber-shee-ner
beans	**bönor**
	b*e*r-nor
beetroot	**rödbetor**
	rerd-bet-or
Brussels sprouts	**brysselkål**
	br*ee*ssel-kawl
carrots	**morötter**
	mo-rert-er
green beans	**haricots verts**
	haree-k*o*-vair
leeks	**purjolök**
	p*e*r-yo-lerk
mushrooms	**svamp**
	svamp
onions	**lök**
	lerk
peas	**ärtor**
	*ai*r-tor
potatoes	**potatis**
	po-t*a*-tis
red cabbage	**rödkål**
	rerd-kawl
spinach	**spenat**
	spay-n*ah*t
tomatoes	**tomater**
	to-m*a*-ter

A bunch of . . .	**En knippa . . .**
	en k-nip-pa . . .
parsley	**persilja**
	per-sil-ya
radishes	**rädisor**
	raidee-sor
A garlic	**En vitlök**
	en veet-lerk
A lettuce	**Ett salladshuvud**
	ett sal-lads-hoov-od
A cauliflower	**Ett blomkålshuvud**
	ett blom-kawls-hoov-od
A cabbage	**Ett kålhuvud**
	ett kawl-hoov-od
A cucumber	**En gurka**
	en gurka
Like that, please	**Sån där, tack**
	sawn dair tak

Vegetables and fruit which may not be familiar:

kantareller	chanterelles (a type of mushroom –
kan-ta-rel-ler	yellow and funnel-shaped)
murklor	morels (type of mushroom)
murk-lor	

[*For other essential expressions, see 'Shop talk' p. 266*]

Meat

ESSENTIAL INFORMATION

- Key words to look for:
  KÖTT (meat)
  KÖTTAFFÄR (butcher's)
  SLAKTARE (butcher)
- Larger supermarkets usually have special meat departments.
- The diagrams opposite are to help you make sense of labels on counters, windows and supermarket displays, and decide which cut or joint to have.

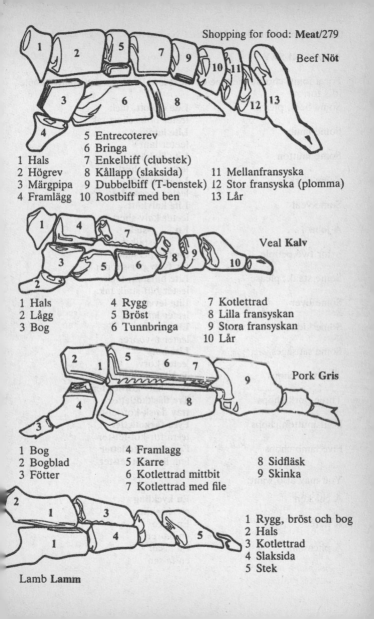

Beef **Nöt**

5 Entrecoterev
6 Bringa

1 Hals   7 Enkelbiff (clubstek)
2 Högrev   8 Kållapp (slaksida)   11 Mellanfransyska
3 Märgpipa   9 Dubbelbiff (T-benstek)   12 Stor fransyska (plomma)
4 Framlägg   10 Rostbiff med ben   13 Lår

Veal **Kalv**

1 Hals   4 Rygg   7 Kotlettrad
2 Lågg   5 Bröst   8 Lilla fransyskan
3 Bog   6 Tunnbringa   9 Stora fransyskan
                               10 Lår

Pork **Gris**

1 Bog   4 Framlagg
2 Bogblad   5 Karre   8 Sidfläsk
3 Fötter   6 Kotlettrad mittbit   9 Skinka
                7 Kotlettrad med file

1 Rygg, bröst och bog
2 Hals
3 Kotlettrad
4 Slaksida
5 Stek

Lamb **Lamm**

WHAT TO SAY

For a joint, choose the type of meat and then say how many people it is for:

Some beef, please	**Lite oxkött, tack**
	leeter ooks-shert tak
Some lamb	**Lite lamm**
	leeter lam
Some mutton	**Lite fårkött**
	leeter for-shert
Some pork	**Lite griskött**
	leeter grees-shert
Some veal	**Lite kalvkött**
	leeter kalv-shert
A joint . . .	**En . . . -stek**
	en . . . staik
for two people	**för två personer**
	fer tvaw per-sooner
Some steak, please	**Lite biffstek, tack**
	leeter biff-staik tak
Some liver	**Lite lever**
	leeter laiver
Some kidneys	**Lite njure**
	leeter n-yoorer
Some sausages	**Lite korv**
	leeter korv
Two veal chops	**Två kalvkotletter**
	tvaw kalv-kot-let-ter
Three pork chops	**Tre fläskkotletter**
	tray flaisk-kot-let-ter
Four mutton chops	**Fyra fårkotletter**
	feera for-kot-let-ter
Five lamb chops	**Fem lammkotletter**
	fem lam-kot-let-ter

You may also want:

A chicken	**En kyckling**
	en sheekling
A hare	**En hare**
	en ha-rer
A pheasant	**En fasan**
	en fa-san

| A tongue | **En tunga** |
| | en t*oo*nga |

Other essential expressions [*see also p. 266*]:

Please can you . . .	**Kan ni . . .**
	kan nee . . .
mince it?	**mala det?**
	m*a*-la det
slice it?	**skiva det?**
	sh*ee*va det
trim the fat?	**ta bort fettet?**
	ta bort f*e*t-tet

Fish

ESSENTIAL INFORMATION

- The place to ask for: **EN FISKAFFÄR** (a fishmonger's).
- Markets and large supermarkets usually have fresh fish stalls.

WHAT TO SAY

Purchase large fish and small shellfish by weight:

½ kilo of . . .	**Ett halv kilo . . .**
	ett halvt kilo . . .
cod	**torsk**
	torsk
eel	**ål**
	awl
haddock	**kolja**
	k*o*l-ya
herring	**sill**
	sill
pike	**gädda**
	y*e*d-da

½ kilo of . . .	**Ett halv kilo . . .**
	ett halvt kilo . . .
plaice	**rödspätta**
	rerd-spet-ta
turbot	**piggvar**
	pig-var
mussels	**musslor**
	moos-lor
crayfish	**kräftor**
	kref-tor
shrimps	**räkor**
	raikor
One slice of . . .	**En skiva . . .**
	en sheeva . . .
salmon	**lax**
	laks
tuna	**tonfisk**
	toon-fisk

For some shellfish and 'frying pan' fish specify the number you want:

A crab, please	**En krabba, tack**
	en kra-ba tak
A lobster	**En hummer**
	en hoom-mer
A whitefish	**En sik**
	en seek
A trout	**En forell**
	en for-rell
A sole	**En sjötunga**
	en sher-toonga
A mackerel	**En makrill**
	en mak-rill

Other essential expressions [*see also p. 266*]:

Please can you . . .	**Kan ni . . .**
	kan nee . . .
take the heads off?	**ta bort huvudena?**
	ta bort hoov-od-en-ah
clean them?	**tvätta dem?**
	tvet-ta dem
fillet them?	**filéa dem?**
	feelay-ah dem

Eating and drinking out

Ordering a drink

ESSENTIAL INFORMATION

- The places to ask for:
  EN BAR
  EN RESTAURANG
  ETT KONDITORI
- You must be aged over 18 years to order alcoholic drinks and strong beers **starköl** (alcoholic content above 2.8%).
- Wine, spirits and strong beers are only sold through the state-owned monopoly, **systembolaget**, and the minimum age limit for buying alcoholic beverages is 20 years.
- The most popular drinks in Sweden are the lager and pilsner-type of beers. They come in two strengths – ordinary beer **folköl** (maximum alcohol content of 2.8%) and light beer **lättöl** (maximum alcohol content of 1.8%).
- **Aquavit** is the local spirit, usually drunk chilled.
- When the bill is presented the amount will be inclusive of service and VAT (**moms**). Tipping is therefore optional.
- Heavy fines are levied on motorists driving under the influence of alcohol and other stimulants. Even a very low level of alcohol in the blood (50 mg/100 ml) is sufficient to lead to prosecution. Two cans of beer may be enough to bring you up to this level. Be careful!
- **Konditori** do not serve alcoholic drinks.

WHAT TO SAY

I'll have . . . please	**Jag ska be att få . . . tack**
	ya ska bay aht faw . . . tak
a cup of coffee	**en kopp kaffe**
	en kop k*a*f-fer
a cup of tea	**en kopp te**
	en kop tay
with milk	**med mjölk**
	med m-yerlk
with lemon	**med citron**
	med see-tr*oo*n

I'll have . . . please	**Jag ska be att få . . . tack** ya ska bay aht faw . . . tak
a glass of milk	**ett glas mjölk** ett glass m-yerlk
a cup of hot chocolate	**en kopp varm choklad** en kop varm shok-la
a glass of chilled chocolate	**ett glas kall choklad** ett glass kall shok-la
a glass of mineral water	**ett glas mineralvatten** ett glass min-nair-ahl-vat-ten
a soft drink	**en läsk** en lesk
a glass of fruit drink	**ett glas saft** ett glass saft
a Coca-Cola	**en Coca-Cola** en coca-cola
an orange juice	**en apelsinjuice** en ap-pel-seen-yoos
an apple juice	**en äppeljuice** en eppel-yoos
a beer	**en öl** en erl
one light beer	**en lättöl** en let-erl
one ordinary beer	**en folköl** en folk-erl
one strong beer	**en starköl** en stark-erl
A glass of . . .	**Ett glas . . .** ett glass . . .
red wine	**rödvin** rerd-veen
white wine	**vitt vin** vitt-veen
rosé	**rosé** rosé
dry/sweet	**torrt/sött** torrt/sert
A bottle of . . .	**En flaska . . .** en flas-ka . . .
sparkling wine	**mousserande vin** moo-sair-ander veen

champagne	**champagne** cham-p*a*n-y
A whisky . . .	**En whisky . . .** en whisky . . .
with ice	**med is** med ees
with water	**med vatten** med v*a*t-ten
with soda	**med sodavatten** med s*oo*da-v*a*t-ten
A gin . . .	**En gin . . .** en yin . . .
and tonic	**och tonic** ock tonic
with lemon	**med citron** med see-tr*oo*n
A brandy/cognac	**En konjak** en kon-y*a*k

The following are local drinks you may like to try:

brännvin bren-veen	aquavit
besk besk	bitter-tasting aquavit
glögg glerg	sweet, hot Christmas punch

Other essential expressions:

Cheers!	**Skål!** skawl
The bill, please	**Notan, tack** n*oo*-tan tak
How much does that come to?	**Hur mycket blir det?** hoor m*ee*-ket bleer det
Is service included?	**Är dricksen inräknad?** air dr*i*ck-sen *i*n-raik-nad
Where is the toilet, please?	**Var ligger toaletten?** var l*i*g-ger toh-ah-l*e*t-ten

Ordering a snack

ESSENTIAL INFORMATION

- Look for any of these places:
  CAFETERIA (snack bar)
  GRILLBAR (grilled meat, fish and sausages)
  GRILLKIOSK (hamburger and sausage stall)
  KORVKIOSK (sausage stall)
  HAMBURGERBAR (hamburger bar)
- For cakes, see p. 270.
- For ice-creams, see p. 272.
- For picnic-type snacks, see p. 274.

WHAT TO SAY

I'll have . . . please	**Jag ska be att få . . . tack**
	ya ska bay aht faw . . . tak
a cheese sandwich	**en ostsmörgås**
	en *oo*st-smer-gaws
a ham roll	**en småfranska med skinka**
	en sm*aw*-fran-ska med sh*i*nka
a hamburger	**en hamburgare**
	en h*a*m-boor-ya-rer
an omelet	**en omelett**
	en ommel-*et*
with mushrooms	**med svamp**
	med svamp
with ham	**med skinka**
	med sh*i*nka
with cheese	**med ost**
	med *oo*st

These are some other snacks you might like to try:

en räksmörgås	a shrimp sandwich
en r*ai*k-smer-gaws	
en grillkorv	a hot dog
en gr*i*ll-korv	
. . . med bröd	. . . with bread
. . . med brerd	
. . . med pommes frites	. . . with french fries
. . . med pom frit	

. . . **med potatismos**	. . . with mashed potatoes
. . . med po-*tatis*-moos	
. . . **med senap/ketchup**	. . . with mustard/ketchup
. . . med sain-*ap*/ketchup	
ett stekt ägg med skinka	a fried egg with ham
ett staikt egg med sh*i*nka	
en halstrad råbiff	a grilled beef steak tartare
en h*a*l-strad r*a*w-bif	
en smörgås med leverpastej	a sandwich with liver paste
en smer-gaws med l*ai*ver-pastay	
en grönsakssoppa	a vegetable soup
en grern-saks-sop-pa	
en tomatsoppa	a tomato soup
en to-m*aht*-sop-pa	
en ärtsoppa	a pea soup
en *ai*rt-sop-pa	

[*For other essential expressions, see 'Ordering a drink', p. 283*]

In a restaurant

ESSENTIAL INFORMATION

- The place to ask for: **EN RESTAURANG** [*see p. 238*].
- You can eat at the following places:
  RESTAURANG
  VÄRDSHUS (an inn)
  HOTELL/MOTELL
  PUB (sometimes serves food)
- A service charge is always added to the bill. Tipping is therefore optional.
- Some 250 restaurants and inns around Sweden offer a 'Tourist Menu' at a fixed price during the period mid-June to mid-September.
- Swedes tend to eat earlier e.g. restaurants serve lunch from 11.30 a.m. and if you're touring and looking for a hotel or evening meal don't leave it much later than 6 p.m.

Swedish

- Alcohol is served from 12 p.m. onwards.
- **Smörgåsbord**, the famous Swedish cold table: offers a variety of dishes from appetizers to cold meats, smoked and pickled fish and usually a hot dish – meatballs or omelette. Followed by fruit salad, cheeses and of course crispbreads.

WHAT TO SAY

May I book a table?	**Kan jag få beställa ett bord?**
	kan ya faw bestel-la ett boord
I have booked a table	**Jag har beställt ett bord**
	ya har bestellt ett boord
A table . . .	**Ett bord . . .**
	ett boord . . .
for one	**för en**
	fer en
for three	**för tre**
	fer tray
The menu, please	**Matsedeln, tack**
	mat-said-eln tak
What's today's set menu?	**Vad är dagens rätt?**
	var air dahg-ens ret
Do you have a menu in English?	**Har ni en matsedel på engelska?**
	har nee en mat-saidel paw eng-el-ska
What's this, please?	**Var är det här?**
[point to menu]	vad air det hair?
The wine list	**Vinlistan**
	veen-listan
A glass of wine	**Ett glas vin**
	ett glass veen
A half-bottle	**En halv flaska**
	en halv flaska
A bottle	**En flaska**
	en flaska
A litre	**En liter**
	en lee-tair
Red/white/rosé/house wine	**Rött/vitt/rosé/husets vin**
	rert/veet/rosé/hoos-ets veen
Some more bread, please	**Lite mera bröd, tack**
	leeter maira brerd tak
Some more wine	**Lite mera vin**
	leeter maira veen

Some salad dressing	**Lite salladsås**
	l*ee*ter s*a*l-lads-saws
With/without garlic	**Med/utan vitlök**
	med/*oot*-an v*ee*t-lerk
Some water	**Lite vatten**
	l*ee*ter v*a*t-ten
How much does that come to?	**Hur mycket blir det?**
	hoor m*ee*-ker bleer det
Is service included?	**Ingår dricks?**
	in-gor dricks
Waiter!	**Hovmästaren!**
	h*o*v-mais-taren
The bill, please	**Notan, tack**
	n*oo*-tan tak

Key words for courses, as seen on some menus [*Only ask this question, if you want the waiter to remind you of the choice*]

What have you got in the way of . . .	Vad har ni för . . .
	vad hahr nee fer . . .
STARTERS?	**FÖRRÄTTER?**
	fer-rait-ter
SOUP?	**SOPPA?**
	s*o*p-pa
EGG DISHES?	**ÄGGRÄTTER?**
	egg-rait-ter
FISH?	**FISK?**
	fisk
MEAT?	**KÖTT?**
	shert
GAME?	**VILT?**
	veelt
FOWL?	**FÅGEL?**
	f*a*wg-el
VEGETABLES?	**GRÖNSAKER?**
	grern-sa-ker
CHEESE?	**OST?**
	oost
FRUIT?	**FRUKT?**
	frookt
ICE-CREAM?	**GLASS?**
	glass
DESSERT?	**DESSERT?**
	des-s*ai*r

Swedish

UNDERSTANDING THE MENU

- You will find the names of the principal ingredients of most dishes on these pages:

Starters see p. 275   Fruit see p. 276
Meat see p. 278   Cheese see p. 275
Fish see p. 281   Ice-cream see p. 272
Vegetables see p. 277 Dessert see p. 271

- Used together with the following lists of cooking and menu terms, they should help you decode the menu.
- These cooking and menu terms are for understanding – not for speaking aloud.

Cooking and menu terms

aladåb	aspic
ångkokt	steamed
aptitlig	savoury
blandad	mixed
blodig	underdone
bräserad	braised
buljong	bouillon
filéad	filleted
förlorat ägg	poached
fylld	stuffed
garnerad	garnished
genomstekt	well-done
glacerad	glazed
gratinerad	au gratin
gravad	cured (salmon and herring)
grillad	grilled
halstrad	grilled
i gelé	jellied
kokad	boiled
kräm	cream
kryddad	spiced
lagom	medium
marinerad	marinated
mosad	mashed
osträtter	cheese dishes
panerad	dressed with eggs and breadcrumbs
rimmad	lightly salted (salmon)

riven	grated
rostad	toasted
rotmos	mashed
rå	raw
rökt	smoked
sallad	salad
saltad	salted
sås	gravy
smörfräst	sautéed
söt	sweet
stekt i gryta	braised
stekt	fried
stuvad	stewed
sufflé	soufflé
sur	sour
tillaga	dressed
ungsbakad	baked
ungstekt	roasted
välstekt	well-done

Further words to help you understand the menu

äggröra	scrambled eggs
älg	elk
and	duck
ansjovis	anchovies
avacado	avocado
bakad potatis	baked potatoes
bönor	beans
bröst	breast
bruna bönor med fläsk	sauce of brown beans served with thick bacon
färs	minced meat
färsk potatis	new potatoes
fasan	pheasant
fisksoppa	fish soup
fläskpannkaka	thick pancake with bacon
fruktsallad	fruit salad
gås	goose
gräddfil	sour cream
gröna ärter	peas
gryta	casserole

Swedish

hare	hare
haricots verts	string beans
kalla rätter	cold dishes
kalops	chunks of beef braised with bouillon, onions, allspice and bay leaves
kalvkött	veal
kokt potatis	boiled potatoes
kotlett	cutlet
kotletter	chops
kroppkakor	potato dumplings (stuffed with mince pork and onions)
köttbullar	meatballs
kroppkakor	potato dumplings (stuffed with mince pork and onions)
kyckling	chicken
pannbiff	mince beef cooked in a casserole or fried
paprika (fylld)	green/red paprika (stuffed)
persilja	parsley
purjolök	leeks
pytt i panna	chunks of meat, sausages, fried potatoes served with a fried egg and pickled beetroot
rådjur	venison
rapphöna	partridge
ren	reindeer
ripa	ptarmigan
ris	rice
rotmos	mashed turnips
saltgurka	pickled gherkins
skaldjurssoppa	seafood soup
stekt potatis	fried potatoes
stekt strömming med potatismos	fried herring with mashed potatoes
surkål	sauerkraut
tonfisk	tuna fish
vinbär: svarta, röda, vita	currants: black, red, white
vinbärsgelé	currant jelly
vispgrädde	whipping cream

Health

ESSENTIAL INFORMATION

- For details of reciprocal health agreements between the UK and Sweden ask for leaflet SA 30 at your local Department of Health and Social Security a month before leaving or ask your travel agent.
- In addition, it is preferable to purchase a medical insurance policy through the travel agent, a broker or a motoring organization.
- Take your own 'first line' first aid kit with you.
- If you fall ill, you will be charged for each visit to a hospital clinic (though not for a stay in hospital) and there is also a prescription charge.
- For finding your own way to a doctor, dentist, chemist or Health and Social Security Office (for reimbursement) see p. 237, 239.
- If you need a doctor look for the following words in the telephone directory or on signs:
  SJUKHUS (hospital)
  AKUTMOTTAGNING (casualty department of a hospital)
  DISTRIKTSLÄKARE (district medical officer)
- In case of an emergency, dial 90 000 (applicable for all three emergency services).

What's the matter?

I have a pain . . .	Jag har ont . . .
	ya har oont . . .
in my ankle	i min vrist
	ee min vrist
in my arm	i min arm
	ee min arm
in my back	i min rygg
	ee min reeg
in my belly/tummy	i min buk
	ee min book
in my bowels	i min tarm
	ee min tarm
in my breast/chest	i mitt bröst
	ee mitt brerst

Swedish

I have a pain . . .	**Jag har ont . . .**
	ya har oont . . .
in my ear	**i mitt öra**
	ee mitt er-ra
in my eyes	**i mina ögon**
	ee meena erg-on
in my foot	**i min fot**
	ee min foot
in my head	**i mitt huvud**
	ee mitt hoov-od
in my heel	**i min häl**
	ee min hail
in my jaw	**i min käke**
	ee min shaiker
in my leg	**i mitt ben**
	ee mitt bain
in my neck	**i min nacke**
	ee min nacker
in my penis	**i min penis**
	ee min penis
in my shoulder	**i min axel**
	ee min ak-sel
in my stomach/abdomen	**i min mage**
	ee min mahg-er
in my testicle	**i min testikel**
	ee min test-ik-el
in my throat	**i min hals**
	ee min hals
in my vagina	**i min vagina**
	ee min vag-eena
in my wrist	**i min handled**
	ee min hand-laid
I have a pain here [*point*]	**Jag har ont här**
	ya har oont hair
I have a toothache	**Jag har tandvärk**
	ya har tand-vairk
I have broken . . .	**Jag har haft sönder . . .**
	ya har haft sern-der . . .
my dentures	**min tandprotes**
	min tand-pro-tais
my glasses	**mina glasögon**
	meena glass-ergon

I have lost . . .	**Jag har tappat . . .** ya har tap-pat . . .
my contact lenses	**mina kontaktlinser** meena kon-takt-linser
a filling	**en plomb** en plomb
My child is ill	**Mitt barn är sjukt** mitt barn air shookt
He/she has pain in his/her . . .	**Han/hon har ont i sin . . .** han/hon har oont ee sin . . .
ankle [see list above]	**vrist** vrist

How bad is it?

I'm ill	**Jag är sjuk** ya air shook
It's serious	**Det är allvarligt** det air al-var-ligt
It's not serious	**Det är inte allvarligt** det air inter al-var-ligt
It hurts (a lot)	**Det gör (mycket) ont** det yer (mee-ket) oont
I've had it for . . .	**Jag har haft det i . . .** ya har haft det ee . . .
one hour/one day	**en timme/en dag** en tim-mer/en da
It's a . . .	**Det är en . . .** det air en . . .
sharp pain	**skarp smärta** skarp smairta
dull ache	**dov värk** dov vairk
nagging pain	**molande smärta** mool-ander smairta
I feel . . .	**Jag känner mig . . .** ya shen-ner may . . .
dizzy/sick	**yr/sjuk** eer/shook
weak/feverish	**svag/febrig** svag/fay-brig

Already under treatment for something else?

I take . . . regularly [*show*]	**Jag tar regelbundet . . .** ya tar ra*i*g-el-boon-det . . .
this medicine	**den här medicinen** den hair medi-*cee*-nen
these pills	**de här pillren** day hair p*i*ll-ren
I have . . .	**Jag har . . .** ya har . . .
a heart condition	**hjärtfel** y*ai*rt-fail
haemorrhoids	**hemorrojder** hemmo-r*oy*-der
rheumatism	**reumatism** ray-ooma-t*i*sm
I think I have . . .	**Jag tror jag har . . .** ya troor ya har . . .
food poisoning	**blivit matförgiftad** bl*ee*v-it m*a*t-fer-yeeft-ad
sunstroke	**fått solsting** fawtt s*oo*l-sting
I'm . . .	**Jag är . . .** ya air . . .
diabetic	**diabetiker** deeab*ai*t-eeker
asthmatic	**astmatiker** ast-m*a*-tik-er
pregnant	**gravid** gr*a*-veed
allergic to penicillin	**allergisk mot penicillin** al-*ai*rg-isk moot penicillin

Other essential expressions

Please can you help?	**Kan ni hjälpa till?** kan nee y*e*lpa til
A doctor, please	**En doktor, tack** en d*o*k-tor tak
A dentist, please	**En tandläkare, tack** en t*a*nd-laik-arer tak
I don't speak Swedish	**Jag talar inte svenska** ya t*a*-lar *i*nter sven-ska

What time does . . . arrive?	**När kommer . . .**
	nair kom-mer . . .
the doctor	**doktorn**
	doktorn
the dentist	**tandläkaren**
	tand-laik-aren

From the doctor: key sentences to understand

Take this . . .	**Ta de här . . .**
	ta det hair . . .
every day/hour	**varje dag/timme**
	var-yer da/tim-mer
four times a day	**fyra gånger om dagen**
	feera gong-er om dahg-en
Stay in bed	**Stanna i sängen**
	stan-na ee saing-en
Don't travel . . .	**Res inte . . .**
	rais inter . . .
for . . . days/weeks	**på . . . dagar/veckor**
	paw . . . dahg-ar/vaikor
You must go to hospital	**Du måste till sjukhuset**
	doo mos-ter til shook-hoos-et

Problems: complaints, loss, theft

ESSENTIAL INFORMATION

- Problems with:
  camping facilities, see p. 246.
  household appliances, see p. 264.
  health, see p. 293.
  the car, see p. 303.
- If the worst comes to the worst, find a police station.
  To ask the way, see p. 236.
  Look for: **POLIS**

- If you lose your passport, report the loss to the nearest police station and go to the British Consulate.
- In an emergency dial 90 000 if you require assistance from the police, fire brigade or ambulance. If dialling from a phone box, the call is free.

COMPLAINTS

I bought this . . .	**Jag köpte den här . . .** ya sherp-ter den hair . . .
today	**idag** ee-da
yesterday	**igår** ee-gor
on Monday	**i måndags** ee mon-dags
It's no good	**Den är inte bra** den air inter bra
Look	**Titta** tit-ta
Here [point]	**Här** hair
Can you . . .	**Kan ni . . .** kan nee . . .
change it?	**byta den?** beeta den
mend it?	**laga den?** la-ga den
Here's the receipt	**Här är kvittot** hair air kvit-tot
Can I have a refund?	**Kan jag få pengarna tillbaka?** kan ya faw peng-ar-na til-ba-ka

LOSS
[See also 'Theft' below: the lists are interchangeable]

I have lost . . .	**Jag har tappat . . .** ya har tap-pat
my bag	**min väska** min vaiska
my bracelet	**mitt armband** mitt arm-band

my camera	**min kamera**
	min k*a*-mera
my car keys	**mina bilnycklar**
	m*ee*na b*ee*l-neeklar
my car logbook	**mina bilpapper**
	m*ee*na b*ee*l-pap-per
my driving licence	**mitt körkort**
	mitt sher-kort
my insurance certificate	**mina försäkringshandlingar**
	m*ee*na fer-s*ai*k-rings-handling-ar

THEFT
[See also 'Loss' above: the lists are interchangeable]

Someone has stolen . . .	**Någon har stulit . . .**
	n*aw*-gon har st*oo*l-it . . .
my car	**min bil**
	min beel
my money	**mina pengar**
	m*ee*na peng-ar
my purse	**min portmonnä**
	min port-mon-n*ay*
my tickets	**mina biljetter**
	m*ee*na bil-yet-ter
my travellers' cheques	**mina resecheckar**
	m*ee*na r*ai*ser-checkar
my wallet	**min plånbok**
	min pl*aw*n-book
my watch	**min klocka**
	min kl*o*cka
my luggage	**mitt bagage**
	mitt ba-g*a*sh

LIKELY REACTIONS: key words to understand

Wait	**Vänta**
	v*e*nta
When?	**När?**
	nair
Where?	**Var?**
	var
Name?	**Namn?**
	namn

Swedish

Address?	**Adress?**
	ah-dress
I can't help you	**Jag kan inte hjälpa dig**
	ya kan inter yelpa day
Nothing to do with me	**Det har inget med mig att göra**
	det har ing-et med may aht yer-ra

The post office

ESSENTIAL INFORMATION

- To find a post office, see p. 236.
- Key words to look for:
  POST
  POSTKONTOR
  or look out for this sign:
- For stamps look for the word **FRIMÄRKEN** (stamps) or **BREV** (letters).
- Stamps can be obtained at a stationer's or a tobacconist, provided postcards are also sold there.
- Post offices are open 9 a.m. to 6 p.m. weekdays and 9 a.m. to 1 p.m. on Saturdays.
- Letter boxes are yellow.

WHAT TO SAY

To England, please	**Till England, tack**
	till eng-land tak
[Hand letters, cards or parcels over the counter]	
To Australia	**Til Australien**
	till ah-oost-ra-lee-en
To the United States	**Till Amerika**
[For other countries, see p. 318]	till amair-reeka
Airmail	**Flygpost**
	fleeg-posst
I'd like to send a telegram	**Jag vill skicka ett telegram**
	ya vill shik-ka ett tele-gram

Telephoning

ESSENTIAL INFORMATION

- Public phone boxes, **TELEFONKIOSK**, are painted grey or green, or they are in glass with red frames.
- Instructions on how to use the phone are printed in several languages. Foreign calls can be made from most boxes.
- For a call to the UK dial 00944, followed by the STD code (omitting the first 0) and then the subscriber's number. The code to the USA is 0091.
- For calls to countries which cannot be dialled direct go to a telegraph office, **TELEGRAF STATION** and write down the country, town and number you want on a piece of paper. Add **PERSONLIGT SAMTAL** if you want a person to person call or **MOTTAGAREN BETALAR** if you want to reverse charges.
- Post offices do not have telephone facilities.
- To ask the way to a public telephone, see p. 239.

WHAT TO SAY

I'd like this number . . .	**Jag vill ha det här numret . . .**
[show number]	ya vill ha det hair n*oo*m-ret . . .
in England	**i England**
	ee *ø*ng-land
in Canada	**i Kanada**
[For other countries, see p. 319]	ee k*a*n-ah-da
Can you dial it for me, please?	**Kan ni slå numret åt mig?**
	kan nee slaw n*oo*m-ret awt may
May I speak to . . .?	**Kan jag få tala med . . .?**
	kan ya faw t*a*-la med . .
Extension . . .	**Anknytning . . .**
	ank-n*ee*t-ning
Do you speak English?	**Talar ni engelska?**
	t*a*-lar nee eng-el-ska
Thank you, I'll phone back	**Tack, jag ringer tillbaka**
	tak ya ring-er till-b*a*-ka

LIKELY REACTIONS

That's (4 crowns)	**Det blir (fyra kronor)**
	det bleer (f*ee*ra kr*oo*n-or)

Cabin number (3)	**Kiosk nummer (tre)**
[*For numbers, see p. 313*]	shee-*osk* n*oo*m-mer tray
Don't hang up	**Häng inte upp**
	haing *i*nter oop
I'm trying to connect you	**Jag försöker anknyta dig**
	ya fer-*serker* ank-n*ee*ta day
You're through	**Du är anknuten**
	doo air *an*-knooten
There's a delay	**Det är en försening**
	det air en fer-s*ai*ning
I'll try again	**Jag försöker igen**
	ya fer-*serker* ee-yen

Changing cheques and money

ESSENTIAL INFORMATION

- Finding your way to a bank or change bureau, see p. 237.
- Look for these words or signs on buildings:
  BANK (bank)
  VÄXLINGSKONTOR (change bureau)
- Banks are open from 9.30 a.m. to 3.00 p.m. on weekdays. In many large cities banks close at 6.00 p.m. All banks are closed on Saturdays and Sundays.
- Change bureaux at frontier posts and airports are usually open outside regular banking hours.
- Exchange rate information might show the pound as:
  £ LONDON, ENGLAND (GR BR) or the British flag.
- Have your passport ready.

WHAT TO SAY

I'd like to cash . . .	**Jag vill växla in . . .**
	ya vill v*ai*k-sla in . . .
this travellers' cheque	**den här resecheken**
	den hair r*ai*ser-checken

these travellers' cheques	**de här resecheckarna**
	day hair r*ai*ser-check-arna
this cheque	**den här checken**
	den hair ch*e*cken
I'd like to change this into crowns	**Jag vill växla det här till kronor**
	ya vill v*ai*k-sla det hair till kr*oo*nor

For excursions into neighbouring countries

I'd like to change this . . . [*show banknotes*]	**Jag vill växla de här . . .**
	ya vill v*ai*k-sla day hair . . .
into Danish crowns	**till danska kronor**
	till d*a*n-ska kr*oo*n-or
into Norwegian crowns	**till norska kronor**
	till n*o*r-ska kr*oo*n-or

LIKELY REACTIONS

Passport, please	**Passet, tack**
	p*a*sset tak
Sign here	**Skriv under här**
	skreev *oo*n-der hair
Go to the cash desk	**Gå till kassan**
	gaw till k*a*s-san

Car travel

ESSENTIAL INFORMATION

- Finding a filling station or garage see p. 238.
  Is it a self-service station? Look out for
  TANKA SJÄLV
- Grades of petrol:
  93 OKTAN (regular)
  96 OKTAN (normal)
  98 OKTAN (super)
  DIESEL OLJA (diesel)

Swedish

- 1 gallon is about 4½ litres (accurate enough up to 6 gallons.)
- In country areas, petrol stations usually close at 6 p.m.
- Many petrol stations also have automatic pumps. Watch for **NATT-ÖPPET SEDELAUTOMAT**.
- Filling stations are usually able to deal with minor mechanical problems. For major repairs you have to find a garage.
- In Sweden the driver and the passenger in the front seats must wear safety belts, and dipped headlights are obligatory at *all* times when driving.
- Drinking and driving see 'Ordering a drink' p. 283.

WHAT TO SAY
[*For numbers, see p. 313*]

(Nine) litres of . . .	**(Nio) liter . . .**
	(*nee*-oo) lee-t*air* . . .
(100) crowns of . . .	**(Hundra) kronor . . .**
	(h*oo*nd-ra) kr*oo*n-or . . .
Fill it up, please	**Full tank, tack**
	full tank tak
Will you check . . .	**Kan ni kontrollera . . .**
	kan nee kon-troll-*air*a . . .
the oil?	**oljan?**
	*oo*l-yan
the battery?	**batteriet?**
	bat-ter-r*ee*-et
the radiator?	**kylarn?**
	sh*ee*l-arn
the tyres?	**däcken?**
	d*ai*ken
I've run out of petrol	**Jag är utan bensin**
	ya air *oo*t-an ben-seen
Can I borrow a can, please?	**Kan jag få låna en bensindunk?**
	kan ya faw l*a*wna en ben-*see*n-doonk
My car has broken down	**Min bil har gått sönder**
	min beel har got s*er*n-der
Can you help me, please?	**Kan ni hjälpa mig?**
	kan nee y*e*lpa may
Do you do repairs?	**Gör ni reparationer?**
	yer nee ray-pa-ra-sh*oo*ner
I have a puncture	**Jag har punktering**
	ya har poonk-t*ai*ring

I have a broken windscreen	**Jag har trasig vindruta** ya har trais-eega vind-roota
I think the problem is here . . . [point]	**Jag tror problemet är här . . .** ya troor prob-laimet air hair . . .
Can you . . .	**Kan ni . . .** kan nee . . .
repair the fault?	**reparera felet?** ray-pa-raira failet
come and look?	**komma och titta?** kom-ma ock tit-ta
estimate the cost?	**kalkylera kostnaden?** kal-keel-aira kost-na-den
write it down?	**skriva ner det?** skreeva nair det
How long will the repairs take?	**Hur lång tid tar reparationerna?** hoor long teed tar ray-pa-ra-shoon-erna
This is my insurance document	**Det här är mitt försäkringsbevis** det hair air mitt fer-saikrings-bay-vees

HIRING A CAR

Can I hire a car?	**Kan jag få hyra en bil?** kan ya faw heera en beel
I need a car . . .	**Jag behöver en bil . . .** ya bay-herver en beel . . .
for five people	**för fem personer** fer fem per-sooner
for a week	**för en vecka** fer en vaika
Can you write down . . .	**Kan ni skriva ner . . .** kan nee skreeva nair . . .
the deposit to pay?	**deponeringssumman?** dep-on-airings-soom-man
the charge per kilometre?	**priset per kilometer?** prees-et per kilo-maiter
the daily charge?	**priset per dag?** prees-et per da
the cost of insurance?	**försäkringskostnaden?** fer-saik-rings-kost-naden
Can I leave it in (Malmö)?	**Kan jag lämna den i (Malmö)?** kan ya laim-na den ee mal-mer
What documents do I need?	**Vilka dokument behöver jag?** vilka docooment bay-herver ya?

Swedish

LIKELY REACTIONS

I don't do repairs

Jag gör inte reparationer
ya yer *in*-ter ray-pa-ra-sh*oo*ner

Where is your car?

Var är din bil?
var air din beel?

What make is it?

Vilket märke är det?
*vi*lket m*ai*r-ker air det

Come back tomorrow/on
   Wednesday [*For days of
   the week, see p. 315*]

Kom tillbaka imorgon/på onsdag
kom till-b*a*-ka *ee*-morron/paw
   *oo*ns-da

We don't hire cars

Vi hyr inte ut bilar
vee heer *in*ter oot b*ee*lar

Your driving licence, please

Ert körkort, tack
airt sher-kort tak

The mileage is unlimited

Milsträckan är obegränsad
m*ee*l-straik-an air *oo*bai-grainsad

Public transport

ESSENTIAL INFORMATION

* Finding the way to a bus station, a bus, a tram stop, the railway station and a taxi rank, see p. 236.
* It is less usual to hail a taxi in the street: go instead to a taxi rank or telephone a taxi station.
* These are the different types of trains, graded according to speed:
   EXPRESSTÅG (stops at a few stations)
   SNÄLLTÅG (stops at many stations)
   LOKALTÅG (stops at all stations)
   PENDELTÅG (stops at all stations)
* There is generally a standard price ticket which entitles you to travel as far as you like. In Stockholm and Gothenburg you may purchase a 1 or 3 day tourist ticket which entitles you to travel as often as you like during the given period.
* Swedish State Railways (**SJ**) offers a 'low-price card' entitling the passenger to a reduction of 45% on all railway journeys within

Sweden (valid for 12 months on all routes except Fridays and Sundays).

- Three family members travelling together pay the low-price fare without having to buy the 'low-price card' and can also travel on Fridays and Sundays.
- Children aged between 6–16 pay half price and under 6 travel free of charge.
- The 'Nordic Railpass' – a 21 day or one month ticket entitles you to unlimited travel in Sweden and the rest of Scandinavia.
- Key words on signs:
  BILJETTER (tickets, ticket office)
  INGÅNG (entrance)
  UTGÅNG (exit)
  FÖRBJUDET (forbidden)
  PERRONG/PLATTFORM (platform)
  VÄNTSAL (waiting room)
  HITTEGODS (left luggage)
  SJ (initials of Swedish Railways)
  SL (initials of Stockholm Local Traffic)
  BUSSHÅLLPLATS (bus stop)
  TIDTABELL (timetable)

WHAT TO SAY

Where does the train for (Malmö) leave from?	**Var går tåget till (Malmö)?** var gor t*a*w-get till (m*a*l-mer)
At what time does the train for (Malmö) leave?	**När går tåget till (Malmö)?** nair gor t*a*w-get till (m*a*l-mer)
At what time does the train arrive in (Malmö)?	**När kommer tåget fram till (Malmö)?** nair k*o*m-mer t*a*w-get fram till (m*a*l-mer)
Is this the train for (Malmö)?	**Är det här tåget till (Malmö)?** air det hair t*a*w-get till (m*a*l-mer)
Where does the bus for (Arlanda) leave from?	**Var går bussen till (Arlanda)?** var gor b*oo*ssen till (*a*r-landa)
Is this the bus for (Arlanda)?	**Är det här bussen till (Arlanda)?** air det hair b*oo*ssen till (*a*r-landa)
Do I have to change?	**Måste jag byta?** m*o*s-ter ya b*ee*-ta
Can I book a seat?	**Kan jag få en platsbiljett?** kan ya faw en pl*a*ts-bill-yet
A single	**En enkel** en *e*n-kel

A return	**En tur och retur**
	en toor ock ray-toor
First class	**Första klass**
	fersta klass
Second class	**Andra klass**
	an-dra klass
One adult	**En vuxen**
	en vooksen
Two adults	**Två vuxna**
	tvaw vooks-na
and one child	**och ett barn**
	ock ett barn
and two children	**och två barn**
	ock tvaw barn
How much is it?	**Hur mycket kostar det?**
	hoor mee-ket kostar det

LIKELY REACTIONS

Over there	**Där borta**
	dair borta
Here	**Här**
	hair
Platform (1)	**Plattform (ett)**
	plat-form (ett)

[*For times, see p. 315*]

Change at (Helsingborg)	**Byt i (Helsingborg)**
	beet ee (hel-sing-bory)
This is your stop	**Det här är din station**
	det hair air din sta-shoon
There's only first class	**Det finns bara första klass**
	det finss ba-ra fersta klass
There's a supplement	**Där är ett tillägg**
	dair air ett till-egg

Leisure

ESSENTIAL INFORMATION

- Finding the way to a place of entertainment, see p. 238, 239.
- For times of day, see p. 315.
- No smoking in cinemas, theatres or concert halls, and in some restaurants.
- Cinemas always show films in the original language with Swedish subtitles.
- It is customary to leave one's coat in the cloakroom in theatres and concert halls.

WHAT TO SAY

At what time does . . . open?	**När öppnar . . .** nair *erp*-nar
the museum	**museet?** moo-*say*-et
At what time does . . . close?	**När stänger . . .** nair steng-er . . .
the skating rink	**skridskobanan?** skr*ee*-skoo-ban-an
At what time does . . . start?	**När börjar . . .** nair ber-yar . . .
the cabaret	**kabarén?** ca-ba-ra*in*
the concert	**konserten?** kon-s*air*t-en
the film	**filmen?** f*i*lm-en
the match	**matchen?** m*a*tch-en
the play	**pjäsen?** pee-*ais*-en
the race	**tävlingen?** t*ai*v-ling-en
How much is it . . .	**Hur mycket kostar det . . .** hoor m*ee*-ket k*o*star det
for an adult/child?	**för en vuxen?/ett barn?** fer en v*oo*ksen/ett barn

Stalls/dress circle	**Parkett/första raden**
[State price, if there's a choice]	par-kett/fersta ra-den
Do you have . . .	**Har ni . . .**
	har nee . . .
a programme?	**ett program?**
	ett pro-gram
a guide book?	**en guidebok?**
	en guide-book
I would like a lesson in . . .	**Jag skulle vilja ha en lektion i . . .**
	ya skool-ler vil-ya ha en laik-shoon ee . . .
skating	**skridskoåkning**
	skree-skoo-awk-ning
water skiing	**vattenskidor**
	vat-ten-sheedor
sailing	**segling**
	saigling
Can I hire . . .	**Kan jag få hyra . . .**
	kan ya faw heera . . .
a boat?	**en båt?**
	en bawt
a fishing rod?	**ett metspö?**
	ett mait-sper
a windsurfing board?	**en vindsurfingbräda?**
	en veend-surfing-braida
a pair of skis?	**ett par skidor?**
	ett par sheedor
the necessary equipment?	**nödvändig utrustning?**
	nerd-vain-dig oot-roost-ning
How much is it . . .	**Hur mycket kostar det . . .**
	hoor mew-ker kostar det . . .
per day/per hour?	**per dag/per timme?**
	per da/per tim-mer
Do I need a licence?	**Behöver jag licens?**
	bay-herver ya lee-sence

Asking if things are allowed

ESSENTIAL INFORMATION

- May one smoke here?
  May we smoke here?
  May I smoke here?   **Kan man röka här?**
  Can one smoke here?   kan man rerka hair
  Can we smoke here?
  Can I smoke here?
- All these English variations can be expressed in one way in Swedish. To save space, only the first English version (May one . . .?) is shown below.

WHAT TO SAY

Excuse me, please	**Ursäkta mig**
	yoo-shek-ta may
May one . . .	**Kan man . . .**
	kan man . . .
camp here?	**campa här?**
	kampa hair
come in?	**komma in?**
	kom-ma in
dance here?	**dansa här?**
	dan-sa hair
fish here?	**fiska här?**
	fiska hair
get a drink here?	**få en drink här?**
	faw en drink hair
get out this way?	**komma ut den här vägen?**
	kom-ma oot den hair vaig-en
leave one's things here?	**lämna sina saker här?**
	laim-na seena sak-er hair
look around?	**se sig omkring?**
	say sig om-kring
park here?	**parkera här?**
	park-aira hair
picnic here?	**ha picnic här?**
	ha picnic hair

sit here?	**sitta här?**
	sit-ta hair
smoke here?	**röka här?**
	rerka hair
swim here?	**simma här?**
	sim-ma hair
telephone here?	**ringa här?**
	ringa hair
wait here?	**vänta här?**
	venta hair

LIKELY REACTIONS

Yes, certainly	**Ja, visst**
	ya veesst
Help yourself	**Var så god**
	var saw goo
I think so	**Jag tror det**
	ya troor det
Of course	**Naturligtvis**
	na-toor-lit-vees
Yes, but be careful	**Ja, men var försiktig**
	ya men var fer-sik-tig
No, certainly not	**Nej, naturligtvis inte**
	nay na-toor-lit-vees inter
I don't think so	**Jag tror inte det**
	ya troor inter det
Not normally	**Normalt inte**
	nor-malt inter
Sorry	**Tyvärr**
	tee-vair

Reference

NUMBERS
Cardinal numbers

0	**noll**	noll
1	**ett**	ett
2	**två**	tvaw
3	**tre**	tray
4	**fyra**	f*ee*ra
5	**fem**	fem
6	**sex**	sex
7	**sju**	shoo
8	**åtta**	*o*t-ta
9	**nio**	n*ee*-oo
10	**tio**	t*ee*-oo
11	**elva**	*e*ll-va
12	**tolv**	tollv
13	**tretton**	tret-ton
14	**fjorton**	f-yor-ton
15	**femton**	f*e*m-ton
16	**sexton**	s*e*x-ton
17	**sjutton**	sh*oo*-ton
18	**arton**	*a*r-ton
19	**nitton**	n*i*t-ton
20	**tjugo**	ch*oo*-go
21	**tjugoett**	choo-go-*e*tt
22	**tjugotvå**	choo-go-tv*a*w
23	**tjugotre**	choo-go-tray
24	**tjugofyra**	choo-go-f*ee*ra
25	**tjugofem**	choo-go-f*e*m
26	**tjugosex**	choo-go-s*e*x
27	**tjugosju**	choo-go-sh*oo*
28	**tjugoåtta**	choo-go-*o*t-ta
29	**tjugonio**	choo-go-n*ee*-oo
30	**trettio**	tray-t*ee*-oo
31	**trettioett**	tray-tee-*e*tt
35	**trettiofem**	tray-tee-f*e*m
40	**fyrtio**	fer-t*ee*-oo
41	**fyrtioett**	fer-tee-*e*tt
50	**femtio**	fem-t*ee*-oo

Swedish

51	**femtioett**	fem-tee-ett
60	**sextio**	sex-tee-oo
70	**sjuttio**	shoo-tee-oo
80	**åttio**	ot-tee-oo
81	**åttioett**	ot-tee-ett
90	**nittio**	nit-tee-oo
95	**nittiofem**	nit-tee-fem
100	**hundra**	hoon-dra
101	**hundraett**	hoon-dra-ett
102	**hundratvå**	hoon-dra-tvaw
125	**hundratjugofem**	hoon-dra-choo-go-fem
150	**hundrafemtio**	hoon-dra-fem-tee-oo
175	**hundrasjuttiofem**	hoon-dra-shoo-tee-fem
200	**tvåhundra**	tvaw-hoon-dra
300	**trehundra**	tray-hoon-dra
400	**fyrahundra**	feera-hoon-dra
500	**femhundra**	fem-hoon-dra
1000	**tusen**	too-sen
1100	**elvahundra**	ell-va-hoon-dra
3000	**tretusen**	tray-too-sen
5000	**femtusen**	fem-too-sen
10,000	**tiotusen**	tee-oo-too-sen
100,000	**hundratusen**	hoon-dra-too-sen
1,000,000	**en miljon**	en mill-yoon

Ordinal numbers

1st	**första**	fersta
2nd	**andra**	an-dra
3rd	**tredje**	traid-yer
4th	**fjärde**	f-yair-der
5th	**femte**	fem-ter
6th	**sjätte**	shet-ter
7th	**sjunde**	shoon-der
8th	**åttonde**	ot-ton-der
9th	**nionde**	nee-on-der
10th	**tionde**	tee-on-der
11th	**elfte**	ellf-ter
12th	**tolvte**	tollv-ter

TIME

What time is it?	**Vad är klockan?**
	vad air klock-an
It's . . .	**Den är . . .**
	den air . . .
one o'clock	**ett**
	ett
two o'clock	**två**
	tvaw
three o'clock	**tre**
	tray
noon	**tolv på dagen**
	tollv paw dahg-en
midnight	**tolv på natten** or **midnatt**
	tollv paw naht-en meed-naht
It's . . .	**Den är . . .**
	den air . . .
five past five	**fem över fem**
	fem erver fem
ten to six	**tio i sex**
	tee-oo ee sex
twenty to six	**tjugo i sex**
	choo-go ee sex
five past five	**fem över fem**
	fem erver fem
twenty past five	**tjugo över fem**
	choo-go erver fem
At what time . . . (does the train leave)?	**När . . . (går tåget)?**
	nair . . . (gor taw-get)
At . . .	**Klockan . . .**
	klock-an . . .
13.00	**tretton nollnoll**
	tret-ton noll-noll
18.25	**arton och tjugofem**
	ar-ton ock choo-go-fem
23.50	**tjugotre och femtio**
	choo-go-tray ock fem-tee-oo

DAYS

Monday	**måndag**
	mon-da
Tuesday	**tisdag**
	tees-da
Wednesday	**onsdag**
	oons-da
Thursday	**torsdag**
	toors-da
Friday	**fredag**
	fray-da
Saturday	**lördag**
	ler-da
Sunday	**söndag**
	sern-da
last Monday	**förra måndagen**
	fer-ra mon-dahg-en
next Tuesday	**nästa tisdag**
	nais-ta tees-da
on Wednesday	**på onsdag**
	paw oons-da
until Friday	**till fredag**
	till fray-da
before Saturday	**före lördag**
	fer-er ler-da
after Sunday	**efter söndag**
	efter sern-da
the day before yesterday	**förrgår**
	fer-gor
two days ago	**för två dagar sedan**
	fer tvaw-da-gar say-dan
yesterday	**igår**
	ee-gor
yesterday morning	**igår morse**
	ee-gor morsay
yesterday afternoon	**igår eftermiddag**
	ee-gor efter-mid-da
last night	**igår kväll**
	ee-gor kvaill
today	**idag**
	ee-da

this morning	**i morse**
	ee mor-ser
this afternoon	**i eftermiddag**
	ee efter-mid-da
tonight	**ikväll**
	ee-kvaill
tomorrow	**imorgon**
	ee-morron
tomorrow morning	**i morgon bitti**
	ee morron bit-tee
tomorrow afternoon	**i morgon eftermiddag**
	ee morron efter-mid-da
tomorrow evening	**i morgon kväll**
	ee morron kvaill
the day after tomorrow	**i övermorgon**
	ee erver-morron

MONTHS AND DATES

January	**januari**
	yan-noo-ah-ree
February	**februari**
	feb-roo-ah-ree
March	**mars**
	marsh
April	**april**
	ah-prill
May	**maj**
	my
June	**juni**
	yoonee
July	**juli**
	yoolee
August	**augusti**
	ah-goos-tee
September	**september**
	september
October	**oktober**
	ock-toober
November	**november**
	november
December	**december**
	day-cember

last month	**förra månaden**	
	fer-ra maw-na-den	
this month	**den här månaden**	
	den hair maw-na-den	
next month	**nästa månad**	
	nais-ta maw-nad	
in spring	**på våren**	
	paw voren	
in summer	**på sommaren**	
	paw som-mar-en	
in autumn	**på hösten**	
	paw herst-en	
in winter	**på vintern**	
	paw vin-tern	
this year	**i år**	
	ee or	
last year	**förra året**	
	fer-ra or-et	
next year	**nästa år**	
	nais-ta or	
in 1985	**nittonhundraåttiofem**	
	nit-ton-hoon-dra-ot-tee-fem	
It's the 6th of March	**Det är den sjätte mars**	
	det air den shait-ter marsh	

Public holidays

● Shops, schools and offices are closed on the following dates:

1 January	**Nyårsdagen**	New Year's Day
. . .	**Trettondagen**	Epiphany
. . .	**Långfredagen**	Good Friday
. . .	**Påskdagen**	Easter Day
. . .	**Annandag påsk**	Easter Monday
1 May	**Första maj**	Labour Day
. . .	**Kristi Himmelfärdagen**	Ascension Day
. . .	**Pingstdagen**	Whit Sunday
. . .	**Annandag pingst**	Whit Monday
. . .	**Midsommardagen**	Midsummer's Day
. . .	**Alla helgons dag**	All Saints' Day
25 December	**Juldagen**	Christmas Day
26 December	**Annandag Jul**	Boxing Day

COUNTRIES AND NATIONALITIES
Countries

America   **Amerika**
am*ai*r-reeka

Australia   **Australien**
ah-oost-r*a*-lee-en

Austria   **Österrike**
*e*rster-reeker

Belgium   **Belgien**
b*e*ll-yen

Britain   **Storbrittanien**
st*oo*r-brit-tan-ee-en

Canada   **Kanada**
kan-ah-da

Czechoslovakia   **Tjeckoslovakien**
checko-slov*a*-kee-en

Denmark   **Danmark**
dan-mark

East Germany   **Östtyskland**
*e*rst-teesk-land

Eire   **Irland**
*ee*r-land

England   **England**
*e*ng-land

Finland   **Finland**
f*i*n-land

France   **Frankrike**
fr*a*nk-reeker

Greece   **Grekland**
gr*ai*k-land

Iceland   **Island**
*ee*s-land

India   **Indien**
*i*ndee-en

Italy   **Italien**
eet*a*-lee-en

Luxembourg   **Luxemburg**
lux-em-b*oo*ry

The Netherlands   **Nederländerna**
n*ai*der-lainder-na

New Zealand	**Nya Zeeland**
	n*ee*-ah z*ai*land
Pakistan	**Pakistan**
	pa-kee-st*ah*n
Poland	**Polen**
	p*o*-len
Portugal	**Portugal**
	porto-gal
Scotland	**Skottland**
	sk*o*t-land
South Africa	**Sydafrika**
	s*ee*d-af-ree-ka
Spain	**Spanien**
	sp*a*n-yen
Switzerland	**Schweiz**
	shvaitz
Wales	**Wales**
	wales
West Germany	**Västtyskland**
	v*e*st-tesk-land
Yugoslavia	**Jugoslavien**
	yugo-sl*a*v-ee-en
Norway	**Norge**
	n*o*r-yer

Nationalities
[Use the first alternative for men, the second for women]

American	**amerikan/amerikanska**
	am-ree-k*ah*n/am-ree-k*ah*n-ska
Australian	**australiensare/australianska**
	ah-oost-ra-lee-*en*-sa-rer/ah-oost-ra-lee-*en*-see-ska
British	**britt/brittiska**
	britt/br*i*ttee-ska
Canadian	**canadensare/canadensiska**
	kan-ah-d*e*n-sa-rer/kan-ah-d*e*n-see-skah
Danish	**dansk/danska**
	d*a*nsk/d*a*n-ska
English	**engelsman/engelska**
	*e*ng-els-man/*e*ng-el-ska

Finnish	**finsk/finska**
	finsk/fín-ska
German	**tysk/tyska**
	teesk/tee-ska
Icelander	**isländare/isländska**
	ees-lainda-rer/ees-lain-ska
Norwegian	**norsk/norska**
	norsk/nor-ska
Scots	**skotte/skottska**
	skot-ter/skott-ska
South African	**sydafrikan/sydafrikanska**
	seed-af-ree-kahn/
	seed-af-ree-kahn-ska
Swedish	**svensk/svenska**
	svensk/sven-ska
Yugoslavian	**jugoslav/jugoslaviska**
	yugo-slav/yugo-slav-ee-ska

Do it yourself

Some notes on the language

This section does not deal with 'grammar' as such. The purpose here is to explain some of the most obvious and elementary nuts and bolts of the language, based on the principal phrases included in the book. This information should enable you to produce numerous sentences of your own making, although you will obviously still be fairly limited in what you can say.

There is no pronunciation guide in the first part of the section, partly because it would get in the way of the explanations and partly because you have to do it yourself at this stage if you are serious – work out the pronunciation from all the earlier examples in the book.

THE

All nouns in Swedish belong to one of two genders: common or neuter, irrespective of whether they refer to living beings or inanimate objects.

the	common	neuter	plural
the address	adressen		adresserna
the apple		äpplet	äpplena
the bill	räkningen		räkningarna
the cup of tea	koppen te		kopparna te
the glass of beer		glaset öl	glasen öl
the key	nyckeln		nycklarna
the luggage		bagaget	bagaget
the menu	matsedeln		matsedlarna
the newspaper	tidningen		tidningarna
the sandwich	smörgåsen		smörgåsarna
the suitcase	resväskan		resväskorna
the telephone directory	telefon-katalogen		telefon-katalogerna
the timetable	tidtabellen		tidtabellerna

Important things to remember

- There is no way of telling if a noun is common or neuter. You have to learn and remember its gender.
- *The* in Swedish is tagged on to the end of the word so that instead of *the apple* they say *apple the*. The most common endings are -en or -n after common nouns: **tidningen resväskan, nyckeln**, and -et or -t after neuter nouns: **äpplet**.
- Does it matter? Not unless you want to make a serious attempt to speak correctly and scratch beneath the surface of the language. You would be understood if you said **tidninget** or even **resväskat** , providing your pronunciation was good.
- The most common ending in the definite plural is -**na**, but first you must get the word right in the indefinite plural:
  newspapers **tidningar**
  the newspapers **tidningarna**
  suitcases **resväskor**
  the suitcases **resväskorna**
- For more about the indefinite plural see *A/an*, p. 324.
- In Swedish as in English 'luggage' has no plural.

Practise saying and writing these sentences in Swedish:

Have you got the key?	**Har ni nyckeln?**
Have you got the luggage?	**Har ni . . .?**
Have you got the telephone directory?	
Have you got the menu?	
I'd like the key	**Jag ska be att få nyckeln**
I'd like the luggage	**Jag ska be att få . . .**
I'd like the bill	
I'd like the keys	
Where is the key?	**Var är nyckeln?**
Where is the timetable?	**Var är . . .?**
Where is the address?	
Where is the suitcase?	
Where are the keys?	**Var är nycklarna?**
Where are the sandwiches?	**Var är . . .?**
Where are the apples?	
Where are the suitcases?	
Where is the luggage?	**Var är . . .?**
Where can I get the key?	**Var kan jag få tag på nyckeln?**
Where can I get the address?	**Var kan jag få tag på . . .?**
Where can I get the timetables?	

Swedish

A/AN

a/an	common	neuter	plural
an address	en adress		adressen
an apple		ett äpple	äpplen
a bill	en räkning		räkningar
a cup of tea	en kopp te		koppar te
a glass of beer		ett glas öl	glas öl
a key	en nyckel		nycklar
a menu	en matsedel		matsedlar
a newspaper	en tidning		tidningar
a sandwich	en smörgås		smörgåsar
a suitcase	en resväska		resväskor
a telephone directory	en telefon-katalog		telefon-kataloger
a timetable	en tidtabell		tidtabeller

Important things to remember

- *A* or *an* is en before a common noun and ett before a neuter singular noun.
- The indefinite plural is formed according to one of the five declensions.

	singular	indefinite plural	definite plural
a suitcase	en resväska	resväskor	resväskorna
a sandwich	en smörgås	smörgåsar	smörgåsarna
an address	en adress	adresser	adresserna
an apple	ett äpple	äpplen	äpplena
a glass	ett glas	glas	glasen

- The plural *some* or *any* is **några** in Swedish. The singular is **någon** (common nouns) or **något** (neuter nouns).

Practise saying and writing these sentences in Swedish:

Have you got a bill?	**Har ni en räkning?**
Have you got a menu?	
I'd like a telephone directory	**Jag ska be att få en . . .**
I'd like some sandwiches	**Jag ska be att få några . . .**

Where can I get some newspapers?	**Var kan jag få tag på några . . .?**
Where can I get a cup of tea?	
Is there a key?	**Finns det en nyckel?**
Is there a timetable?	**Finns det en . . .?**
Is there a telephone directory?	
Is there a menu?	
Are there any keys?	**Finns det några nycklar?**
Are there any newspapers?	**Finns det . . .?**
Are there any sandwiches?	

Now make up more sentences along the same lines. Then try these new phrases:

Jag vill ha . . . (I'll have . . .)
Jag behöver . . . (I need . . .)

I'll have a glass of beer	**Jag vill ha ett glas öl**
I'll have a cup of tea	**Jag vill ha . . .**
I'll have some apples	
I need a cup of tea	**Jag behöver en kopp te**
I need a key	**Jag behöver . . .**
I need some newspapers	**Jag behöver några tidningar**
I need some keys	**Jag behöver . . .**
I need some addresses	
I need some sandwiches	
I need some suitcases	**Jag behöver . . .**

SOME/ANY

In cases where *some* or *any* refer to things that can be counted, **några**, **någon**, or **något** are used. In cases where *some* refers to a part of a whole thing or an indefinite quantity, the word **lite** can be used.

the bread	**brödet**	**lite bröd**	some bread
the butter	**smöret**	**lite smör**	some butter
the cheese	**osten**	**lite ost**	some cheese
the coffee	**kaffet**	**lite kaffe**	some coffee
the ice-cream	**glassen**	**lite glass**	some ice-cream
the lemonade	**lemonaden**	**lite lemonad**	some lemonade
the pineapple	**ananasen**	**lite ananas**	some pineapple

Swedish

the sugar	**sockret**	**lite socker**	some sugar
the tea	**tet**	**lite té**	some tea
the water	**vattnet**	**lite vatten**	some water
the wine	**vinet**	**lite vin**	some wine

Practise saying and writing these sentences in Swedish:

Have you got some ice-cream? **Har ni lite glass?**

Have you got some pineapple?

I'd like some butter **Jag ska be att få lite smör**

I'd like some sugar

I'd like some bread

Where can I get some cheese? **Var kan jag få lite ost?**

Where can I get some ice-cream?

Where can I get some water?

Is there any water? **Finns det lite vatten?**

Is there any lemonade?

Is there any wine?

I'll have some beer **Jag vill ha lite öl**

I'll have some tea

I'll have some coffee

THIS AND THAT

The following words can be used when pointing:

(this) **den här** (refers to a common noun)
 det här (refers to a neuter noun)
(that) **den där** (refers to a common noun)
 det där (refers to a neuter noun)

In order to correctly decide whether you should use **den** or **det**, you must first decide on the gender of the noun. However, don't worry too much about it, you will be understood even if you use the wrong one.

If you don't know the Swedish name for an object, just point and say:

Jag ska be att få den där	I'd like that
Jag vill ha den här	I'll have this
Jag behöver det här	I need this

15 stamp	**frimärke** (*n*)	**frimärken**
16 station	**station** (*c*)	**stationer**
17 sunglasses	**solglasögon** (*n*)	**solglasögon**
18 telephone	**telefon** (*c*)	**telefoner**
19 ticket	**biljett** (*c*)	**biljetter**

Index

Conversion tables

Read the centre column of these tables from right to left to convert from metric to imperial and from left to right to convert from imperial to metric e.g. 5 litres = 8.80 pints; 5 pints = 2.84 litres

pints		litres		gallons		litres
1.76	1	0.57		0.22	1	4.55
3.52	2	1.14		0.44	2	9.09
5.28	3	1.70		0.66	3	13.64
7.07	4	2.27		0.88	4	18.18
8.80	5	2.84		1.00	5	22.73
10.56	6	3.41		1.32	6	27.28
12.32	7	3.98		1.54	7	31.82
14.08	8	4.55		1.76	8	36.37
15.84	9	5.11		1.98	9	40.91

ounces		grams		pounds		kilos
0.04	1	28.35		2.20	1	0.45
0.07	2	56.70		4.41	2	0.91
0.11	3	85.05		6.61	3	1.36
0.14	4	113.40		8.82	4	1.81
0.18	5	141.75		11.02	5	2.27
0.21	6	170.10		13.23	6	2.72
0.25	7	198.45		15.43	7	3.18
0.28	8	226.80		17.64	8	3.63
0.32	9	255.15		19.84	9	4.08

inches		centimetres		yards		metres
0.39	1	2.54		1.09	1	0.91
0.79	2	5.08		2.19	2	1.83
1.18	3	7.62		3.28	3	2.74
1.58	4	10.16		4.37	4	3.66
1.95	5	12.70		5.47	5	4.57
2.36	6	15.24		6.56	6	5.49
2.76	7	17.78		7.66	7	6.40
3.15	8	20.32		8.65	8	7.32
3.54	9	22.86		9.84	9	8.23

miles		kilometres
0.62	1	1.61
1.24	2	3.22
1.86	3	4.83
2.49	4	6.44
3.11	5	8.05
3.73	6	9.66
4.35	7	11.27
4.97	8	12.87
5.59	9	14.48

A quick way to convert kilometres to miles: divide by 8 and multiply by 5. To convert miles to kilometres: divide by 5 and multiply by 8.

fahrenheit (°F)	centigrade (°C)		lbs/ sq in	k/ sq cm
212°	100° boiling point		18	1.3
100°	38°		20	1.4
98.4°	36.9° body temperature		22	1.5
86°	30°		25	1.7
77°	25°		29	2.0
68°	20°		32	2.3
59°	15°		35	2.5
50°	10°		36	2.5
41°	5°		39	2.7
32°	0° freezing point		40	2.8
14°	−10°		43	3.0
−4°	−20°		45	3.2
			46	3.2
			50	3.5
			60	4.2

To convert °C to °F, divide by 5, multiply by 9 and add 32.
To convert °F to °C, take away 32, divide by 9 and multiply by 5.

CLOTHING SIZES

Remember – always try on clothes before buying.
Clothing sizes are usually unreliable.

women's dresses and suits

Europe	38	40	42	44	46	48
UK	32	34	36	38	40	42
USA	10	12	14	16	18	20

men's suits and coats

Europe	46	48	50	52	54	56
UK and USA	36	38	40	42	44	46

men's shirts

Europe	36	37	38	39	41	42	43
UK and USA	14	14½	15	15½	16	16½	17

socks

Europe	38–39	39–40	40–41	41–12	42–13
UK and USA	9½	10	10½	11	11½

shoes

Europe	34	35½	36½	38	39	41	42	43	44	45
UK	2	3	4	5	6	7	8	9	10	11
USA	3½	4½	5½	6½	7½	8½	9½	10½	11½	12½

All these books are available at your local bookshop or newsagent, or can be ordered direct from the publisher. Indicate the number of copies required and fill in the form below.

Send to: **CS Department, Pan Books Ltd., P.O. Box 40, Basingstoke, Hants.   RG21 2YT.**

or phone: 0256 469551 (Ansaphone), quoting title, author and Credit Card number.

Please enclose a remittance* to the value of the cover price plus: 60p for the first book plus 30p per copy for each additional book ordered to a maximum charge of £2.40 to cover postage and packing.

*Payment may be made in sterling by UK personal cheque, postal order, sterling draft or international money order, made payable to Pan Books Ltd.

Alternatively by Barclaycard/Access:

Card No.

―――――――――――――――――――――――――――
Signature:

Applicable only in the UK and Republic of Ireland.

While every effort is made to keep prices low, it is sometimes necessary to increase prices at short notice. Pan Books reserve the right to show on covers and charge new retail prices which may differ from those advertised in the text or elsewhere.

NAME AND ADDRESS IN BLOCK LETTERS PLEASE:

....

Name ―――――――――――――――――――――――――

Address ――――――――――――――――――――――――

―――――――――――――――――――――――――――

―――――――――――――――――――――――――――

―――――――――――――――――――――――――――

3/87